ICT Law and Internationalisation

Law and Electronic Commerce

Volume 10

ICT Law and Internationalisation

A Survey of Government Views

Edited by

Bert-Jaap Koops
Corien Prins
Hielke Hijmans

KLUWER LAW INTERNATIONAL
THE HAGUE · LONDON · BOSTON

Library of Congress Cataloging-in-Publication Data

ISBN 90-411-1505-6

Published by Kluwer Law International,
P.O. Box 85889, 2508 CN The Hague, The Netherlands.

Sold and distributed in North, Central and South America
by Kluwer Law International,
675 Massachusetts Avenue, Cambridge, MA 02139, U.S.A.

In all other countries, sold and distributed
by Kluwer Law International, Distribution Centre,
P.O. Box 322, 3300 AH Dordrecht, The Netherlands.

Printed on acid-free paper

Kluwer Law International incorporates the publishing programmes of
Graham & Trotman Ltd, Kluwer Law and Taxation Publishers,
and Martinus Nijhoff Publishers.

Printed in the Netherlands.

Foreword

In recent years, the Netherlands government has worked hard to develop views on the many different issues arising from what usually is called the development towards an information society.

The Ministry of Justice has drafted a policy regarding the effects of these developments on the role of the legislator. The main result of all these efforts can be found in the 1998 Memorandum *Legislation for the Electronic Highways.* In this book, you will find an updated version of the summary of this memorandum.

However, the emphasis of this book is on a more specific subject: internationalisation and ICT law in the information society. I find it extremely important to think about the consequences for the sovereignty of a national state, seen from the perspective of a fundamentally international environment like the Internet. And I do not want to stop there, but I would also wish to try and find solutions, which, as we all know, is not that simple.

Recently, I sent a memorandum on the subject of internationalisation to the Netherlands Parliament. An important objective of this memorandum is to facilitate cooperation between countries, within and among international organisations, and between the public and the private sectors. The memorandum itself already is an example of cooperation between the public and the private sector, in this case between government and a university. The quality of the paper would never have been as high as it is now if we had not been able to cooperate closely with a research team of Tilburg University. The comparative-law study by this research team shows us how some countries work and think on the subject of law and the information society. And this knowledge about the work in other countries has helped us to formulate our position. You will find the results, both the Memorandum and the comparative study, in this book.

I am glad to have the opportunity to bring the Netherlands point of view to the attention of people outside the Netherlands, within government, but also within other circles.

With this book, I hope and expect to contribute to the international debate on the highly important matters of ICT law in the information society. This may help others to formulate or to reformulate their position. And by doing so, it will help us as well.

The Minister of Justice,

A.H. Korthals

Legislation for the Electronic Highways
Management Summary
MINISTRY OF JUSTICE
February 1998

Internationalisation and Law
in the Information Society
MINISTRY OF JUSTICE
May 2000

Governments on
Internationalisation and ICT Law
The Positions of Germany, France, the United Kingdom, and the United States
TILBURG UNIVERSITY
July 2000

Table of Contents

Part A

The Netherlands

Legislation for the Electronic Highways Management Summary

Ministry of Justice
The Hague

February 1998

Legislation for the Electronic Highways

Management Summary

Editors' note

This is a translation of the management summary of the 1998 Memorandum Legislation for the Electronic Highways. In the footnotes, we have updated this memorandum to indicate the state of affairs (as of July 2000) of the activities and legislation announced in this document. Therefore, all the footnotes are ours. Parliamentary documents and bills are indicated as TK (Tweede Kamer, Lower House) and EK (Eerste Kamer, Upper House). One should note that, although the main principles in the Memorandum still form the basis for the policy of the Dutch government, the principles themselves have evolved over time. The result of these changes can be found in the Memorandum on Internationalisation and Law in the Information Society of May 2000.

1. General principles

1. This memorandum is designed to:

- provide a legitimisation for government action during the transition towards the information society, insofar as the instrument of legislation can play a role in that process;
- to spell out that legitimisation in the form of an appraisal system for use by the legislator;
- to indicate the differences between the physical world and the electronic environment in important areas;
- to make proposals in respect of concrete issues stemming from technological developments.

The conclusions and intentions contained in the memorandum provide a building block for the revision of the National Action Plan Electronic Highways.[1] The document takes account of international developments: a comparative-law survey provides one of the foundations for the document.[2]

2. Subject to these objectives, the memorandum generates the following products:

---

1 This Action Plan has been followed by the 1999 policy paper *The Digital Delta*, <http://www.info.minez.nl/ezenglish>.

2 *Netiquette or Legiquette* by Tilburg University, Van der Hof a.o. 1997.

- a common frame of reference for the Cabinet for legislative issues concerning the electronic highway (see points 19ff of this summary);
- proposals for the preparation, amendment, or withdrawal of legislation and for discussion in international consultative forums and for associated activities (the most important proposals are set out in points 8-18 of this summary).

3. Subject:
The subject of this memorandum is the electronic highway, i.e., the complex of technical infrastructures and services providing the basis for communication and the processing, storage, and distribution of information. The 'electronic highway' is a metaphor for the transition to an information society.

The electronic highway may be conceptualised in terms of three layers, each of which could call for a different response on the part of the legislator: a network layer (i.e., the operation of the infrastructure), a communication layer (the link between infrastructure and user), and a content layer (value-added services).

The electronic highway could conceivably evolve at three different levels: first, as a 'luxury good', in which electronic services serve a supplementary, entertainment function; second, 'complementarity', in which electronic services are of major social and economic significance but in which there is no 'displacement' of traditional means of communication; and, third, 'displacement' itself, when it ceases to be possible for the citizen to function without access to the most common forms of electronic infrastructure and services as the traditional means of communication have lost their significance. The memorandum assumes that the electronic highway will operate at the 'complementarity' level. In addition, the document indicates what the legislator's tasks will need to be if a level of displacement is achieved in respect of certain services.

4. Three particular aspects[3] of the developments outlined in the document call for more detailed orientation by the government. These are:

- *dematerialisation*: knowledge, services, and information that are not laid down in tangible form constitute the engine of the economy. The digital recording of information is no longer tied to a particular physical storage device or place. Digitally recorded information is also inexhaustible, as it can be infinitely copied without loss of quality or destruction of the original;
- *internationalisation*: the information society is above all an open society. Information is barely tied to place or status, and it can penetrate many corners of society very rapidly. To an even greater extent than in the past, economic and social developments will have their origin in sources beyond the purview of the national government;
- *technological turbulence*: new information techniques and products are succeeding one another rapidly or are converging into new media. The developments in the tech-

[3] Recently, in the debate on the information society, the government has extended this list with three particular aspects: horizontalisation, transparency, and vulnerability. The Dutch government no longer speaks of 'technological turbulence', but, more generally, of 'turbulence', since it is not only technology but also society that is turbulent.

nology, the use made of it by the public, and the social and legal problems thrown up as a result are highly unpredictable and have a high rate of turnover.

5. The advent of the information society involves far-reaching changes but does not entail a radical break with the past. For the time being, the central role of the government remains confined to that of regulation. With respect to the electronic highway, the government has two main tasks.

- Guaranteeing a number of fundamental values and norms in an electronic environment. This concerns the protection and regulation of fundamental rights, ensuring law enforcement, and the provision of legal certainty.
- Facilitation of electronic communication. This is a matter of promoting a transparent and accessible market, promoting the reliability of electronic communication, eliminating obstacles within the existing legal infrastructure, promoting standardisation, and providing or encouraging support facilities.

The starting point in implementing these tasks is that the legal rules governing the physical world should also be applicable in the electronic domain: what applies offline should also apply online. It is conceivable that the electronic domain will generate social renewal. In that case, what applies online can apply offline. But then too, the legal rules must be the same in both these areas.

Outside these two main tasks, the government has a third task, namely that of guaranteeing widespread accessibility to the basic facilities required for the social functioning of citizens and businesses. This third task does not yet call for the deployment of a set of legal instruments.

6. If signs of displacement should begin to occur in various fields in the future (see point 3), the translation of traditional norms and frameworks will in all probability no longer suffice, as these have generally been developed for the physical world. In those circumstances, one will have to consider the need for totally new standards and frameworks. In addition, the government will need to implement its third task by the deployment of a set of legal instruments.

7. The memorandum concludes that the existing legal frameworks are generally applicable to the electronic highway, if necessary after some amendment. An important qualification is, however, in order: the international nature of the electronic highway does not sit easily with territorially organised government, as physical barriers are not a factor in the electronic highway.[4] The memorandum concludes that there is no all-embracing solution to this problem, although it can be substantially reduced by a combination of solutions. To this end, the memorandum proposes a pragmatic multi-track approach (see point 14), on the basis of existing national sovereignties.

---

4 This conclusion prompted the Dutch Lower House to ask the Minister of Justice to present a more specific paper on the effects of internationalisation. The resulting paper is the ILIS Memorandum, included in this book.

For the time being, the proposed measures must create sufficient legal certainty. It will depend on the further development of the electronic highway whether in the longer term, a more fundamental approach is required in which these sovereignties will need to be breached.

2. Legal fields

8. The memorandum discusses how the three traditional legal fields – private law, administrative law, and criminal law – apply to the electronic highway. In addition, a number of special legal areas are examined, insofar as interesting developments are taking place that have a bearing on the electronic highway.

9. Private law is to a significant extent formulated in technology-independent terms and can therefore largely be applied effectively to the electronic highway. Generally speaking, there are, for example, no procedural requirements for the formation of legal acts: they need not come about in writing. Similarly, the law of evidence generally does not create obstacles.

Legal requirements do, however, apply for a number of legal acts, e.g., to protect legal certainty or the weaker party. The 'electronic performance of legal acts' project (a part of the national program *Market Forces, Deregulation, and Legislative Quality*)[5] – which is expected to be reported on in March 1998[6] – examines the extent to which one can adapt such procedural requirements that constitute an obstacle to electronic legal matters.

In order to promote electronic legal matters, the Cabinet proposes:

- the inclusion in the Civil Code of general provisions. These must provide the courts with a frame of reference for applying property law to the electronic highway. One of the relevant points of departure is the 1996 UNCITRAL Model Law on Electronic Commerce;
- to examine whether proven statutory obstacles to electronic legal matters can and must be eliminated;[7]
- to create a legal framework for 'Trusted Third Parties' (confidential value-added services that, for example, guarantee the authenticity of electronic signatures) that is also supportive with respect to substantive law and the law of evidence. In setting up

5 A description of this program can be found at <http://www.info.minez.nl/mdw> (in Dutch).

6 The report *Electronic Performance of Legal Acts* (*Elektronisch verrichten van rechtshandelingen)* was presented to Parliament in May 1998, available in Dutch at <http://info.minez.nl/pdfs/12.pdf>.

7 These two proposals must now be seen in the perspective of the Directive 2000/31/EC ("Directive on electronic commerce"), *OJ* L 178/1, 17 June 2000, <http://europa.eu.int/eur-lex/en/dat/2000/l_178/l_17820000717en00010016.pdf>. The Dutch government will give priority to the implementation of the directive in national law, including the examination of statutory obstacles (required by art. 9). Later on, the Dutch government will work on the inclusion of general provisions.

this framework, account is taken of the memorandum on 'Trusted Third Parties' being prepared by the Ministers of Transport, Public Works and Water Management, and Economic Affairs.[8]

Private international law issues must be resolved on the basis of existing criteria in private international law. Priority must be assigned to drawing up specific private-international law rules tailored to the electronic highway.

Finally, the concept of tort is, in principle, suitable for the electronic highway; consideration is not being given to a specific civil-liability regulation for intermediaries such as Internet providers.

10. The general administrative law of the General Administrative Law Act, which relates to the preparation, performance, and execution of decisions, prescribes a written form in a number of respects. These statutory obstacles to electronic decision-making need to be eliminated as far as possible without detriment to legal certainty and the care of decision-making. Given the speed of technological change, it is not yet possible to spell out precisely the requirements that electronic decision-making must fulfil. The memorandum suggests the inclusion in the General Administrative Law Act of an experimental provision under which electronic documents can, in certain circumstances, be treated on an equal footing with written documents. This would permit administrative bodies to experiment with, for example, electronic licence applications.[9]

In special administrative law, rules on goods and services (and the trade therein) are particularly important. Examples include rules on gambling and the offering of medicine. Electronic commerce makes it easy for foreign suppliers to offer goods or services directly and so to circumvent licensing requirements in national or European legislation. Where this occurs, a specific provision will need to be included in the legislation aimed at suppliers outside the European Union. These suppliers must be obliged to appoint a representative within the European Union. Licensing requirements can then be imposed on that representative. Further research is still being conducted into the implications of this proposal, while the compatibility of the proposal with existing and future European Union and WTO regulations is also being examined.

11. Substantive criminal law is to a large extent formulated in technology-independent terms. This means that it can in general be readily applied to the electronic highway.

An important underlying principle in the formulation of penal provisions is that it is not really possible to assign ownership of electronic information; digitally stored information can be copied without limit and is therefore not unique. Criminal law must therefore concentrate, not on the information itself, but on providing protection against the infringement of technical facilities that protect information, such as encryption.

---

8 TK 1998-1999, 26 581 (*Nationaal TTP-project*), no. 1.

9 The idea of an experimental provision has not led to a legislative proposal. Rather, the Dutch government is now working on a more permanent amendment of the General Administrative Law Act, which will give electronic data traffic between government and citizens a status equivalent to that of paper data traffic. Part of the proposal will be that the citizen will not be obliged to use electronic means. The drafting of this proposal is not yet finished.

Dematerialisation and internationalisation create a requirement for the effective regulation of the liability borne by intermediaries, such as Internet providers, for illegal information disseminated as the result of their intervention, in that it is often difficult to go beyond the intermediary to identify, let alone punish, the perpetrator. In addition, clarity is desirable for the intermediary with respect to his liability. The Computer Crime II Bill imposes an obligation on intermediaries to take action against illegal information disseminated as a result of their intervention and of which they are aware.[10]

In spelling out the responsibility of intermediaries in greater detail, a significant role also needs to be assigned to self-regulation, comparable, for example, with the Internet Hotline for the Disclosure of Child Pornography[11]. Care must also be taken to provide adequate government support in the field of law enforcement.

When it comes to investigation powers on the electronic highway, criminal-procedure law is in a state of flux. The Special Investigation Powers Bill[12] is being considered by the Lower House; the Computer Crime II Bill, of which the preliminary draft was submitted for consultation in January 1998, lays down a number of specific matters in respect of the electronic highway.[13]

The Code of Criminal Procedure must draw a clear distinction between:

- powers with respect to existing and future information. Investigations concerned with future information – e.g., tapping wireless telephone conversations – must be subject to time-limits;
- electronic searches with respect to individuals and indefinite groups of individuals, or what is known as 'data mining'. Restrictions on investigation must be imposed with respect to data mining.

In addition, the memorandum puts forward a number of proposals for technical amendments of criminal and criminal-procedure law.

12. The memorandum also discusses developments in a number of special legal fields, the most notable of which are the following.

- In the media field, considerable attention has been devoted to the protection of young people. Measures will, as far as is possible, need to be introduced by means of self-regulation and at the European level.

---

10 TK 1998-1999, 26 671, nos. 1-3 (*Computercriminaliteit II*). The provisions on ISP liability were eventually removed from the bill because they contradicted the regulation of the European Electronic Commerce Directive. The Bill is still pending in parliament.

11 See <http://www.meldpunt.org>.

12 TK 1996-1997, 25 403, nos. 1-3. The Bill was approved in 1999, published in the *Staatsblad* 1999, 245, and entered into force on 1 February 2000. It regulates, for example, observation, infiltration, pseudo-purchase, oral interception, and wiretapping.

13 TK 1998-1999, 26 671, nos. 1-3 (*Computercriminaliteit II*).

- Article 7 of the Constitution will be brought into line with technological developments.[14]
- The feasibility in the longer term of technical distinctions in the new Telecommunications Act needs to be investigated.
- Copyright law can generally be applied effectively to the electronic highway. There are doubts about the use of collective solutions ('reprography rights') to the use of new media.

3. Central topics

13. The memorandum has five central topics. The first of these concerns the most fundamental issue posed by the electronic environment for the legislator: internationalisation and jurisdiction (see 7 above). The next three topics are substantive in nature and indicate the policy objectives for government involvement in the information society: the facilitation of reliable communication between citizens, safeguarding privacy, and ensuring the effective operation of the information market to which citizens have access. The fifth theme deals with the final piece of the legislative process, namely enforcement of the law.

14. The theme of 'internationalisation and jurisdiction' goes to the heart of the most awkward problem thrown up by the electronic highway, i.e., the inherent incompatibility of governments organised on a territorial basis with the world-wide nature of the electronic highway (see point 7). In the electronic environment, physical distance and political boundaries are much less significant. The place where someone is located is no longer automatically the same as that where the activities are carried out. In some cases, indeed, it is not possible to locate the place at all.

No all-embracing solution has been found to this problem. The memorandum adopts a pragmatic approach, based on:

- a substantial difference in comparison with the pre-electronic situation;
- the international nature of the problem, which sets limits on the room for manoeuvre for the Netherlands.

This multi-track approach comprises the following elements.

- International harmonisation of substantive standards should be pursued where this is likely to succeed, as in the case of private law, legislation regulating economic activity, property offences, and specific computer offences.
- Harmonisation is not rejected out of hand for other kinds of legislation, which is often based on cultural differences, such as offences relating to the freedom of expression.

[14] See the May 2000 report of the *Commissie Grondrechten in het digitale tijdperk* (Committee Fundamental Rights in the Digital Era), available in Dutch at <http://www.minbzk.nl/gdt/artikelen/rapport_gdt_5-00.pdf>. Art. 7 defines the freedom of speech.

- Rules must be introduced on the scale of jurisdiction, with agreements on which jurisdiction should take priority. The 'due process doctrine' in existing private international law can play a role in this regard.
- Rules must be introduced for cooperation between enforcement agencies.
- It must be possible to depart in certain circumstances from the requirement of double criminality, which is currently a precondition for international cooperation in criminal cases.
- The effective international regulation of civil and criminal liability of intermediaries is desirable. In the case of criminal law, the solution introduced in the Computer Crime II Bill (see point 11) could provide a model for international consultations.[15]
- International self-regulation that is comprehensive and enforceable and that contains the necessary safeguards should be encouraged. Priority should be given to self-regulation for satellite communication and a code of conduct for information providers.

Preference should in all cases be given to global regulation. Among other things, this could be feasible for property law and intellectual-property law. In many cases, however, global regulation will not be feasible. In these circumstances, agreements between a group of industrialised countries, for example within the OECD or the Council of Europe, can be an acceptable alternative. In some cases, it will be necessary to make do with regulation at the European Union level.

15. The protection of personal data – the first part of the 'privacy' theme – is the subject of the Data Protection Act that is being tabled in the Lower House in February 1998.[16] This act is designed to implement an EC directive.[17] The Telecommunications Bill also lays down rules on personal data in the Telecommunications sector. On the basis of these legislative proposals, the Cabinet will pay particular attention to:

- the promotion of transparency of data processing for citizens;
- the amplification of general legal standards by means of self-regulation;
- international harmonisation outside the European Union as well, and certainly within the OECD.

The use of biometric data – the second element of this theme – is related to article 11 of the Constitution (i.e. the inviolability of the human body). This means that for the use of such data:

- a statutory basis is required;
- the consent of the individual concerned is required.

The protection of communication of a closed nature – the third element – is dominated by article 13 of the Constitution, for which a legislative proposal[18] was accepted in the

---

[15] See, however, note 10.

[16] This act (*Wet bescherming persoonsgegevens*) was adopted in 2000 (*Staatsblad* 2000, 302) and will come into force in the beginning of 2001.

[17] The Data Protection Directive (95/46/EC).

[18] TK 1997-1998, series 25 443. The Bill, however, met with severe criticism in the Upper House, upon which a Committee was installed to suggest revisions of the Constitution in the light of

Lower House on 21 January 1998. In the case of the electronic highway, the debate concerns the question as to whether e-mail is covered by this protection. The question is answered in the affirmative: in practice, e-mail can always be protected by means of a password, and it is safeguarded by the proposed article 13. The criminal-law protection of e-mail is also taken further in the draft Computer Crime II Bill.[19] Among other things, this proposes:

- making the inspection by Internet service providers of e-mail stored by them an offence;
- rendering the criminal investigation of e-mail subject to the same requirements as those that apply to the criminal investigation of postal items.

Anonymity on the electronic highway – the fourth element – is a relative concept. People always leave behind traces that say something about their person, without necessarily disclosing their identity. In order to prevent the disclosure of unnecessary data on individuals, the Cabinet will promote the use of privacy-enhancing technologies, e.g., through the provision of information. On the other hand, a duty of identification must be introduced for the use of biometry linked to the individual (see 16 below).

16. Responsibility for a reliable technical infrastructure – forming part of the 'reliability' theme – resides first and foremost with providers and users of the electronic highway themselves. In this regard, the minimum requirements are adequately covered by the new Telecommunications Act.

A survey does, however, need to be conducted into the applicability to the electronic highway of the durability requirements for the preservation of documents.

The responsibility for reliable legal matters resides to a greater extent with the government. This certainly applies to:

- instances in which the citizen does not have a free choice as to whether or not to use the electronic highway (the level of displacement, see point 3);
- relationships between the citizen and the government itself, as regulated, for example, in administrative law.

This responsibility for reliable legal matters is reflected in a number of intentions. The Cabinet will:

- investigate whether article 350a of the Criminal Code needs to be amended in order to render the manipulation of the electronic transfer of data a punishable offence;[20]
- encourage self-regulation with respect to deception on the electronic highway, by way of supplementing the rules in the Civil Code;

---

the digital era. The Committee's report of May 2000 (see note 14) is to lead to a new legislation proposal. The Dutch government will present its view to parliament later on in 2000.

19 TK 1998-1999, 26 671, nos. 1-3 (*Computercriminaliteit II*).

20 Article 350a Dutch Criminal Code penalises damaging stored data (e.g., by altering or deleting data, or by spreading a virus). The Computer Crime II Bill (see note 10) proposes to also penalise damaging data in transit.

- arrange electronic access to public registers in accordance with the memorandum on the Accessibility of Government Information;[21] the privacy risk generated by the technical linking of digital information needs to be taken into account;
- promote international agreements on biometry;
- conduct further research into issuing biometrically-protected electronic proof of identity;
- propose the extension of the Compulsory Identification Act with a view to electronic identification.

'Trusted Third Parties' are important for reliable legal matters. Self-regulation plays a key role when such parties are appointed, without prejudice to the legal framework referred to in point 9. Some form of government supervision is desirable (in concurrence with the memorandum of the Ministers of Transport, Public Works and Water Management, and Economic Affairs referred to in point 9).[22]

17. With respect to the topic of 'markets', the conclusion is that information and communication markets are of a special nature. The rapid technological developments and the process of internationalisation, combined with the fact that information – as required for the functioning of a constitutional democracy – is the subject, call for alertness on the part of government, as it is important for information to be widely available in society. The effectiveness of the new statutory instruments – and the supervision by the Netherlands Competition Authority and by the Independent Post and Telecommunications Authority[23] – will need to be evaluated regularly. In addition, the standardisation of technical standards and interfaces is important for the functioning of markets. The Cabinet will promote self-regulation and devote attention to the choice of a suitable public-law safeguard.

As soon as the development of the electronic highway has reached a level at which displacement is taking place (see point 3), accessibility for the citizen will need specific attention. This applies all the more if communication between the government and citizen takes place to a significant extent by electronic means.

Application of the regime of universal service to e-mail and the Internet is not yet appropriate. The government can, however, play a role in the allocation of addresses and domain names on the electronic highway. Transparency of such allocation will enhance accessibility. The Cabinet is considering to provide support for the present system of self-regulation by the Internet Domain Registration Foundation[24].

---

[21] The 1999 Action Program on Electronic Government (*De elektronische overheid*), TK 1998-1999, 26 387, no. 1, gives the framework for these activities, available in Dutch at <http://www.minbzk.nl>.

[22] The government originally intended to have a TTP Chamber (*TTP-kamer*) supervise TTPs who voluntarily submit to an accreditation regime. The European Electronic-Signature Directive, however, suggests a somewhat different form of supervision, so that the government now intends to have the OPTA (the Dutch Independent Post and Telecommunications Authority) function as the supervisory body for TTPs.

[23] See, respectively, <http://www.nma-org.nl/> and <http://www.opta.nl>.

[24] See <http://www.domain-registry.nl>.

Nor does the multiformity provide a reason for intervention by the legislator at the present time. In this respect, it should be noted that the anarchic structure of the Internet in fact generates multiformity. Grounds for intervention could arise as soon as:

- new media displace the traditional ones;
- media that are important for forming an opinion disappear 'behind the modem'.

The techniques are converging, and the possibilities for providing information are increasing substantially. These developments call for the renewed coordination of the various regimes – especially the Telecommunications Act and the Media Act. This coordination will need to be reviewed in several years' time.

18. The fifth topic is law enforcement. Technological developments are rendering law enforcement more difficult, but they are also creating certain opportunities. In assigning criminal-law enforcement powers, the following principles need to be weighed.

- Effective enforcement on the electronic highway has primacy; the electronic highway may not become a legal vacuum.
- Any infringement of citizens' privacy as a result of enforcement activities should be kept to a minimum.
- The development of the market must be encouraged. In this regard, the fewest possible restrictions should be imposed on the admission and use of technologies.
- The costs for electronic-highway users must not be disproportionately high.

More specifically:

- the use of cryptography remains unrestricted;
- measures are being proposed whereby the tapping of telecommunications will remain possible in a changing telecommunications market. This must not result in disproportionate costs or in a distortion of competition among telecommunication providers;
- within the framework of the Council of Europe, agreements need to be reached on specific jurisdictional issues with respect to investigation on the Internet;
- research is being conducted into the use of data mining as an investigation technique;
- the Lower House will receive more detailed information by the summer of 1998 on the intentions concerning the organisation of the police and judicial system with a view to criminal-law enforcement on the electronic highway.[25]

Private-law enforcement on the electronic highway imposes new evidentiary requirements. The Cabinet intends to introduce new regulations concerning digital signatures. This is based on a proposal for an EC directive expected in the spring of 1998.[26] Attention must also be devoted to the law of seizure, based as it is on physical goods that can be impounded. Nevertheless, the present law provides means of safeguarding rights in the

[25] In this field, several initiatives have been taken. On a national scale, a team of *cybercops* work within the Central Criminal Intelligence Agency (*Divisie Centrale Recherche Informatie)*, and research is being done within the Netherlands Forensic Institute (*Gerechtelijk Laboratorium*). On a local scale, there are many activities.

[26] The EC Directive on electronic signatures (1999/93/EC). The directive will be implemented in the Civil Code, the Code of Civil Procedure, and the Telecommunications Act. The implementation will have to be completed by July 2001.

electronic environment. For the present, the development of the law can therefore be left to the courts.

4. Towards an appraisal system for legislation

19. In summary form, the central features of the electronic highway (see point 4) present the government with the following problems.

Dematerialisation influences:

- *transport and storage*: there is no longer any self-evident distinction, a legal fiction is required;
- *authenticity*: information can be copied flawlessly and without limit;
- *anonymity versus identifiability*: identifiability of the opposite party is highly desirable but conflicts with the desire of anonymity and privacy;
- *open and closed communications*: there is no longer any self-evident distinction.

Internationalisation was discussed under 14 above. Solutions were advanced for:

- jurisdictional conflicts;
- divergence of substantive standards;
- difficulties of enforcement.

Technological turbulence has consequences for:

- *technology-independence*: on account of the rapid succession and convergence of techniques, regulations on the basis of concrete media or techniques do not provide an adequate frame of reference in the longer term. This can also result in legal inequality between the use of old and new techniques and in discrepancies between online and offline communications.
- *flexibility*: the process of formal legislation calls for careful decision-making and may therefore take too long to keep up with the turnover rate of new ideas. Legislation is at risk of being out of date before it even hits the statute book.
- *effectiveness*: the legislator often lacks the necessary technical expertise and insight into the social applications of a particular technique to regulate certain areas in advance.

20. The memorandum develops an appraisal system for the legislator, set out under point 22. This appraisal system is directed towards the actors in the legislative process. These include those negotiating on behalf of the Netherlands at the European or international levels on the introduction of legislation. The appraisal system must enable them to make consistent judgements in preparing and drawing up regulations. More particularly, the appraisal system is aimed at ensuring that the choices made are properly substantiated, particularly when they depart from the principal rules set out in the appraisal system.

The appraisal system is not coercive in nature and, in view of the complexity of the issues in question, cannot be so. Furthermore, for certain issues, not just one specific instrument but a combination of the aforementioned instruments will be the most suitable.

21. Some prior comments.

- For regulations related to the electronic highway, the appraisal system provides a special case of the Instructions for Government Regulations[27] (especially instructions 6ff).
- Instruction 6 states: "new regulations will only be introduced once a need has been clearly established." For the electronic highway, this means that a regulation must implement a government task referred to under point 5.
- The three characteristics (see points 4 and 19) result in a marked preference for alternatives to formal legislation. On the other hand, the uncertain nature of the electronic highway calls for legal certainty in certain instances. This dilemma is reflected in all solutions.
- Technology-independent legislation is to be preferred. In many cases, this achieves equivalence between the offline and the online world. Technology-independent legislation is also better equipped to deal with technological turbulence. In some cases, however, technology-dependence is precisely what is required. The need for legal certainty could, for example, create a need for technology-dependent legislation (see also point 19).
- In the short term, self-regulation is to be preferred but also entails risks. The preference for self-regulation does not apply where fundamental values and standards of the constitutional democracy are at issue. In addition, the memorandum lays down a number of requirements for self-regulation as an alternative to government regulation. The government will safeguard the observance of those requirements.
- In the longer term, there could in fact prove to be a reason for government regulation. This could be the case if:
  - a level of development arises in which there is displacement (see point 3). In those circumstances, the government will need to provide guarantees for accessibility;
  - the technological developments reach calmer waters, and a period of stability is ushered in. In order to promote legal certainty, there could be a case for the codification of the standards arrived at by self-regulation.

5. The appraisal system

22. The appraisal system looks as follows.

1.1 The rules and regulations should preferably be introduced at a global level, or at any event together with as many countries as possible. Particularly private law lends itself to this, as do standardisation and other legislation in the field of economic regulation, as well as other issues in which cultural attitudes do not differ markedly.

---

[27] Regulation (1992) by the Prime Minister (published in the *Staatscourant* 1992, 230), as amended in 1995 and 1998.

If this is not feasible, legislation in a more limited international context, such as the OECD or the Council of Europe, provides a good alternative. If that alternative is also not feasible, the European Union will then be considered.

1.2 Legislation at the national level may be considered:
- to protect standards and values;
- if legislation at international level is not feasible or would take too long;
- to strengthen the competitive position of the Netherlands;
- as a model for the development of international law.

2.1 As an alternative to government regulation, other solutions should first be explored, with particular emphasis on self-regulation. This certainly applies as long as:
- there is no 'displacement' of traditional forms of communication, and
- there is technological turbulence.

In addition, technology itself can in certain instances come up with solutions to problems of technological origin, e.g., filtering systems to protect young people from undesirable material.

2.2 Such self-regulation must satisfy the following preconditions.
- The target groups at issue are sufficiently organised.
- The relevant social interests are being promoted and protected on an equal basis.
- There is sufficient linkage between all the parties.
- Compliance with the agreements is sufficiently assured.

2.3 The government is responsible for the observance of the conditions referred to in 2.2. Among other things, it may use the following instruments to that end:
- the promotion of insufficiently represented interests;
- the drafting of supporting legislation;
- threatening legislation if self-regulation does not measure up;
- supervision;
- cooperating in enforcement.

2.4 Government action will in all cases be called for if fundamental norms and values of the constitutional democracy are under threat. In the case of the electronic highway, this applies in particular to the protection of classical fundamental citizen rights and the prevention and investigation of serious violations of the rule of law and state security.

3.1 On account of the turbulent nature of the developments in the electronic highway, government intervention should be as flexible, adequate, and timely as possible. This must be weighed against the interests of legal certainty.

3.2 It will be established whether the existing statutory norms provide a sufficient frame of reference, so that the development of the law can be left to the courts.

3.3 It will be established whether government intervention can take place by administrative means. This might include:
- providing a model for the way in which the electronic highway should be used;
- information;
- voluntary agreements.

Insofar as such administrative action limits the freedom of private individuals, a statutory basis must be provided.

3.4 It will be established whether private law should be further elaborated with a view to the electronic highway in order to eliminate the legal uncertainty in legal relationships.

3.5 If none of the aforementioned forms or a combination thereof is adequate, government intervention will need to take place in the form of or within the framework of formal public-law legislation. In doing so, alternatives to substantive norms in the law will be explored. The formal law only lays down general standards, unless:
- more specific standards are required in order to safeguard the protection of classical fundamental rights;
- the conditions are laid down under which the government can violate those rights.

3.6 It will be examined whether technologically-independent legislation is possible. Technology-independent rules are not suitable:
- as a definition for the scope of a regulation;
- if legal subjects – in connection with complicated technology – have a requirement for insight into the technology;
- if technology-independent rules would provide legal subjects with insufficient guidance on their rights and obligations;
- if conditions are laid down under which the government may violate those rights.

The preference for technology-independent legislation can result in the non-inclusion of substantive standards in specific, technical legislation. For example, privacy rules could all be included in a general privacy law and not in various sector-specific acts based on technology.

3.7 In implementing general standards, a choice will be made between:
- self-regulation;
- leading matters to the courts;
- an Order in Council or a ministerial order;
- a combination of these instruments.

6. Implementation of the memorandum

23. The appraisal system outlined above will be applied with immediate effect in the preparation and determination of regulations and for the Dutch input in international consultative forums. The appraisal system will be grounded in the Instructions for Government Regulations. For implementation purposes, the remaining proposals in the memorandum have been clustered into a number of follow-up projects, each of which can be taken up individually. The memorandum provides for progress control over the implementation, coordinated by the Minister of Justice, if possible within the framework of a second National Action Plan Electronic Highways[28]. Finally, it is proposed that the memorandum be updated every two years.[29]

[28] The Minister of Justice sent a progress report to parliament on 15 September 1999 (TK 1998-1999, 25 880, no. 8).

[29] This update is now scheduled for the beginning of 2001.

Internationalisation and Law in the Information Society

Ministry of Justice
The Hague

May 2000

Letter from the Dutch Minister of Justice

To the Chairman of the Lower House of the Dutch States General

The Hague, 18 May 2000

During the discussions of the proposed Legislation for the Electronic Highways on 12 April 1999, I promised to elaborate in further detail the Dutch position on the various legal dossiers in relation to the information society.

In respect of this promise I am herewith sending you, on behalf of the State Secretary of Foreign Affairs, the memorandum *Internationalisering en recht in de informatiemaatschappij* (*Internationalisation and Law in the Information Society*). The memorandum also serves as a reply to questions that came up during the general discussions with the State Secretary of Foreign Affairs in preparation for the internal-market council held on 7 December 1999.

The memorandum leads to the conclusion that the Cabinet will continue on the road it has chosen, one in which the body of thought from the memorandum *Legislation for the Electronic Highways* is the guiding principle. In doing so, the Cabinet opts for a recognisable policy line, one that has met with appreciation on many fronts. To make it more readily recognisable, the Cabinet has now worked out this policy line in a limited number of practical working principles. In formulating the working principles, consideration was given to developments that have taken place since the publication of the Memorandum on Legislation for the Electronic Highways.

It is of the utmost importance that an adequate legal infrastructure is developed for the information society. This leads to an active and constructive attitude in international negotiations. The legal infrastructure reserves an important role for self-regulation. In addition, another aspect deserves special attention: the government must ensure that proper protection is provided for citizen interests that sometimes tend to recede into the background in a market environment. The interests of citizens may vary with the dossier. For instance, they may be constitutional interests, but they may also be the interests of the economically weaker party. Apart from this, the protection of fundamental standards and values continues to be a responsibility of the legislator.

The Dutch position is concretely set forth in the following working principles.

- The level of protection 'online' must be the same as the level of protection 'offline'.

- The due care exhibited in social and economic life and other general legal principles that apply 'offline' form the guiding principle for the position taken up in negotiations.
- Where possible, the design of specific rules for the electronic environment occurs as a 'functional equivalent' of rules for the 'offline' world.
- One of our aims is to bring about co-regulation and to stimulate self-regulation at the international level.
- One of our aims is to create a framework for alternative dispute resolution. The use of alternative dispute resolution is stimulated.
- A starting point is that rules are technology-neutral.
- A starting point is the harmonisation of regulations.
- A starting point is the 'country-of-origin principle'.
- One of our aims is to develop rules that allow for the tracking of 'perpetrators' on the Internet, in the context of enforcement.
- Rules relating to the exercise of jurisdiction must avoid as much as possible an overlap in the exercise of powers by different states.
- It is no longer one of our aims to abandon double criminality.
- The contribution at the EU level will be geared to arrangements and starting points that apply in a broader international context.

Furthermore, the memorandum announces some specific actions. The memorandum itself will be brought to international attention. The memorandum will form the guiding principle for the Netherlands in evaluating the privacy directive. The use of self-regulation will be promoted in various fields. Finally, the Cabinet will give impetus to international judicial developments by encouraging an international academic debate, in order to seek solutions to issues of enforcement and jurisdiction.

As a basis for the memorandum, Tilburg University has conducted a comparative-law study. I enclose herewith a copy of that study[30]. This study will be published as Volume 39 of the publication series of the National Programme for Information Technology and Law (*ITeR*), and it is also available on the Internet (e.g., via <http://www.digitaal.nl> and <http://rechten.kub.nl/crbi/rapport.pdf>).

The Minister of Justice,
A.H. Korthals

---

30 A copy has been deposited at the Parliamentary Documentation Department (*afdeling Parlementaire Documentatie*) for inspection. A translated and updated version of this study is included as part B of this book. *(Editors)*

1. Introduction

1.1 Object and background

The object of this memorandum is to determine the Dutch position with regard to the numerous international dossiers in the field of legislation and the information society[31].

The memorandum results from the Memorandum *Wetgeving voor de elektronische snelweg* (*Legislation for the Electronic Highways*) (hereafter: LEH Memorandum) published in February 1998. The LEH Memorandum suggests that – in the discussion of the topic of internationalisation and jurisdiction – jurisdiction is generally territorially oriented; this interferes with the international character of the information society, where physical boundaries play no role. This is regarded as the most fundamental problem for the legislator in the information society. In order to get to grips with this problem, the LEH Memorandum recommends a number of possible solutions[32] that serve as guidelines for the position taken by the Netherlands in the various international relations.

In April 1999, I promised the Lower House during the consultation on the LEH Memorandum, to work out the Dutch position and the coherence between the different activities in the various international relations in a memorandum. This memorandum is the result of that promise. In addition, this memorandum answers several questions posed to the Deputy Minister of Foreign Affairs by the members of the parliamentary committees for European Affairs and for Economic Affairs during the general consultation meeting in preparation of the internal-market council of 7 December 1999. The reason for asking these questions was the EC Directive on Electronic Commerce to be discussed during the internal-market council. This memorandum does not focus on fiscal regulations, given the fact that specific solutions need to be created for that area, for instance, in the context of the OECD.

On some points this memorandum contains an elaboration of the solutions suggested in the LEH Memorandum. First, the issue is looked at from a wider perspective. In view of the position in an international framework, attention has also been given to more general legislative issues not directly related to jurisdiction. Furthermore, the feasibility of the solutions offered in the LEH Memorandum has been tested against the starting points adopted by several other important countries and international organisations. For this

[31] Although the memorandum *Wetgeving voor de elektronische snelweg* (*Legislation for the Electronic Highways*) refers to the concept of electronic highway throughout the text, it is more common policy nowadays to speak of the information society.

[32] See pages 8, 121, 122, 205, 206 of the LEH Memorandum.

purpose, Tilburg University has conducted a comparative-law study. In addition, the information gathered so far has been brought up to date. Account has been taken of the developments that have occurred since the publication of the LEH Memorandum. Finally, the solutions offered have been worked out in more concrete detail. To further an (even more) clear-cut policy on the part of the government, this memorandum lays down that policy in the form of a limited number of practical working principles.

The memorandum anticipates the general bringing up-to-date of the information provided in the LEH Memorandum, which is due to be published before the end of 2000,[33] in which also the consequences of the information society for national legislation will be dealt with. In bringing the LEH Memorandum up-to-date, the advice of the *Commissie grondrechten in het digitale tijdperk* (Committee Fundamental Rights in the Digital Era), to be published shortly,[34] will be taken into consideration as well.

For a proper understanding of the meaning of this memorandum, I wish to make several comments on the elaboration of the Dutch position in this memorandum.

Firstly, I would point out the following. It is evident that the Netherlands, due to its size, can only exert marginal influence in international negotiations. The Dutch *position* is not necessarily the *outcome* of these negotiations. Nevertheless, we must continue to enhance the quality of our position; a relatively small country may still be able to exert substantial influence by following a clearly recognisable line of approach and making a high-quality contribution.

Secondly, we must keep in mind that the information society is developing rapidly. In this respect, I wish to mention one aspect in particular. The structure of the information offered on the Internet, notably the World Wide Web, is extended by a new type of web pages (called portals) which contain mainly references (hyperlinks) to other sites giving information on the Internet. This adds a new dimension to the dematerialised and international character of the Internet: the determination of the place where information can be found – and the relevance thereof – becomes even more complex. The question whether the law should also look at the location of a hyperlink or whether only the place of the information itself – as far as this can be established – is of importance, still needs to be answered.

A third question focuses on the role the government should play in an information society. First and foremost, I believe that the government should provide an adequate legal infrastructure. This implies that the government must protect those interests that are in peril in a market-dominated environment. It is the government that should protect these vulnerable interests. However, it does not automatically mean that such protection should take the form of legislation.

In this respect, I would refer to the Cabinet policy document *De digitale delta* (*The Digital Delta*) outlining a stimulating role – apart from the legal infrastructure – for the government. This role as 'promoter' is closely linked to the importance of the use of the

---

33 This update is now scheduled for the beginning of 2001. *(Editors)*

34 This advice was presented on 24 May 2000, see <http://www.minbzk.nl/gdt> (in Dutch).

Internet – particularly electronic commerce – for economic growth and more job opportunities, as well as for social participation.

1.2 Perspective of the memorandum

The developments leading to a full-fledged information society are rapid. Obviously, this does not only concern the technological developments but also the development of the law.

This memorandum looks at the situation on the basis of four themes, which are also at the centre of international discussions. These are the following.

1. Regulation. On the one hand, this refers to the conclusions of the LEH Memorandum that, generally speaking, self-regulation is to be preferred to legislation, and on the other hand, to the level of regulation, in which regard there is a clear preference for world-wide solutions.
2. The basic principle that equal standards should apply 'online' as well as 'offline'.
3. The enforceability of regulations in an international environment. Alternative forms of resolving disputes are discussed here as well.
4. Issues concerning jurisdiction and applicable law. The LEH Memorandum argues that more than one legal system could apply to a large number of Internet operations.

These themes are worked out in chapter 2. Chapter 3 outlines the Dutch position. Chapters 4-6 discuss the state of affairs of the most important international dossiers.

2. Themes

2.1 General

The scope for Dutch efforts is significantly determined by the international opinion on legislation for the electronic environment as expressed in a number of key policy documents.

Since 1994, there has been great political attention for developments in the electronic environment, which often concentrates on how the economic potential of the information society can be put to best use. For a number of years now, there has been consensus that the private sector has taken the lead and that the role of the government involves supporting developments and ensuring a clear and stable framework of legislation.[35]

2.1.1 Policy documents of the OECD and the EU

The more general policy documents of the OECD and the EU often regard establishing trust[36] as the main aspect of the role of the government. Here, legislation is one of the instruments. In the terms of the memorandum *Legislation for the Electronic Highways*, legislation should primarily serve to facilitate and the legislator should make every effort to take a reserved approach. In such general visions of the information society, there is less attention for the other main role that the LEH Memorandum sees for the legislator, namely safeguarding fundamental values and norms, such as civil rights, in an electronic environment. However, this attention plays an important role in the results of the ministerial conference in Bonn of July 1997,[37] which dedicated detailed passages to freedom of speech and to the protection of minors.

---

35 See the European Commission's Communication dated 19 July 1994, *Europe's way to the information society: An action plan.*

36 As reads the main conclusion of the OECD Ministerial Conference in Ottawa (7-9- October 1998) on *Building trust for users and consumers.*

37 Global Information Networks, Ministerial Conference Bonn, 6-8 July 1997, see <http://www.ispo.cec.be/bonn/final.html>. This conference was attended by ministers of the EU Member States.

2.1.2 The Lisbon Summit

In the meantime, attitudes to the Internet itself seem to have changed. I refer to the European summit held in Lisbon on 23 and 24 March 2000, where the use of ICT (access and skills) and developments towards a competitive, dynamic, knowledge-based society were central themes.[38] The law must, above all, not be an obstacle to electronic commerce in Europe, which it should make every effort to support. For this, the "rules for electronic commerce (...) should be predictable and instil confidence in trade and industry and in consumers". Thus, the bodies were called upon to realise a legislative framework as soon as possible in 2000.[39]

The final conclusion of the OECD Conference in Paris[40] emphasises the responsibility of national governments, "notably to protect vulnerable groups". The importance the international community attaches to the realisation of the Cybercrime Convention in the Council of Europe contributes to an information society in which rules hold sway (and which is thus not a legal vacuum).

Another important tendency I (again) deduce from the conclusions of the European Council in Lisbon, indicates that the speed of technological changes could demand a new and more flexible approach in the field of legislation in the future. Thought is also being given to alternative dispute resolution systems as an instrument for regulation in the electronic environment.[41] The comparative-law survey of Tilburg University shows that thinking about legislation for the electronic environment is undergoing rapid change. The new and more flexible approach in the field of legislation is gradually taking shape. What is striking is that a number of general starting points of the last few years taken from international policy documents – and also from the LEH Memorandum – seem to become more subtle. Such aspects include the widespread preference for self-regulation and the equality of standards that apply to 'online' and 'offline'. The researchers at Tilburg University here draw the conclusion that ICT law is reaching maturity.

2.2 Regulation

The theme of regulation governs the degree to which and the way in which rules are laid down: at the international or the national level, by the government or via self-regulation. The technological developments in the Internet environment demand special attention in this regard. Detailed rules are often dependent on technology and can thus hinder developments. By contrast, global rules often create insufficient legal certainty, primarily because in an international context, there is often no court that can safeguard a uniform

38 The summit took place under the title "Employment, economic reform and social cohesion – Establishing a European area of Research and Innovation".

39 See points 10 and 11 of the Presidency's conclusions, <http://europa.eu.int/council/off/conclu/mar2000/mar2000_en.pdf>.

40 OECD 1999, p. 13.

41 See once again points 10 and 11 of the Presidency's conclusions.

interpretation. In relation to the speed of technological advances, technology-independence is preferable – the interests of legal certainty must be safeguarded.

2.2.1 Regulation versus self-regulation?

Starting point
In general terms, the LEH Memorandum states a preference for self-regulation, which can also include technical solutions. The rules must take sufficient consideration of the various interests involved, particularly the more vulnerable interests. The regulations must be plausibly enforced. It is the role of the government to assure that these conditions can be met. Even then, there are limits to the possibilities of self-regulation. The LEH Memorandum introduces an important subtlety: self-regulation is not appropriate when it concerns the fundamental principles of the rule of law. Then, the government should itself take regulatory action.

Developments
Due to its inherent nature, the instrument of self-regulation can be applied primarily in the sphere of private law. In a number of private-law dossiers, there is a preference for self-regulation. Many countries support this preference, particularly by encouraging the development of codes of conduct. The accent is increasingly shifting towards co-regulation. In co-regulation, the government takes a somewhat directing role in the interests of legal certainty and confidence. Nevertheless, a number of European directives seem to contain detailed rules that must be converted into national legislation by the member states: the directive on electronic commerce, the directive on electronic signatures and the (draft) copyright directive in the information society.[42] These more detailed rules are drawn up to encourage the confidence of suppliers and customers and to remove obstacles for the market.

In the criminal-law context, there is, in principle, no role for self-regulation, given the responsibility of the government for enforcing criminal law. However, certain forms of self-regulation can encourage compliance with statutory norms. In the field of liability in particular, self-regulation can support the investigating authorities to enforce criminal law, by way of setting up hotlines.

Where suppressing the offer of harmful – not illegal – content is concerned, self-regulation is considered an excellent instrument in the context of the European Union. This nevertheless does involve the government. The European countries consider the protection of privacy primarily a government task: the European directives give clear frameworks. Self-regulation can sometimes play a role in supplementing these frameworks. So it does in the telecoms sector and in the field of data exchange with countries outside the European Union. In the United States, the protection of personal data is done through self-regulation in many important sectors.

---

[42] These dossiers are discussed more extensively in chapters 4-6, which also include links.

The example of privacy protection expresses the starting point of the LEH Memorandum – like in the EU in general – that the protection of basic norms and values is the task of the legislator.

Here, I conclude that in international trade and industry, there are contrasting schools of thought when it comes to self-regulation. Often, a call is made on the government to ensure legal certainty and consumer trust through (private-law) legislation, while people reject government intervention to protect privacy or to investigate offences. There are also thoughts within the business community on a suitable balance between the general preference for self-regulation and the areas in which the legislator should provide preconditions that are more in line with my view as mentioned above.

International context

Internationally, there is a high degree of consensus on the importance of self-regulation. The ministerial meeting in Bonn led to the following statement: "Ministers stress the role which the private sector can play in protecting the interests of consumers and in promoting and respecting ethical standards, through properly functioning systems of self-regulation in compliance with and supported by the legal system."[43] In the meantime, international thinking is developing. During the OECD Conference in Paris,[44] a new concept became visible. Legislation and self-regulation should no longer be seen as a dichotomy but as complements of each other. A much-used term was 'co-regulation', or an integrated approach: "the regulatory environment should be a balance between self-regulation by industry and regulation by government and international bodies developed cooperatively by government, business and the public voice."[45] In this approach, government legislation provides a legal infrastructure with a number of basic norms. This is supplemented by social parties in the form of codes of conduct, among other things. According to the OECD, room should primarily be given to innovation and competition. Co-regulation also has the advantage of speed and flexibility, but it also enables specific rules for specific sectors.

Current approach

In an international context, the accent is increasingly shifting from self-regulation (the government at a distance) to co-regulation (the government involved). I consider co-regulation a constructive alternative to the instrument of self-regulation, because it offers the government the option of setting preconditions in the interests of legal certainty. However, the concept of co-regulation should be elaborated further. The term co-regulation is confusing, given that it seems to indicate voluntary agreements while this is (often) not the intention. It seems that the concept of co-regulation is interpreted differently in different countries, depending on the national tradition of legislation and cultural backgrounds. Seen from the Dutch legislative tradition, I distinguish co-regulation in the

---

43 Recommendation 19 of the Ministerial Conference's declaration (Bonn 6-8 July 1997), <http://www.ispo.cec.be/bonn/final.html>.

44 OECD 1999.

45 OECD 1999, p. 11.

following points from the more traditional forms of self-regulation that serve to supplement basic legal standards:

- The rules are realised in a dialogue between the government and the private sector. Here, the government at least formulates the policy starting points and ensures that all the relevant parties are also involved, including potential newcomers to the market and consumers.
- The government retains responsibility, which can be expressed, if necessary, in the realisation of legislation as part of the regulatory system.
- Co-regulation is not non-committal. Where this is agreed between the government and the business community, taking part in the system can also be compulsory, possibly after the intervention of the legislator. An alternative to strict enforceability is to grant (procedural) benefits to taking part in the co-regulation system.

The dialogue of the government with the private sector has the added advantage of being able to curb the rules from springing up at random. Codes of conduct in the field of electronic commerce and standard clauses for the protection of privacy help to encourage a uniform approach. I am keen to stimulate this development. However, we must keep in mind that the government should conclude agreements with representative representatives of the market. This representativeness is often more difficult to measure internationally than nationally, and it can also change very quickly.

For the sake of clarity, I note that applying the instrument of self-regulation depends on the legal field and on the actual circumstances. People should realise that for (large sections of) electronic commerce, the market comprises many small businesses and there are few obstacles to join this market. This market structure places extra demands on self-regulation. After all, we can never be sure that all parties will comply with codes of conduct and the like.

With an overview of all these aspects, I continue to champion an international policy that stimulates self-regulation and brings about co-regulation. That policy must pay attention to the preconditions for self-regulation mentioned in the appraisal system of the LEH Memorandum. In addition, the government will need to work with market parties to bring about a coherent system of private and public rules. Protecting fundamental norms and values continues to be a task for the legislator, in which consensus has been reached within the European Union.

2.2.2 The level of regulation

Starting point

The international character of electronic traffic means a preference for international – and preferably global – legislation, according to the LEH Memorandum. In the electronic environment, (conflicting) national legislation is not particularly appropriate. In general, there is little point in holding on to national characteristics in national legislation when communications are increasingly becoming international. This is more strongly the case in electronic commerce. An international market evolves; such a market also requires an international legal context.

Developments / International context

Many international dossiers concern regulation initiatives in the context of the EU. Parallel to this, there are often also advances in wider international fora such as in the Council of Europe where negotiations are taking place to establish a Cybercrime Convention, in the UN (UNCITRAL), and in the OECD for private-law topics and also privacy aspects. These developments interfere with each other, because solutions found in one forum are then argued for in another. Another important forum is the World Trade Organisation (WTO). The discussion at the WTO focuses on the question how different treaty provisions relate to electronic commerce. This analysis should show the degree to which amended and/or supplementary WTO rules are required, with the ultimate goal of promoting electronic commerce.

The approach differs per organisation, partly depending on the point of view taken and its international legal status. It is good to understand that in the context of the first pillar of the EU Treaty, the European Commission primarily focuses on manifesting the internal market. It sees the realisation of legislation such as the directive on electronic commerce primarily as an instrument of bringing this goal closer. The drafting of a model act on electronic commerce in the context of UNCITRAL is, by contrast, mainly directed at international uniformity through removing improper legal obstacles. Standard provisions are being developed that can be incorporated by the member states in their national legislation. However, they are not compelled to do so. Harmonising legislation demands patience and is limited. In the area of criminal law, experiences with the Cybercrime Convention show that harmonising content-related offences on the Internet is not viable because of national characteristics. The only area in which this seems to succeed is child pornography. But this does not mean that it is not possible to make progress in criminal-procedure law and mutual legal assistance. The Netherlands plays an active role in realising the various regulations in the context of the Council of Europe and the European Union. The development of criminal-procedure contexts in the Cybercrime Convention has been particularly stimulated by Dutch legislation.

A general problem in realising international legislation is that it can take many years before an international convention is realised and comes into force. Naturally, this similarly applies to EC directives that require a term for conversion into national legislation.

Current approach

Because of the cross-border, global nature of the Internet, the Netherlands is in principle an advocate of regulation at global level which leaves room for solutions geared to national practice such as in conformity with the preference of the LEH Memorandum. However, this approach is still not always feasible – as stated in the LEH Memorandum. The question thus becomes: how desirable is European legislation? At the level of the European Union, many initiatives are being developed. I assess these initiatives from a constructive position.

Attention must be given to the limited efficacy of European legislation in the electronic environment. Sometimes, European legislation can even have a counter-productive effect on the world-wide information market if the EU selects measures that are not applied elsewhere.

Given the fact that specific topics are dealt with in parallel in different fora, good mutual coordination is essential.

I opt for reticence in preparing national legislation particularly if this can hamper the development of the information society. Sometimes, national legislation will however be necessary, for example, because of the fact that international legal developments do not lead to sufficient legal certainty or to sufficient protection of vulnerable interests. And national initiatives in the field of (self-)regulation can serve as a model, such as in the case of criminal-procedure law where the Dutch legal developments inspired parts of the Cybercrime Convention. The code of conduct in the Netherlands developed by ECP.NL for electronic commerce can also acquire such a function. When developing initiatives, attention is in any case required for interaction between national and international developments.

2.3 'Online' equals 'offline'

Starting point

In the LEH Memorandum, the Cabinet assumes the starting point that 'online' and 'offline' should, in principle, be subject to the same norms. This starting point arises from the thought that Internet may well be a new phenomenon but does not actually create an entirely new world. Actions making use of the Internet are, from a legal perspective, not by definition any different to other actions. However, the current legal context may not be applicable 'online' or may serve as a barrier. Sometimes, a 'technical' conversion of norms to the 'online' situation may suffice; sometimes, it concerns an issue that has no parallel in the 'offline' situation. Then new norms will have to be developed. This involves a sliding scale: once 'online' is less comparable with 'offline' the legislation will assume a character of its own. The starting point 'online' is 'offline' is thus not a dogma but an approach.

The legislator must ensure that an adequate legal context is achieved with respect to legal certainty. This legal context must be practicably applicable in the electronic environment and must also be enforceable. This task of the legislator firstly concerns removing obstacles that have actually been ascertained, such as certain requirements of form. This secondly concerns drawing up specific legislation for the electronic environment with an eye to actually realising equality between 'online' and 'offline'.

Developments

Many international policy documents concerning the Internet take the starting point that 'online' and 'offline' should be governed by the same norms.

The starting point 'online' is 'offline' is reflected in the criminal-law dossiers. Even in the penalisation of so-called CIA crimes,[46] where a direct analogy with the 'offline' situation is not possible, the chosen solutions are derived from general notions of criminal law.

---

[46] The computer-related crimes concerning confidentiality, integrity, and availability.

In the field of liability law, in the context of the directive on electronic commerce, the European Commission has chosen for a solution that is not entirely in line with the approach for the 'offline' situation. By aiming at promoting the internal market, the directive imposes less far-reaching liabilities on the Internet provider than on comparable professional groups in the 'offline' world. However, in practice, the difference will be minimal. For other topics, too, the European Commission opts (to a limited extent) for proposing specific legislation for the Internet. Although at global level in the WIPO, no distinction is made between 'online' and 'offline', in the draft directive on copyright in the information society, the Commission has opted for a divergent new provision on private copying. Because it is extremely detailed, this is relatively technology-dependent, but, given the ease of copying 'online', it is essential in the view of the Commission. When exchanging personal data, an interesting phenomenon occurs: the distinct advances of electronic commerce and, with this, of international digital data traffic compels concluding international agreements on protecting privacy. The regulations are not differentiated in terms of data storage devices. The issue of 'online' here leads to rules that also lead to stronger privacy protection 'offline' as well.

International context

The starting point that 'online' is 'offline' should be the same has its restrictions. New situations can demand new legal contexts. Sometimes, the application of 'old law' is possible, but it is in the interest of a uniform application of the law and of effective law enforcement to draft legislation for 'online'. One example is the desired harmonisation of the penalisation of child pornography in the Cybercrime Convention. Without such harmonisation, there is no double criminality, which is required for the provision of legal assistance in criminal cases. A second example of the need for a specific legal context for the 'online' situation concerns the development of specific forms of alternative dispute resolution for (private-law) conflicts in the electronic environment.

There seems to be an increasing need to depart from this starting point. The rules designed for the physical world cannot be translated to the 'online' world in all cases. I provide the following examples.

- Sometimes, new phenomena are created on the Internet, such as breaking into networks or interfering with the usual course of the information. The law must be able to respond to such cases.
- The lack of trust in electronic legal matters, often resulting from unfamiliarity, can demand a specific legal framework, where similar issues in the physical world would be left more to the courts.
- Harmonisation of legislation can reduce problems with law enforcement 'online', even in areas where comparable law-enforcement problems – arising from differences in national legislation – do not exist 'offline'. From the 'online' perspective, pressure to harmonise can arise – a harmonisation that is probably not required 'offline'. Here, I think of content-related offences under general criminal law, where deep-rooted differences may exist between descriptions of such offences in various countries that would hamper law enforcement 'online' but not 'offline'. Harmonisation can be

needed 'online' to realise double criminality, which is required for judicial cooperation.
- The desirability of specific forms of (alternative) dispute resolution for conflicts in the electronic environment can lead to the need for a specific legal framework.

International advances have shown that the starting point that 'online' is 'offline' is gradually losing value. It is sometimes more constructive to look at the differences between the 'online' world and the physical world than to constantly work from the perspective of similarity. The starting point that 'online' and 'offline' should be the same naturally does remain a benchmark for the legislator.

Current approach
In my opinion, in international talks, the Netherlands should be open to nuances when interpreting the starting point that 'online' and 'offline' are the same. Having said this, the level of protection offered by the law 'online' and 'offline' must be the same. The starting point remains that the Internet is not a domain governed by different values and norms than the physical society. When elaborating concrete topics, new rules are sometimes introduced for the digital world, of which copyright law is an example. Although at the international level, no distinction is made between 'online' and 'offline' by the WIPO, the European Commission opts for creating new, specific technology-dependent legislation for the Internet. The protection level this directive offers must not deviate from the 'offline' protection level.

In addition, we must be reticent in using legislation purely as an instrument for stimulating electronic commerce, possibly even at the expense of traditional commerce. The legal framework should be neutral.

In conclusion: when drawing up international rules for the information society, attention should be given to both the similarities and differences between the physical world and the electronic world. With this, a specific legal context for the Internet can become topical again in the long run.

2.4 Enforceability

Starting point
The enforcement of (national) law on the Internet is a complex business. The problem is that the Internet is by nature a cross-border phenomenon, while jurisdictions are restricted to territorial boundaries. In addition, the immaterial nature of communications over the Internet means that it is difficult to ascertain precisely where an action has taken place.

International cooperation is required to reduce a lack of enforceability. In this way, the identity of persons on the Internet can be traced in cases that require this with a view to their possible liability. A condition for this is that those who act can be traced; that it is possible to follow the electronic trail to the source with a view to law enforcement. This not only applies to the competent authority that must enforce public law, but also applies in private law to the party whose interests have been violated. The Internet provider can be asked to play and important role in this. His cooperation will, after all, be frequently required to be able to trace the person who committed the act and – if this cannot be ascertained or if undesirable information is already widely distributed over the network – to terminate infringements of the law.

These matters are closely related to the territorial effect of the law and of law enforcement, particularly in public law. In a situation in which boundaries are becoming increasingly irrelevant, from the perspective of an effective operation of the law, it will be necessary that law enforcement is also able to take place in networks 'physically' located outside the Netherlands. Given that the need for cross-border law enforcement also exists in other countries, agreements between states are required. In such agreements, national sovereignty is always at issue.

Effective authority is continually required. The Netherlands Scientific Council for Government Policy (*Wetenschappelijke Raad voor het Regeringsbeleid*) report *Governments Losing Ground (Staat zonder land)*[47] goes into this topic in depth.

Developments

Here, it is useful to draw a distinction between the developments in the sphere of public law, and more in particular in criminal law on the one hand and private law on the other.

Criminal law often concerns international criminal cooperation: in principle, the legal power of states is territorially bounded, and gathering data abroad (or having data gathered) requires the offence in question to be punishable in that country, too. Although harmonisation of substantive law is difficult, this requirement of double criminality does not seem a point of discussion in an international context. The solution can be found in agreements on providing mutual assistance.

Clarity on investigation powers 'online' and their cross-border application makes an immediate contribution to enforceability. In the negotiations on the Cybercrime Convention, several difficulties still need to be resolved, particularly forced use of authorisations and the (un)intended collection of data abroad. As far as the latter point is concerned, the Netherlands takes the position that the country concerned should be notified and that this country should be able to refrain from agreement with the cross-border criminal investigation and the use of the data acquired. With this, the Cabinet elects to take a fairly strict, rule-of-law approach.

In the private-law area, enforcing legislation takes place via the national court of the supplier or the customer or before the judge of a third country chosen by the parties, based on the rules of private international law. The EC directives on electronic commerce and electronic signatures do not impair the rules of private international law. However, within the European Union, diverse EC directives attempt to improve enforceability in international disputes via harmonising national legislation.

The EC directive on electronic commerce also contains an instruction to ensure effective enforcement directed at the member state of the country of the supplier. Within the European Union, this is a useful solution for enforcement in the electronic environment,

---

47 WRR 1998.

assuming that the country of the supplier can always be established. The directive must ensure that this is also the case for electronic commerce. To this end, the directive also contains a number of obligations, such as providing a physical address. However, outside the European Union and outside the field of electronic commerce, this solution is still not sufficient. Certainly when the authority of a state is not up to the mark or when it is not effective in enforcing certain legal standards, enforcement by the country of the supplier does not provide sufficient guarantees. This problem is, however, not exclusive to the 'online' world.

Enforcement in the private-law area does not automatically mean that disputes are brought to the courts. Arbitration, mediation and other terms of alternative dispute resolution can enable a better resolution of the dispute under certain circumstances. In the context of private law, a great deal of experience has already been gained with this in the 'offline' world. In this regard, I conclude that there is a strongly growing attention for the development of international forms of electronic alternative dispute resolution, certainly for the field of private law.

The EC Electronic Commerce Directive aims at encouraging the realisation of and use of these types of mechanisms. The European Commission also considers the out-of-court arbitration of disputes in general as the main element of its policy. Work is also being done in this field in connection with the OECD: the implementation of guidelines in the field of consumer protection in the context of electronic commerce.

A new form of enforcement is the application of technical security (encryption) against misuse such as illicit access to or illicit use of services or protected material. EC Directive 98/84/EC on conditional access and the proposal for the EC directive on copyright in the information society determine that breaking technical security set up by 'online' suppliers of services or by music and film producers is illegal. Technical protection can be a useful supplement to more traditional forms of enforcement.

International context

It is striking that the comparative-law survey shows that few initiatives are taken in the countries researched to safeguard law enforcement in the electronic environment. Even in areas that are potentially difficult to enforce, often in the sphere of public law, there are no coherent visions. The sense of urgency to tackle the enforcement shortfall is not yet manifest.

I concluded earlier that there is already rapidly growing attention for alternative dispute resolution mechanisms, which also come to the fore in the comparative-law study.

Current approach

In my opinion, international legal developments could use an added boost when it comes to enforceability. I am not referring here to the many negotiations taking place in sub-areas where rapid results cannot be expected given that solutions easily touch on the sovereignty of states.

In the first instance, I want to stimulate academic debate at an international level, partly by making use of the context of the subsidy programme Information Technology and Law (*ITeR*). In the near future I will decide on the setting up of a virtual international legal knowledge centre.[48] This centre could also play a role here.

Criminal enforcement of offences on the Internet demands rapid action. Simplifying the usual legal-assistance procedures by setting up national contact points is not enough. Clarity is required on the cross-border application of powers by authorities that prosecute offences committed 'online'. The Cabinet is continuing the relatively strict, rule-of-law line mentioned earlier.

I also attach importance to developing international forms of alternative (electronic) resolution of disputes, certainly in the field of private law. So, I appreciate that the OECD, together with the Hague Conference for Private International Law and the International Chamber of Commerce will also be organising a workshop in The Hague in the autumn of 2000 on the development of global mechanisms for alternative means of resolving disputes.

2.5 Jurisdiction

Starting point

The same problem can also be seen from the perspective of the jurisdiction of states. The LEH Memorandum concluded that there is often an accumulation of jurisdictions on the Internet. Given that an unlawful or punishable act on the Internet often has legal consequences in a series of countries, these countries are well served if they are able to exercise jurisdiction regarding actions that were not physically performed in their territories but which do have an impact there. Most countries, including the Netherlands, find that the latter provides sufficient leads for exercising jurisdiction. Because of its effect, they assume that the offence is (also) perpetrated on their territory.

In the theme of jurisdiction, a distinction between private law and public law is clearly required. In private law, obvious solutions are available through the rules of private international law, whereby parties often have a choice of law and forum. In principle, parties can make private-law agreements on the law that concerns them, in which case jurisdiction is no problem. Rules on the matter, such as in the EC directives on electronic commerce and electronic signatures that are based on the 'country-of-origin' principle, can be defined as default rules meant to set a basic standard for situations where the parties involved have not previously entered into an agreement. Sometimes, private law rules are mandatory law. Parties cannot deviate from the law, nor from the legal system or the court the law allocates to them. In public law, rules are by definition mandatory law and must be upheld by states.

The Netherlands Scientific Council for Government Policy report *Governments Losing Ground* formulates the problem of jurisdiction as follows: "This (deterritorialisation) gives rise not just to practical problems (enforcement) but also to problems of a more fundamental nature (...). Deterritorialisation may mean that actions can no longer be

---

48 This implements a motion by Parliament initiated by MP Wagenaar, TK 1998-1999, 25 880, no. 4.

attributed to a particular national legal regime. When this occurs, we end up as it were with 'governments losing ground'".[49]

The principle of territoriality, which is certainly the main rule for establishing jurisdiction in public law, is not always applicable on the Internet.[50] This involves two aspects. Firstly, as regards actions on computer networks, the territory of the state in which the perpetrator is located can still not be ascertained with any certainty. If, for instance, investigation takes place in a computer network, the investigating officer often does not know where the information to which he has access is physically stored, nor can he always know this. Secondly, the place is not always relevant. On the Internet, the same information is often available in many different places. The problem of jurisdiction is reinforced because the referral structure of websites on the Internet is becoming increasingly complex and, moreover, because websites are extremely dynamic.

Developments

Not all countries maintain these same starting points. Some countries feel that all networks directly accessible from their country fall under their jurisdiction; other countries proceed from the starting point of the physical location of a certain computer, with which they restrict their jurisdiction.

For criminal law, the broad position has another side. If investigating officers carry out actions in networks located in the territory of another state, with this, they could be violating the constitutional rights of the other state without the infringement being protected by the necessary guarantees for the citizens. This argues for a limited view of (criminal law) jurisdiction.

In private law, the following developments are under way. The proposed directive on the distance-selling of financial services determines that the consumer may not waive the protection granted to him by the directive. Normally, the usual place of residence of the consumer determines the applicability of the directive. The European Directives on electronic commerce and electronic signatures are based on the country-of-origin principle. This means that the law of the country of the supplier applies to the pre-contractual stage in case of 'business-to-business' conflicts and that member states ensure the compliance of companies based in their territory. Exceptions to the country-of-origin principle are made for the benefit of public order, security, and consumer protection, among other things. Conflicts in the contractual stage, where freedom of contract in particular plays a key role, remain predominantly in the domain of private international law.

International context

Responsibility for law enforcement on their territory leads to reticence of states to accept infringements of their jurisdiction, and with this, of their sovereignty. Experiences in negotiations on the Cybercrime Convention confirm this.

It is acknowledged that a convergence of jurisdiction is inescapable and that, as a result, attention should pre-eminently be directed at resolving possible disputes. In the

---

[49] WRR 1998.

[50] For more details, see Van der Net 2000.

private-law area, there is still no structural mechanism, and possible frictions must be dealt with through joint consultation between the countries involved. Agreements on jurisdiction are being sought.

Against this backdrop, territoriality can be concluded to be losing ground as the key clue for jurisdiction. Where, on the one hand, jurisdiction overlaps, on the other it demands international criminal-law collaboration – once jurisdiction is established. Attention is mainly given to the latter, whereby traditional legal assistance is not longer the sole variant. Attention should be directed at the intention to make use of authorisations in foreign computers, the order to preserve traffic data, and the tapping of networks.

The EC directive on electronic commerce opts for the starting point – for public law and for parts of private law – of the country-of-origin principle, provided the transaction takes place within the European Union. The legislation of the country in which the supplier is physically located applies to supplies over the World Wide Web originating from a member state of the European Union. This supplier is also bound to make its location known (with an announcement on its website). This system creates clarity for the suppliers in the information society on the applicable jurisdiction. Such a system only works if there is effective enforcement.

Here, I also remark that an identification obligation – which is what the directive's system for the supplier of information actually boils down to – is primarily suited to commercial transactions on the Internet, where the supplier benefits by being transparent, thereby gaining consumer confidence.

Current approach

For the sake of clarity, it is emphasised that the Netherlands is not attempting to realise universal jurisdiction: Dutch jurisdiction is only desired if there is a clear impact on Dutch public order. In an international context, I will argue for a restricted view of (criminal) jurisdiction, among other things, to safeguard against infringement of civil rights in the Netherlands without this infringement being underpinned by the necessary guarantees for the citizen.

In criminal law, the principle of territoriality is often seen in coherence with the principle of double criminality. Cooperating on criminal proceedings undertaken by another country only takes place with regard to offences that are also punishable in the other country. The comparative-law survey showed that a cautious differentiation of this principle – under extremely strict conditions to fight crime on the Internet – receives no support and even evokes resistance.

The harmonisation of substantive legislation can considerably reduce the jurisdiction issue. However, harmonisation offers no complete solution. As long as the application of the harmonised rules takes place in the context of national legal systems – with supervision by the national courts – differences between states can continue to exist. It is self-evident that this problem arises to a lesser extent within the European Union, given the nature of European law and the position of the European Court of Justice.

It is constructive to further elaborate in an international context, the choice of the EC directive for electronic commerce for the law of the country of origin, so that this will be suitable for application in a larger area. Such an elaboration can take place along the following lines.

- At the international level, harmonisation takes place via a number of basic norms.
- In addition, the country-of-origin principle applies.
- The country-of-origin principle gives the obligation to actually supervise and therefore cooperate with requests for assistance from other states in individual cases.
- There is mutual recognition of the supervision.

This elaboration is also appropriate for application outside the European Union inasmuch as states could agree on the basic norms and have sufficient confidence in the supervision exercised by others. I will introduce this proposal into the international academic debate that I announced under point 2.4.

The above can have particular importance for supervision in the context of public law. However, there is no intention that with this, the conflict-of-law rules laid down by private international law will be set aside.

3. The Dutch Position

3.1 Starting points for the Dutch position

As has been mentioned in the introduction, the purpose of this policy memorandum is to determine the Dutch position in the many dossiers that play a role in an international context in the field of legislation and the information society. In this position, the following starting points apply.

1. The Cabinet continues on the road taken, using the body of thought contained in the LEH Memorandum as a guideline. This way, the Cabinet chooses a recognisable policy line, which moreover has received high acclaim in many places. For this reason, the Cabinet has laid down that policy line in a set of working principles. The developments that have taken place since the publication of the LEH Memorandum have been taken into account.
2. The Netherlands attaches considerable importance to the development of an adequate legal infrastructure for the information society. This leads to an active and constructive attitude in international negotiations.
3. The position must be effective and feasible. A concentration of effort is desirable. Naturally, attention is focused on the views held by other countries and by the international institutions themselves.
4. There is a concern that the government is withdrawing too one-sidedly and, as a result, leaving the protection of vulnerable citizen interests too much to the market. The vulnerable interests at issue may differ per dossier. They may involve rule-of-law interests, but, for example, also the interest of an economically weaker party. This concern does not diminish the fact that the Cabinet attaches importance to forms of international self-regulation.

So, a policy line is laid down in the form of a set of working principles. In this policy line, the four themes from this policy memorandum play a central role. This means the following.

1. High priority is given to the creation of co-regulation and the stimulation of international self-regulation for the 'online' environment. In this area, the Cabinet takes several initiatives.
2. The starting point in this is that the level of protection offered by the law must be the same 'online' as 'offline'.

3. Questions of enforcement and jurisdiction are still not receiving enough attention at the international level. The Cabinet wishes actively to promote the legal development in these areas, first of all by sparking off an international debate over this issue.

3.2 Working principles for the Dutch position

This will lead to a set of working principles for the Dutch position. I must point out that these working principles largely correspond to existing practices. The added value of the working principles resides in the fact that for the Cabinet, they form a benchmark in a very rapidly changing technical and social environment. This promotes a consistent contribution from the Netherlands, naturally taking into account the merits of each separate dossier.

The working principles are as follows.

1. *The level of protection 'online' must be the same as the level of protection 'offline'.*
   This does not prevent the creation of specific rules for the information society when these are necessary from the viewpoint of law enforcement or to eliminate obstacles for electronic transactions. In addition, specific rules relating to unfamiliarity with electronic legal transactions are acceptable.
2. *The due care exhibited in social and economic life and other general legal principles that apply 'offline' form the guiding principle for the position taken up in negotiations.*
   The normal rules for due care used 'offline' in social and economic life are the guiding principle for the position. This also applies to the other general legal principles. This defines working principle number 1.
3. *Where possible, the design of specific rules for the electronic environment occurs as a 'functional equivalent' of rules for the 'offline' world.*
   This takes place in accordance with the ideas developed by UNCITRAL.
4. *One of our aims is to bring about co-regulation and to stimulate self-regulation at the international level.*
   Here the prerequisites formulated in the appraisal system of the LEH Memorandum are taken into account.
5. *One of our aims is to create a framework for alternative dispute resolution. The use of alternative dispute resolution is stimulated.*
   Where possible, use is made of electronic means such as knowledge systems. Attention must be given to maintaining the independence of dispute resolution.
6. *A starting point is that rules are technology-neutral.*
   Technology-independent rules must be formulated in such a way as to guarantee sufficient legal security.
7. *A starting point is the harmonisation of regulations.*
   Experience has taught us that when there are culturally-determined differences in legislation, harmonisation is often unsuccessful. This must be taken into account.

8. *A starting point is the 'country-of-origin principle'.*
   This applies within the European Union, but also elsewhere insofar as effective enforcement by the country of origin is guaranteed. The model of the EC directive on electronic commerce can serve an example.
9. *One of our aims is to develop rules that allow for the tracking of 'perpetrators' on the Internet, in the context of enforcement.*
   The purpose of these rules: enforcement. Naturally, account is taken of other interests, such as privacy. Rules that allow for a total control of all citizens – for example, through general requirements allowing cryptography to be broken – are therefore rejected.
10. *Rules relating to the exercise of jurisdiction must avoid as much as possible an overlap in the exercise of powers by different states.*
    Activities via the Internet quickly fall under a large number of jurisdictions. It must be avoided that on the Internet, citizens and companies are faced with an unnecessarily large number of states that want to actually exercise jurisdiction.
11. *It is no longer one of our aims to abandon double criminality.*
    The reason for this is that this aim from the LEH Memorandum has met with a great deal of international resistance.
12. *The contribution at the EU level will be geared to arrangements and starting points that apply in a broader international context.*
    An 'Alleingang' of the European Union should be avoided. However, the European Union must be able to play a major role in stimulating the international legal development.

3.3 Concrete actions

Apart from the working principles, the policy memorandum also provides for several concrete actions. I list these actions here.

On earlier occasions, the Cabinet has brought the LEH Memorandum to the attention of international relations and delegations of other countries. Among those showing an interest were the OECD – during the conferences on electronic commerce – and various sections of the European Commission. I am planning to discuss this policy memorandum in the near future with those involved at the European Commission, the Council of Europe and the OECD in order to create further initiatives. In so doing, I will build on the insights obtained from the research performed by Tilburg University.

Furthermore, the contents of this policy memorandum will serve the Cabinet as a guiding principle in contributing to the evaluation of the EC privacy directive, which, pursuant to directive article 33, must take place as early as 2001.

In addition to this, the Cabinet will actively promote the creation of international forms of self-regulation in the following fields.

- An international code of conduct for electronic commerce. The government will further support ECP.NL in propagating the code of conduct, which can serve as a model and so prevent unbridled proliferation of codes of conduct.
- The results of the national TTP project (TTP.NL) will be propagated within standardisation activities that will take place in order to arrive at an international interoperable TTP infrastructure.
- An international reporting mechanism for Internet providers for illegal content.
- The introduction of rating and filtering systems for content harmful to minors.
- The development of mechanisms for alternative dispute resolution, where possible through electronic means.

As I see it, the government's most important task is to provide protection against illegal content and content harmful to minors. In this area, the aim will be to create co-regulation that meets the description given in section 2.2.1.

Finally, I plan to give the international development of ICT law an impulse, particularly in finding solutions to questions of enforcement and jurisdiction. Many of these solutions are not easy to reach, as they quickly come into conflict with the sovereignty of states. I shall therefore endeavour to first stimulate the academic debate at the international level. In so doing, I shall as much as possible use the possibilities offered by the Information Technology and Law *(ITeR)* subsidy programme. Furthermore, the planned virtual international legal knowledge centre,[51] concerning which I shall soon make a decision, must play a role in this debate.

In order to make a concentrated effort possible, it will regularly be examined what the most important international legal dossiers are in the area of the information society. In connection with these dossiers, it will be examined at an early stage of the negotiation what the significance of the working principles are for the concrete position.

[51] TK 1998-1999, 25 880, no. 4.

4. Current Developments in Criminal Law

4.1 Introduction

In this chapter, the developments in the domain of criminal law occupy centre stage. The enforceability of regulations naturally is an important theme here: criminal-procedure law and the rules for mutual legal assistance directly determine the enforceability of substantive criminal law.

The theme of self-regulation in itself does not fit in the context of criminal law, given the responsibility of the government for criminal-law enforcement. However, specific forms of self-regulation can promote compliance with legal norms. Moreover, self-regulation can ensure that users of the information society can strengthen their (evidence) position in lawsuits.

Below, three dossiers are discussed. In the framework of the Council of Europe, a committee of experts will negotiate a comprehensive convention known as *Crime in Cyberspace*. Some of the topics of this convention are also being discussed in the EU. A treaty on the issue of mutual legal assistance is in preparation. The directive on electronic commerce contains a provision on liability, which also relates to criminal liability. Further, in an action plan, the EU is devoting attention to the spread of illegal and harmful messages on the Internet. Since this does not directly relate to criminal law, it will be considered in chapter 6.

4.2 Most important dossiers

4.2.1 Crime in Cyberspace

In the framework of the Council of Europe, negotiations are being conducted over a convention that usually is called *Crime in Cyberspace*. In a letter of 23 December 1999,[52] you were informed about the Dutch position in these negotiations.

The draft convention contains provisions that require the parties to make punishable in their national legislation specific behaviour. These provisions first of all focus on the protection of information systems themselves, the so-called CIA crimes (confidentiality,

[52] TK 1999-2000, 23 530, no. 40.

integrity and availability) and, second on content-related crimes. CIA crimes include breaking into a computer system, eavesdropping on data traffic via telecommunications from or to a computer system, changing or destroying electronically-stored data, disrupting the functioning of a computer system and trading in passwords and access codes.

Furthermore, the convention introduces an arrangement for harmonising child pornography. Acceptance of the proposed regulation leads to a certain adaptation of the Dutch system, because the depiction of children as sexually desirable objects is made punishable rather than the child's involvement in the production of pornographic material. Regarding other offences, such as inciting racial hatred or disseminating (other forms of) pornography, the European countries and the US appear to have a radically different angle of approach.

Furthermore, there is a certain agreement on a number of issues relating to criminal-procedure law: the status of electronic messages (e-mail) in the exercise of criminal-procedure powers; cross-border use of those powers; preservation of traffic data by network operators; and tapping of telecommunication networks.

In principle, criminal-procedure powers should not be used across borders; legal assistance by the competent authorities of the country in question remains the obvious means to gather information abroad. The intervention of the authorities, however, is not required when the information concerned is accessible to the public on the Internet, or when a person with an authorisation to access a foreign computer voluntarily queries the information at issue and makes it available. There is less unanimity over whether powers must be introduced to compel an authorised person to cooperate when he does not voluntarily cooperate in the acquisition of data by a foreign country. What is more, the countries that are a party to the convention, among others, must create statutory powers to tap public *and* private networks. This is in line with the Dutch system laid down in the Telecommunications Act and the Criminal Code. Finally, mutual-assistance instruments are created to complement existing treaties. In addition, regulations concerning criminal liability are provided for.

Regulation

The draft Cybercrime Convention is a result of negotiations held in the 1980s in the context of the OECD and the Council of Europe. The convention is being prepared in the framework of the Council of Europe, but its purpose is at the same time to determine a global course, given that the US, Canada, Japan and other countries are involved in the drafting. Moreover, also in the context of the G8, with partly the same participants, issues are being discussed that are part of the Cybercrime Convention. The Dutch legislation is partly a result of and partly a source of inspiration for the thoughts formed within the Council of Europe. There is also a distinct relationship with various current activities in the framework of the EU, which will be considered in the next sections. In addition to this, as a result of the European Council in Tampere, there are plans to develop within the EU common definitions, penalisations and punishments in a limited number of important sectors, including high-tech crime. Concrete proposals have not yet been made with respect to this. The various consultation circuits mutually influence one another: when a course has been set in one international body, it can become a standard for another body.

The aim of the Cybercrime Convention is to harmonise substantive criminal law for a number of offences. National idiosyncrasies appear to block a rapid harmonisation of substantive criminal law with respect to content-related offences. In a new domain – as that of CIA crimes – there seems to be more room for harmonisation, because there, (maintenance of) national criminal law plays a less dominant role. In addition to this, regulation is provided for with respect to aspects of criminal procedure. This way, a framework is created for future international cooperation in the field of criminal law.

Apart from that, as indicated in the policy memorandum on Euro Criminal Law,[53] the Netherlands does not see the harmonisation of substantive criminal law as a goal in itself, but only considers it necessary if practice shows that differences lead to bottlenecks in law enforcement (in the area of international cooperation in particular). In addition, there are a number of principles of Dutch criminal law that must be respected in the harmonisation, including the principle that we reject minimum penalties.

'Online' is 'offline'

The regulation pertaining to child pornography has significance for the starting point of 'online' is 'offline'. Here, the necessity of harmonisation for enforcement 'online' also leads to a harmonisation in the physical world. The CIA penalisations cover specific computer crimes for which there are no direct equivalents in the physical world. Even so, in the proposed penalisation, the 'offline' situation is more or less followed. Take, for example, the offence of computer trespassing (computer hacking, comparable to unlawful entry of a dwelling). As for the issues of criminal procedure, where possible, an analogy with the 'offline' situation has also been chosen.

Enforceability and jurisdiction

Harmonisation of criminal provisions can promote enforceability, for example, in connection with the double-criminality requirement applicable in judicial cooperation. The provisional choices in the domain of criminal-procedure law produce clarity on a number of points as to how enforcement should take place. However, this does not alter the fact that there are still bottlenecks here, especially in the cross-border use of criminal investigation powers via computer networks. There is no unanimity regarding that. Where it concerns investigations with a view to state security, there is a strong inclination to permit further exceptions.

The technical possibilities to collect information across borders and the importance of criminal-law enforcement can generate a certain pressure on the principle of territoriality. This underlines the importance of adequate mutual-assistance procedures in situations in which a power to initiate cross-border action is lacking.

Naturally, it might happen that more than one state want to institute criminal proceedings in connection with the same offence. An action on the Internet might involve

[53] TK 1998-1999, 26 656, no. 1.

the applicability of a series of jurisdictions. In that case, mutual consultation is required to determine in which country the criminal proceedings will take place.

4.2.2 Draft Convention on Mutual Assistance in Criminal Matters

As has been reported to the Lower House recently, this convention is now being finalised in the framework of the third pillar of the EU.[54] The convention complements and updates the existing mutual-assistance treaties of the Council of Europe, the Benelux, and Schengen. In pursuance of the agreement, account will in principle be taken of the criminal-procedure requirements that apply in the requesting country. Among other things, cooperation in tapping telecommunications will be regulated more specifically, cooperation is provided for in controlled delivery and infiltration, and there is a general regulation regarding protection of personal data incorporated in the convention. Conditions apply to (assistance in) tapping of telecommunications by the authorities of another country. Further, it is determined that in some situations it must be possible to tap telecommunication networks. In addition to this, cross-border tapping without technical cooperation of the authorities in question is regulated and coupled to the introduction of a duty to notify those authorities.

Regulation
Criminal-law cooperation in the form of mutual legal assistance has of old been on the agenda of the Council of Europe and is moreover a subject of bilateral agreements. For many years now, this theme has also been discussed within the EU framework. The present convention displays a strong affinity with the Cybercrime Convention.

'Online' is 'offline'
The convention as such is not focused on Cybercrime. Where it relates to cooperation in intercepting telecommunications, no specific regulation is created for the 'online' situation.

Enforceability and jurisdiction
Mutual legal assistance in criminal cases is an outstanding means to enhance enforceability. Clear arrangements as laid down in the draft convention can facilitate international cooperation.

The present regulation on the one hand confirms that criminal-procedure powers may not be exercised across borders and, on the other hand, it also legitimises specific exceptions to that. The proposed tapping regulation without technical assistance from the country concerned leads to a more balanced concept of jurisdiction. The country in which the tapping is done can, on the basis of a notification, still prohibit the tapping later on.

[54] The Convention was adopted by the European Council on 29 May 2000: Convention on Mutual Assistance in Criminal Matters between the Member States of the European Union (2000/C197/01), *OJ* 12 July 2000. (*Editors*)

4.2.3 Liability

As I have reported to you in my letter of 7 September 1999,[55] the liability of intermediaries is dealt with in the directive on electronic commerce.

According to the directive, depending on the specific activities of intermediaries, other liability regimes apply in which no distinction is made between civil and criminal liability. It provides for an exclusion of liability in the event information is merely passed on (mere conduit). In the case of storage of information at the request of the consumer (hosting), the party involved is liable if he actually knows that the activities are illegal and/or if he does not take measures the moment he becomes aware of that. There is a hybrid form if the information is stored for technical reasons (caching): the intermediary is not liable for that, providing more technical requirements are complied with.

Regarding the tenor of the provision for the exclusion of liability, there is some vagueness, because in the preamble of the directive it is stated that the liability exclusion only covers a situation in which the intermediary "neither has knowledge nor control of the information that is passed on or stored". Notwithstanding this, the text of the directive implies itself a deviation from current Dutch liability law, which in principle has an open nature both in civil and criminal law: in certain circumstances, it is always possible that somebody is held liable. The legislative proposal Computer Crime II also contained a liability regulation that followed the same pattern. In connection with the creation of the directive, I earlier decided to delete that regulation from the proposal.

Regulation

The liability regulation offers a framework than can reduce legal uncertainty within the EU. Liability law is moreover also a point of discussion outside the EU, in the negotiations over the Cybercrime Convention.

What is striking is that the liability regulation is described in a rather detailed and technology-dependent way. Especially the distinction between the three types of intermediaries may be quickly outdated as a result.

The fact that the directive on electronic commerce also extends to criminal liability included a discussion with the European Commission. The Commission sees the directive as a horizontal regulation, so that the liability regulation also applies to criminal law, whereas in my opinion, it would have been more obvious to regulate criminal liability in the third pillar. Within a legal framework for liability, self-regulation can play a complementary role, for example, through a system of hotlines. Specifically, intermediaries can define their liability in caching and hosting situations by using effective procedures for handling reports on (possible) illegal activities.

'Online' is 'offline'

In the directive, a liability regulation was chosen that does not square with the liability regulation for the 'offline' situation. It must be admitted that the difference in practice

---

[55] TK 1999-2000, 25 880, no. 7.

will probably not be very large, because under current law the courts will not quickly hold an intermediary liable, even though it is possible in certain circumstances.

This does not alter the fact that here, 'online' does not follow 'offline'. The main reason for this is the striving of the Commission – by introducing a broad, horizontal regulation – to provide legal certainty to the new (electronic) players in the internal market. As a result, the formulated regulation gives less room to the specific requirements of criminal-law enforcement.

Enforceability
The creation of an international regulation concerning criminal liability of intermediaries is conducive to criminal-law enforcement, for example, in the area of cross-border criminal investigations. The liability exclusion of intermediaries provided for in the directive does not, however, help criminal law enforcement on the Internet. The preventive impact of the proposed system is less than in an open liability system.

Jurisdiction
The creation of a liability regulation reduces in a material sense the jurisdiction problem within the European Union. Through harmonisation of substantive criminal law (conditions for criminal liability), no problem can occur in the framework of mutual assistance due to the absence of double criminality. No longer can differences among liability regimes stimulate offenders to flee to the country with the lightest regime.

5. Current Developments in Private Law

5.1 Introduction

The focus of private law is the freedom of parties to conclude and to enter into contracts.

An important topic in relation to the information society is electronic commerce. In the directive on electronic commerce, the European Union has chosen to actively promote the internal market. The aim of harmonisation of regulations is to remove legal obstacles. At an international level, general regulations have been drawn up for electronic legal matters in the context of UNCITRAL.

It is important that a good balance is found between the interests of consumers and those of business and industry. Consumer trust is needed for the promotion and development of electronic commerce. This means that the protection of the consumer is an important aspect of electronic commerce.

Copyright law is discussed in the final section. The proposed directive concerning copyright and related rights sets forth detailed rules, starting from the assumption that copyright owners must be protected so as to protect their creative achievements on the Internet and to safeguard their technical security measures (encryption, decoders, copy-protection mechanisms) from being hacked.

The importance of a solid private-law framework is stressed in the conclusions of the Lisbon Summit of 23 and 24 March 2000. Council and Parliament are called upon to enact the proposed legislation as soon as possible, including the directive on electronic commerce and the draft directive on copyright and related rights. It should also be investigated how to strengthen consumer trust in electronic commerce, particularly by employing a system of alternative dispute resolution.[56]

5.2 Private international law

The field of private international law generally must deal with questions as to the competent court and the applicable law. On the one hand, the discussion on jurisdiction is taking place in relation to the draft EC regulation concerning jurisdiction and the recog-

---

56 Conclusions of the Presidency, European Council Lisbon, 23-24 March 2000, <http://europa.eu.int/council/off/conclu/mar2000/mar2000_en.pdf>.

nition and execution of court decisions in civil and trade cases,[57] which is currently in an advanced stage of preparation, and on the other hand, in relation to the draft world-wide convention on the same subject being drawn up in the context of the Hague Conference for Private International Law[58]. This convention is expected to be concluded at a diplomatic conference to be held in 2001.

Competent court

The question about how to regulate jurisdiction internationally in the case of Internet agreements must be answered differently depending on whether or not the receiver of an offer is a consumer. In digital language: is the agreement business-to-business or business-to-consumer?

In business-to-business contracts, the parties are at liberty to set down in their agreement, in accordance with their own insights, which court will be competent. If such a choice of forum has not been made, then the court in the habitual place of residence or establishment of the offering party has jurisdiction. The question arises as to whether it is necessary, in addition to this forum, that a second forum be declared to be competent near the recipient. In 'offline' contracts, this alternative forum is the court in the geographic area where the merchandise is delivered or where the agreed services are performed. The court in the place where the agreement is carried out is deemed to be the most appropriate court to assess whether the agreement was correctly complied with. To the extent that an agreement comes into being 'online', but is complied with 'offline', there is no reason not to make available this alternative forum as well.

In 'offline' consumer agreements, it is presently the case that the court in the habitual place of establishment of the offering party has jurisdiction. In addition, the court in the habitual place of residence of the consumer has jurisdiction if, prior to the conclusion of the agreement, the offering party has made a special proposal or publicity in the national state of the habitual place of residence of the consumer, and if the consumer has performed the actions in that national state that are necessary for the conclusion of the agreement. Deviations from this consumer forum are only permitted if the parties should so agree after the dispute has arisen. In an 'online' situation, a consumer often is not aware of the habitual place of establishment of the offering party. Often, a consumer will have to effect payment prior to delivery. As the economically weaker party, a consumer deserves to be protected against the risks and the costs involved in foreign legal proceedings. For the offering party in the 'online' situation, the consumer forum means that it may ultimately have to deal with very many different courts. This can form an obstacle for medium-sized and small enterprises to enter into electronic commerce. The solution to this dilemma is sought in clearly setting forth the addresses of both the offering party and the purchaser, whether or not the latter is a consumer, in seals of approval, and more particularly, in a form of dispute settlement (on a sector-of-trade basis) – 'online' or 'offline' – similar to the sector dispute committees as they are used in the Netherlands. In

[57] *OJ* C376 E of 28 December 1999, p. 1-17.

[58] Draft of 30 October 1999, published on the Hague Conference website <http://www.hcch.net>.

that case, the aforementioned choice of forum for consumer protection would apply to offering parties that do not wish to subject themselves to dispute settlement.

Problems of jurisdiction also occur in the event of unlawful acts via the Internet: unfair competition, insults, infringements on trademarks, brand and trade names, etc. The rules to decide jurisdiction for 'ordinary' unlawful acts revolve around the jurisdiction of the court in the place where the unlawful act was committed, or at least where the act had its unlawful effect. The virtual nature of an unlawful act via the Internet means it is not always possible to use the 'classic' rule of jurisdiction, because this might result in a large number of courts being declared to have jurisdiction. So far, there is little clarity in the discussion on this topic. A solution for the jurisdiction problems in cases involving electronic commerce might be found in a system of dispute settlement developed by trade and consumer organisations jointly.

Applicable law

There is also little clarity as to the question which rules ought to apply in deciding which law will be applicable to Internet agreements and unlawful acts via the Internet. Although the questions about the applicable law must always be distinguished from those of how to establish the competent court internationally, the two are clearly related. The questions that were asked in the preceding section in relation to the jurisdiction of a court come up in a similar sense in respect of the applicable law. Here, too, the protection that the consumer enjoys in the physical world raises questions in the digital world. Again, alternative dispute resolution can offer a solution to the questions involved in the application of the law of the habitual place of residence of a consumer.

It is clear that it is necessary to make agreements about the applicable law. It will take some time before a regulation is adopted for deciding which law will apply to agreements and unlawful acts within the European Community or on a global basis. Meanwhile, a certain reticence is desired on this topic, so that the groups involved, such as the Confederation of Netherlands Industry and Employers VNO-NCW and the Netherlands Consumer Association, have an opportunity to arrive at appropriate regulations for these topics. On the basis of the outcome of the discussion, I will further refine my position.

5.3 Brief outline of the most important dossiers and their choices

5.3.1 Directive on legal aspects of electronic commerce

The Electronic Commerce Directive[59] forms a supplement to community law that applies to the information society services. One of its focuses is the electronic conclusion of agreements and the liability of intermediaries. The point of departure of the directive is harmonisation in areas in which the existing divergence in national provisions forms an obstacle to the development of the internal market. At the same time, the directive is to

59 Directive 2000/31/EC ("Directive on electronic commerce"), *OJ* L 178/1, 17 June 2000, <http://europa.eu.int/eur-lex/en/dat/2000/l_178/l_17820000717en00010016.pdf>.

prevent unbridled proliferation of national provisions in this field. The directive sets forth an obligation for the provider of services to furnish information; this would increase the transparency of the way in which – and the conditions under which – electronic commerce takes place. More specifically, these aspects are furthered by rules concerning the provision of information that makes it clear to those involved, which contractual obligations they take upon themselves and when. This is of importance to gain and to retain the trust of consumers in electronic commerce.

Regulation

International regulation of these matters is advisable in connection with the cross-border nature of electronic commerce. Working with a variety of national regulations can easily have an adverse effect on competition.

The directive leaves plenty of scope for self-regulation, which is in accordance with the preference of the Netherlands. For example, the directive encourages the drawing up of codes of conduct by professional and consumer associations.

'Online' = 'offline'

In addition to removing legal obstacles, the European Commission aims at an active promotion of the internal market. The directive entails harmonisation of national provisions that are applicable to information society services. This involves such topics as information provision, provider liability and the conclusion of contracts. One consequence is that for harmonised areas, sometimes different rules apply 'online' than 'offline'. For this reason, the Netherlands has spoken out against harmonisation of the way in which and the moment that a contract is concluded. Since other member states had objections as well, during the negotiations in Council the directive has been adjusted on this point.

In the area of liability, the Netherlands has aimed its efforts at a regulation that in any case leaves room to hold intermediaries liable for knowingly and wilfully passing on material that is unlawful or damaging to third parties, if they had a reasonable opportunity to act differently. This puts the focus on the due care and caution that apply in the physical world. The solution does not fully satisfy the Dutch position. However, there seems to be a scope at a national level to take due care and caution as a basis nonetheless.

Enforceability

Once the directive is implemented, its enforcement will take place via the national courts. The directive includes a provision concerning alternative dispute resolution. As for the protection of consumers, the directive leaves the rules of private international law intact.

Jurisdiction

The directive takes as its starting point the country-of-origin principle: the court of a member state where the offering party has his habitual place of establishment supervises the compliance with the law arising from the directive and sees to it that the offer is actually governed by that law. A few exceptions can be found in the appendix, for certain areas of law in the interest of consumers.

5.3.2 UNCITRAL Model Law on E-commerce and Draft Uniform Rules on Electronic Signatures

The attitude of the United Nations Commission on International Trade Law (UNCITRAL) is primarily aimed at removing improper legal obstacles in the market, and not so much at promoting electronic commerce, as is done by the European Commission. The removal of obstacles includes promoting the predictability of the law and increasing its practical applicability. The area covered by UNCITRAL is that of trade law; consumer issues do not come up here. The approach leaves intact the possibility to take national measures to protect consumers.

On the basis of UNCITRAL's abstract model law,[60] which gives rules for electronic legal matters, the draft uniform rules on electronic signatures have been drawn up. These rules are a practical elaboration of articles 7 and 8 of the model law, which relate to the validity of electronic signatures and which state the conditions under which electronic documents are deemed to be originals.

Regulation
UNCITRAL is a global organisation that reports directly to the General Assembly of the UN. Further, the approach involves as light a touch as possible, which leaves plenty of scope for self-regulation. Matters are only regulated if the conviction is held that, on the one hand, it adds something essential in terms of content, predictability, or applicability of existing law, and on the other hand, it does not obstruct or steer technical and economic developments.

'Online' = 'offline'
Without explicitly stating it as a motto, the work adheres to this starting point. The major legal principles of traditional legal matters are followed or respected, and deviations are accounted for. Wherever the applicable law – even if it has been written for traditional legal matters – sufficiently clearly suggests the correct solution, no specific rules are made. The model law is based on the (abstract) criterion of functional equivalence. Functional equivalence concerns the rationale of formal requirements. If an electronic signature provides sufficient guarantees, then it is legally valid. One of the aims is to offer protection to those acting in reasonable faith or trust on the basis of electronic signatures or certificates. What constitutes reasonable faith or trust, of course, depends on the circumstances of the case. In order to give parties in practice more clues on this point, it is attempted to ensure that the rules formulate a number of points of view on the basis of which the reasonableness of the trust can be assessed in concrete cases.

Enforceability and jurisdiction
The model law gives general rules for electronic commerce, but it does not impose any legally binding obligations on the member states. The aim of the rules is to set down a

---

60 UNCITRAL Model Law on Electronic Commerce, General Assembly Resolution 51/162, 16 December 1996, with an additional article 5bis, 1998, <http://www.uncitral.org>.

minimum package of conditions that the parties involved must meet if electronic signatures are to be legally valid. It is left to national law to decide what is right by law if these are violated.

5.3.3 Directive on electronic signatures

The object of the European directive concerning a community framework for electronic signatures[61] is to facilitate the use of electronic signatures and to contribute to their statutory recognition. It is important to note that the directive makes a distinction between 'ordinary' electronic signatures and advanced electronic signatures. Ordinary electronic signatures are, for instance, signatures scanned from paper. Advanced electronic signatures are linked to the signatory in a unique manner: they make it possible to identify the signatory, they are created with means that signatories can keep under their exclusive control, and they are linked to the data to which they relate in such a way that any subsequent change in the data can be detected.

The implementation in Dutch legislation must be completed by 19 July 2001 at the latest. Implementation takes place in the Civil Code (*Burgerlijk Wetboek*), the Code of Civil Procedure (*Wetboek van Burgerlijke Rechtsvordering*) and the Telecommunications Act (*Telecommunicatiewet*).

Regulation
The directive comprises an obligation to develop a system that monitors the service providers that issue qualified certificates to the public and that are established on the territory of a member state. The Netherlands was highly in favour of regulating this supervisory task via self-regulation, which also appears from the TTP policy pursued.[62] This policy favours the exercise of supervision by means of a voluntary accreditation and certification regulation. Partly at the urging of the Netherlands, the directive also leaves scope for this. Moreover, however, the directive obliges the members states to develop supervisory systems for the aforementioned certification service providers that do not affiliate themselves with the aforementioned voluntary regulation. For purposes of this latter supervision, work is presently being done to formulate a registration obligation under public law.[63]

'Online' = 'offline'
The intention of the directive is that the same standards apply 'online' as 'offline'. The appendices to the directive state conditions for certificates, for certification service providers that issue qualified certificates to the public, and for secure means for the production of electronic signatures. An advanced electronic signature based on a qualified certificate, issued by a certification service provider and effected using secure means, is

---

[61] Directive 1999/93/EC concerning a Community framework for Electronic Signatures (EC *OJ* L 2000 13/12).
[62] TK 1998-1999, 26 581, no. 1 (*Nationaal TTP-project*).
[63] Compare note 22. *(Editors)*

completely equated with a hand-written signature and must be allowed as evidence in legal proceedings. Ordinary electronic signatures may not be denied legal validity and they may not be refused as evidence in legal proceedings merely on the grounds of the fact that the signature was made in an electronic form or does not meet the conditions that have been drawn up in the appendices to the directive.

Enforceability
The directive obliges the members states to provide a suitable system of supervision of the certification service providers that are established on their territory and that issue qualified certificates to the public. For the rest, the general rules of property law suffice here.

Jurisdiction
The directive determines that every member state shall apply the national provisions that it determines pursuant to this directive to the certification service providers established on its territory and to the services that they provide. The members states may not restrict the provision of certification services by providers established in other member states in areas that are governed by this directive. Furthermore, the members states must guarantee the free movement in the internal market of products for electronic signatures that satisfy this directive.

5.3.4 Consumer protection in the event of contracts concluded at a distance and the distance selling of financial services

The objective of the European Distance-Selling Directive[64] is to provide consumers with better protection for contracts concluded at a distance (for example, contracts concluded via the Internet, telephone, fax, or e-mail), which will contribute to the realisation of the internal market in this field. For this purpose, the directive includes obligations for suppliers to furnish information, cooling-off periods (time to think the matter over) linked to rights for the consumer to terminate the contract, a provision about fraudulent use of bank cards, and a provision on the use of communications technology by suppliers in communicating with consumers. A bill to implement the directive was submitted to the Lower House on 28 October 1999. A report by the Lower House was issued on this on 14 March 2000.[65] On 1 October 1999, the European Commission submitted a (revised) draft for a directive concerning distance-selling of financial services to consumers.[66] This draft directive fills the gap created by the previous directive for distance-selling, from which financial services were excluded. The proposed directive is in many respects highly similar to this earlier general distance-selling directive. The proposed directive comprises two important complementary provisions: on the one hand, the information obligations

64 Directive 97/7/EC, *OJ* EC L 144.
65 TK 1999-2000, 26 861, no. 4. The Cabinet replied in July 2000. *(Editors)*
66 *OJ* EC C 1999, 279.

for service providers, and on the other hand, the right of consumers to retract an order or assignment.

Regulation
For the Netherlands, reference is made to self-regulation as it is used by the Netherlands Association for Direct Marketing, Distance Selling and Sales Promotion (DMSA). Currently, the State Secretary for Transport, Public Works and Water Management and I are investigating in what way the use of communications technologies by suppliers in their communications with consumers can most effectively be implemented, taking into account the Telecommunications Act. One of the subjects of our investigation is the role self-regulation might play in the implementation.

'Online' = 'offline'
The directive contains the same standards for 'online' and 'offline', on the understanding that, if a contract was concluded at a distance, the provision to the consumer of the information described in the directive must take place either in writing or through some other durable medium that is available to and easily accessible for the consumer.

Enforceability
The directive obliges the members states to ensure that suitable and effective means are available to ensure compliance with the provisions of the directive in the interests of consumers. One of these means is the collective legal action.

The draft directive on distance-selling of financial services also urges the member states to create out-of-court dispute resolution bodies for cross-border consumer disputes.

Jurisdiction
In the event of a choice for the law of a third country, the directive entails the obligation for the member states to include in their legislation the provision that consumers cannot be deprived of the protection granted them on the grounds of the directive, if there is a close connection between the agreement and the territory of one or more member states. A close connection may be deemed to be present if a consumer has his habitual place of residence in a national state where the directive applies.

The proposed directive concerning distance-selling of financial services stipulates that suppliers of the financial teleservices must inform consumers about the applicable law and the competent court if the agreement does not link these to the consumers' place of residence. Information on this must reach consumers in written form or through another durable medium in sufficient time before the conclusion of the agreement.

5.3.5 Proposed directive concerning the harmonisation of certain aspects of copyright and related rights in the information society

Since December 1997, work has been done on a directive for the harmonisation of copyright and related rights in the information society,[67] the aim of which is to make it possible for the EU and its member states to join the WIPO treaties of December 1996. In February 1999, the European Parliament advised in the first reading. The European Commission launched an amended proposal in May 1999. The proposal aims to guarantee the application of copyright in a digital environment. The proposal comprises rules about reproduction rights, publication rights, and distribution rights. It also regulates the restrictions member states may impose on these rights. The proposed directive makes it unlawful to crack technical-security measures. Finally, the proposal would make it unlawful to delete or manipulate electronic management information. It is hoped to reach a joint position by May of this year.[68] After that, the European Parliament will discuss the proposal in the second reading. The proposed directive is expected to be accepted around 1 January 2001. The members states then will have two years to convert it into national law.

Regulation

The directive concerns the European implementation of rules that were drawn up at a global level: the WIPO Internet treaties. Copyright law prescribes that permission is required of copyright owners for certain acts: for copying a book, playing a CD in a club, or including an academic article in a workbook. Copyright law therefore invites self-regulation and mutual agreements to define the relationship between price, quantity, and duration of use. Right now, for example, agreements are being made between publishers and libraries or universities. Freedom to adopt self-regulation is to a certain extent limited by conditions or exceptions, as in the case of photocopying or playing music in public spaces. For such cases, certain organisations have been appointed to negotiate exclusively on behalf of the copyright owners.

'Online' = 'offline'

The WIPO treaties make no distinction between 'online' and 'offline'. The EC directive makes an important exception to this, in respect of the freedom existing in many countries (including the Netherlands) for consumers to make copies for private use without prior permission. In other cases, the Netherlands and most other member states of the EU work with systems of levies on unrecorded (blank) media and/or recording equipment. On the grounds of the proposed directive, digital copying for private use will largely come under the control of copyright owners. This refers to cases such as recording digital television broadcasts to watch at a later time and recording a CD to play in the car. The reason why the European Commission feels that a strict regime is necessary has to do

---

[67] *OJ* EC C 108 of 7 April 1998; Amended Proposal of 21 May 1999, *OJ* EC 180 of 25 June 1999.

[68] A joint position was reached on 8 June 2000. (*Editors*)

with the ease of copying on the Internet and the very minor loss of quality this entails. In general, the Commission and a number of member states place much confidence in the possibilities of technical-security measures. However, the way this is related to important principles such as freedom of the press, accessibility of information for all, and privacy protection is not entirely clear or seems to have been neglected.

Enforceability

For the actual enforcement of copyright law, no other factors apply than for enforcement in other legal areas. One place where enforcement is spoken of is in the TRIPs convention (a part of the WTO convention), but there, it is primarily tailored to the physical world. There is a great deal of trust in enforcement of copyright law by using technology, such as encryption, passwords, and copy-control mechanisms. The WIPO treaties also cover this aspect. If technical-protection measures are abused, member states may take suitable measures. The Cabinet feels it is of great importance that, in applying technical measures, a balance is sought between the interests of copyright owners and users. Attention must be devoted to the position of libraries, educational institutions, consumer interests, competition, and free press.

Jurisdiction

In principle, no other problems or solutions apply for copyright law than for other legal fields, on the understanding that copyright law is already to a high degree subject to international regulation, and that at the heart of copyright law lie mutual agreements. These agreements may also decide the applicable law and the question of jurisdiction. The WIPO treaties do not contain any rules on private international law, nor does the European directive. The general rules of private international law are applicable.

6. Other Developments

6.1 Introduction

Two topics that cannot be directly classified under the areas of criminal and private law are discussed in this chapter: privacy regulations and the initiatives to bar harmful content from the Internet.

Another relevant fact is that regulations are being prepared on the infrastructure for electronic communications; this is also known as the ONP review. The European Commission has recently published a Communication, *Towards a new framework for electronic communications infrastructure and associated services. The 1999 communications review*. The State Secretary of Transport, Public Works and Water Management has recently reported to you on this. For the sake of brevity, I refer to this report.

6.2 Most important dossiers

6.2.1 Privacy Directives

European legislation has been drawn up to protect natural persons in connection with the processing of personal data. This legislation primarily consists of a (general) privacy directive[69] and a (special) directive aimed at the telecoms sector[70]. The general privacy directive will be evaluated in 2001. The special privacy directive is specifically applicable to the processing of data by public telecommunications networks and services. With the implementation of these two directives in, respectively, the (future) Data Protection Act[71] and the Telecommunications Act, national privacy law has largely become European in nature.

---

69 Directive 95/46/EC on the protection of individuals with regard to the processing of personal data and on the free movement of such data (*OJ* EC L 281).

70 Directive 97/66/EC of 15 December 1997 concerning the processing of personal data and the protection of privacy in the telecommunications sector (*OJ* EC L 24).

71 This act (*Wet bescherming persoonsgegevens*) was enacted in July 2000 (*Staatsblad* 2000, 302) and will come into force in the beginning of 2001. *(Editors)*

The general privacy directive[72] assumes complete freedom in the exchange of personal data between a person's country of residence and another member state. The following provisions have been set down on data exchange between EU member states and third countries. Member states may only pass on personal data to a third country if that country offers an adequate level of data protection. This is the case if the data processing meets conditions as to specificity, quality and proportion, transparency, security, and the rights of those registered. If the Commission has determined that a third country has an adequate level of protection, then the exchange of data may not be restricted.

However, the directive also names a number of exceptions to the principle of an adequate protection level.

The privacy directive for the telecoms sector grants rights to subscribers and users of public telecommunications networks and services, as in the matter of forwarding telephone calls to the consumers' connection and direct marketing. It also makes provisions for protection of the lawful interests of subscriber-legal entities by imposing on parties that offer networks and services a general obligation to act with due care and caution in the matter of privacy.

Regulation

Although the rules for privacy are highly European in orientation, this does not detract from the fact that they leave scope for the implementation of European statutory standards by means of self-regulation. The Netherlands is, in particular, a proponent of self-regulation in the telecoms sector, among other things, for data processing for direct marketing purposes.

Self-regulation plays an even more important role in the exchange of data with non-EU member states, since, in the United States in particular, privacy protection largely takes shape via self-regulation in the electronic environment as well. However, this makes it difficult to determine whether there is an adequate level of protection. The general privacy directive takes this into account: the Commission may determine that certain model contracts offer adequate guarantees with a view to privacy. Standard clauses have been formulated in an OECD context with which such guarantees can be built into contracts.

As mentioned above, data exchange with the United States is of particular importance. Extensive negotiations have taken place between the EU and the US about so-called Safe Harbor Principles. These negotiations have brought about a solution: the EU will assume that there is an adequate level of data protection if a US company declares that it will voluntarily adhere to a number of principles formulated by the US government for data protection. The Netherlands feels it is important that the compliance with and enforcement of this agreement is given due consideration.

The foregoing makes it clear that the general directive encourages the development of codes of conduct (such as the standard clauses formulated by the OECD), which might be referred to as co-regulation.

---

[72] I informed you about this in greater detail in my letter dated 9 March 2000.

'Online' is 'offline'
Neither in the general privacy directive nor in the telecoms directive is a distinction made between 'online' and 'offline'. A major focus of the telecoms directive is, naturally, data exchange via the Internet. The negotiations between the EU and the US have also had an important bearing on electronic commerce. Precisely this factor has caused international data traffic to show a strong increase, which has also increased the need for a regulation with the US. This implies that 'online' data traffic has prompted a regulation that would also apply 'offline'.

Enforceability and jurisdiction
The enforceability of the privacy regime is scarcely discussed in the general privacy directive. Conditions are set for the level of compliance, the provision of assistance to citizens who exercise their rights, and compensation for damages. From time to time, the Commission assesses whether the data protection level is still adequate. If, in a concrete case, the protection level in a third country is circumvented, and serious damage threatens as a result, the data exchange may be temporarily suspended.

The question whether the chosen form of self-regulation will result in an adequate implementation of the stipulations of the directive primarily depends on the assessment of whether the enforcement level is adequate.

6.2.2 Barring harmful content

The protection of young persons against harmful content on the Internet has particular attention within the European Union. The Green Paper of the European Commission from 1996 on Illegal and Harmful Content on the Internet, which outlines the problems and suggests possible policy strategies, has led to a resolution of the Telecommunications Council. This led to the European Action Plan to promote a safer use of the Internet, which runs from 1999 to 2002. This action plan provides a good basis for the development of alternatives to legislation and regulations, such as rating and filtering techniques.

The action plan is composed of three lines of action. The first line of action aims to set up an international network of hotlines. This primarily encourages international cooperation, which is a condition for the effectiveness of hotlines on the Internet. Another objective of this line of action is to develop European guidelines for codes of conduct for collaboration between companies. The second line of action encourages the development of internationally compatible rating and filtering systems. This is to lead to, for example, recommendations for international labelling and filtering systems that will observe language and cultural differences, for developing supporting software, improving audit services of producer-labelling of content, and achieving a critical mass among users of these systems. The third line of action aims to increase public awareness. The aim here is to increase the knowledge of users about the dangers of the Internet, in two stages. In the first stage, the effective channels and media will be identified, and the feasibility will be investigated of actions to increase public awareness. The second stage will involve supporting large-scale national initiatives.

Regulation

Dutch policy concerning the offer on the Internet of content that is harmful to young people is currently seeking to join international policy development in this field within organisations such as the OECD and the EU. The members states of the European Union have spoken out in favour of self-regulation and in favour of reticence in enacting legislation to control the problem of harmful and illegal content on the Internet. Support by the Netherlands to the position in favour of giving priority to self-regulation is expressed in the memorandum *Legislation for the Electronic Highways* as well as in the Cabinet memorandum *Not for All Ages. Audio-visual Media and the Protection of Young Persons* (*Niet voor alle leeftijden: audiovisuele media en de bescherming van jeugdigen*).[73]

Existing forms of self-regulation include the hotlines of the NLIP (Netherlands League of Internet Providers) and the founding of the Safe Internet Foundation. The focus of this foundation is a series of security aspects of the Internet, including barring harmful content. It is an alliance of providers of Internet products and services, and government agencies. The intention is that the providers together formulate a package of solutions to increase safety on the Internet. The government participates in this internationally operating organisation.

I feel these are important initiatives that show that it is possible to achieve adequate regulation by means of a good dialogue between government and business and industry. I recognise that protecting youths against taking cognisance of harmful content is an important task of the government. Our choice in favour of self-regulation (or co-regulation) is, in part, based on the fact that international consensus as to which content is harmful is difficult to achieve (see also the discussion of the Cybercrime Convention). National legislation is not very effective.

Enforceability

'Online' enforceability is not without problems, for several reasons. One of these is that it is difficult to determine who is responsible or liable for certain harmful content, because of the hyperlinked structure of websites and the dynamics of websites.

---

[73] In the Netherlands, this system is in line with a legislative proposal to amend, among other laws, the Media Act (*Mediawet*) and the Criminal Code, which aims at protecting juveniles more effectively against audio-visual products deemed harmful to them (TK 1999-2000, 26 841, nos. 1-3).

Part B

Germany, France, the United Kingdom, and the United States

Governments on Internationalisation and ICT Law

The Positions of Germany, France, the United Kingdom, and the United States

Bert-Jaap Koops
Corien Prins
Maurice Schellekens
Serge Gijrath
Eric Schreuders
assisted by Tomas Oudejans

Tilburg University

July 2000

Management Summary

The information society is essentially an international society. This challenges the law, which is still to a large extent nationally-based. How can and should governments regulate information and communications technologies (ICT) and the Internet, given the fundamental influence of internationalisation? This research presents the views on this of the governments of Germany, France, the United Kingdom, and the United States, focusing on a number of general themes and specific issues in private and criminal law. The research was commissioned by the Dutch Ministry of Justice to support their memorandum *Internationalisation and Law in the Information Society* of May 2000. It took place from January through April 2000 by analysing the states' major ICT policy papers and laws and by an international workshop held in Amsterdam[74]. For publication in this book, the research was updated in July 2000.

General themes

Unlike the Dutch government, which published an overall analysis of ICT law in 1998 (*Legislation for the Electronic Highways*), few comprehensive legal policy documents avail in the countries researched; only France has taken a similar effort with its *Policy Paper on the Adaptation of the Legal Framework to the Information Society* of October 1999, which is to lead to a legislative proposal in 2001.

Nevertheless, the general treatment of ICT law in view of internationalisation in Germany, France, the UK, and the US is roughly the same. This holds, for instance, for the first general theme researched, the principle that "what holds offline, should also hold online". This is the basic starting point of Dutch policy. It is also explicitly mentioned in the policy of the UK, whereas it can be inferred implicitly from the policy documents and laws of France and Germany. However, in recent times, the adage has been put under pressure, because legislative initiatives on several specific issues show that it is not always followed. Increasingly, certain interests – such as consumer protection, legal certainty, stimulating electronic commerce – call for specific rules for the online world that differ from those in the offline world. This tendency is also mirrored at the international level, e.g., in the European Union.

It is true that the adage "what holds offline, should also hold online" was a useful concept in the 'early days' of ICT law (in the mid-1990s), when it had to be made clear that the Internet was not a legal vacuum. Now, however, it appears rather a romantic, outdated concept. The complexity of the matter proves that the problems in the online

---

74 A report of the workshop is presented in Appendix IV.

world differ from those in the offline world. Therefore, it is unwise to take as a starting point the concrete rules of the offline world when thinking about regulating the online world. Rather, the levels of protection should be the same in both worlds (as US policy documents mention). Governments should pay more attention to the interests and goals underlying the rules of the offline and online worlds. The question is *why* we have certain rules in the offline world, and *why* such rules should be maintained online. But rather than rely on transposing traditional rules or principles, governments had better forget the adage and be simply creative in finding solutions to the specific problems of the online world. One must also bear in mind the possibility that the adage "what holds offline, should also hold online" may be turned into its reverse: "what holds online, should also hold offline". Thus, the legislature must view the relationship between offline rules and online rules as an interactive one.

The second general theme of this research is self-regulation. The Dutch government has appeared a fervent advocate of self-regulation mechanisms in solving legal uncertainty about the consequences of cross-border electronic communications. In choosing self-regulation, the government hopes to create sufficient flexibility in a time of technological and societal turbulence. Also, self-regulation is, in principle, not bound by borders. Nevertheless, government regulation is still the starting point if fundamental values of the rule of law are at stake – the Dutch government here refers to the classic fundamental civil rights, to preventing and investigating breaches of the rule of law and of state security, as well as to consumer protection, privacy, and the issue of applicable law.

The research shows that self-regulation is likewise a central theme in the various policy documents of the countries as well as of international organisations. Also, more or less the same issues are mentioned when it comes to a preference for government intervention (in particular, fundamental rights and values, consumer protection, law and order, state security).

Despite the broad support for self-regulation, there is a remarkable tendency in all countries. Whereas the governments used to take the point of view that government intervention was, in principle, undesirable and that the market should lead, there is increasing awareness that governments cannot restrict themselves to merely stimulating; shaping e-commerce policy and Internet policy is a task for government and market together. 'Co-regulation' is a term that appears prominently in many recent policy documents. Even in the US, the general opinion seems to tend to a view that the government should play a more guiding role than formerly in shaping the policy. One must bear in mind, however, that the term 'co-regulation' is not interpreted the same way in the various countries. The interpretation depends to a large extent on legislative and cultural traditions. When governments talk about co-regulation, they are therefore prone to talk about different things.

In thinking about the necessity of government intervention, it may be useful to distinguish between regulation that aims at answering practical questions ("Can I use a digital signature to make a transaction?") and regulation that aims at influencing behaviour ("Don't use encryption that hampers law enforcement!"). The first kind of regulation is generally called for and welcomed by the market, whereas the second kind is generally not favoured.

When deciding both what rules should apply in the online world and what level of regulation is most appropriate to shape these rules, the enforcement of the resulting rules is of crucial importance. Especially in an international context, enforcement of regulation is a problematic issue. This, then, is a third general theme that pervades ICT law.

In the policy documents, the question of how to safeguard enforcement is less prominent than the first two general themes. Although governments have put considerable thought to the necessity and options of ensuring enforcement of ICT law in the international context, so far, they have not put forward ideas about an integral approach to enforcement. They simply look for the best approach in each given case, which is in line with the Dutch pragmatic approach in this matter. It is also remarkable that there are few concrete ideas about how to address at an international level those issues generally considered to be potentially difficult to enforce in an international context, such as tax law, privacy, and cryptography. This finding has led the Dutch government to propose in the ILIS Memorandum to stimulate the international academic debate on enforcement, because "international legal developments could use an added boost when it comes to enforceability".

In those areas where the interests to be protected are broadly shared internationally, there will be the best likelihood of an international approach. It is wise to start with small domains on which there is more agreement, e.g., in combating child pornography, for which an international network of hotlines is already at work. Constructions of national contact points are the most promising in the short term to address enforcement internationally. In private-law matters, one can think of an international network of ombudspersons or Chambers of Commerce to play a central part in international alternative dispute resolution. In criminal law, for the time being, states concentrate on an international network of national contact points available 24 hours a day and seven days a week to directly deal with and co-ordinate requests for mutual criminal assistance. This network can give an impetus to further-reaching forms of cross-border cooperation.

Specific issues

Besides these general themes, we researched four specific issues, two in criminal law and two in private law.

The first issue in criminal law is double criminality, which is usually required for mutual assistance in criminal matters. In the memorandum *Legislation for the Electronic Highways*, the Dutch government suggested that this requirement could perhaps be dropped under certain conditions in cases where a state requests another state to provide information in order to be able to follow a digital trace.

There is no indication that other countries think about abandoning the requirement of double criminality. It is true that it is discussed within the Council of Europe, but overall, their draft *Convention on Cyber-Crime* (usually referred to as *Crime in Cyberspace*) does not provide an opening to discarding double criminality. Although the text seems to suggest that the requirement must not or need not be absolute, there is no consensus on this among the participating states. Moreover, the abandonment of double criminality as discussed is restricted to *preserving* data in another country; it does not stretch to *providing* those data, and so, the requirement will at all counts continue effectively to exist.

Likewise, the discussion at the international workshop did not support relinquishing the requirement of double criminality. The foreign experts appeared astonished rather than stimulated to think about the idea. Double criminality seemed to them to be so fundamental, that there is or should be in fact no possibility to undermine it in any way. As a result of this finding, the Dutch government abandoned the idea in their Internationalisation Memorandum.

Given the fact that abandoning double criminality in any way is not favoured internationally, and because of the fact that in most cases it is hardly realistic to harmonise substantive criminal law, the international fight against ICT crime will have to resort to cooperation between enforcement authorities.

The Dutch government's view on this second issue, cooperation between enforcement authorities, is that there must be rules that ensure effective cooperation, especially to regulate investigation powers aimed at foreign Internet providers and to ensure the cooperation of other states to facilitate investigation. In particular, the government stated in its 1998 memorandum that the draft convention *Crime in Cyberspace* should enable judicial authorities to directly address foreign network providers, without prior mediation of investigation authorities in the country of the network provider. Court supervision could take place afterwards.

The necessity of closer cooperation between enforcement authorities is recognised in the other countries. Governments acknowledge that to achieve this, traditional mutual assistance will have to be adapted drastically. They see this primarily as a problem for which solutions have to be found at an international level. Therefore, this issue is discussed mainly in international platforms; on the national level, no conclusive steps are taken before the results of the international discussions become clear.

At a national level, states restrict themselves to short-term measures, like establishing continuously accessible contact points, and to other means available within the present legal framework. The Dutch desire to make it easier to gain access to foreign data seems to be in line with the thinking in other countries, but foreign governments have not yet published positions about the specific desire to get data directly from foreign Internet providers.

Moreover, the draft convention *Crime in Cyberspace* of the Council of Europe does not contain a proposal to this effect. It does propose a new investigation power: a preservation order to telecoms or Internet providers that can be easily given and that safeguards the availability of the data pending the exercise of other investigation powers, such as a search and 'seizure' of data. However, for preserving data stored in another state, authorities will still have to make a traditional request for criminal assistance – a request addressed to foreign providers directly was turned down in the draft convention.

The first specific issue in private law we researched is the topic of private international law in international online contracts. The Dutch government attaches great value to clarifying the rules of private international law. The Dutch government favours establishing a broadly formulated framework of private international law rules that apply to online contracts within the framework of the Hague Conference on Private International Law.

For the time being, this view does not seem to be shared in the countries we researched. In the US, the issue does not seem to play a part in policy-making at the federal level (one should bear in mind that in the US, the issue of applicable law to online contracts can be addressed at the state level). For Germany and the UK, we did not find government positions on this, whereas France has formulated a different position. The European countries seem to want to tie in with the existing rules of the (European) Rome and Brussels Conventions. The Netherlands, then, is leaning more towards a global solution than the other countries. One should note, however, that this approach does not seem to work out particularly smoothly. At a meeting in Ottawa in February 2000, it appeared scarcely realistic to agree upon a draft for adapting the Hague Conference.

The second issue in private law is civil liability of Internet providers. In Dutch law, tort law is sufficiently technology-independent for the government to be able to leave it to the courts to develop this issue. Still, the government supports the European Commission in trying to establish common principles at an international level in order to create a level playing field. However, the Dutch government is not happy with the outcome of provider liability in the E-Commerce Directive. In particular, the Minister of Justice questions the clarity of the distinction between the various categories of service providers (access, caching, and hosting providers). Moreover, he doubts the prudence of excluding in advance access providers from liability regardless of whether they had knowledge of unlawful content.

An analysis of the civil-liability position of Internet providers in the other countries shows that the material criteria used are similar: for instance, involvement with the content, knowledge, and due care. Providers who are involved with the content are fully liable, while those who are not are only liable if they do not conform with duties of care. In some countries, the latter category is further divided into access providers and hosting providers. Generally, (non-content) providers are only liable for illegal content of which they have knowledge, with two exceptions. In Sweden, providers have a pro-active duty to check material; since they can comply with this requirement by establishing a hotline, there is no obligation of result but only one of effort. A second exception is the categorical exclusion, regardless of knowledge, of access providers in the German and European regulations. Finally, a duty of care for service providers encountered everywhere is to remove or block access to illegal content as soon as they gain knowledge of it, at least as far as they are reasonably able to.

It is generally recognised that Internet service providers have a special role and responsibility to identify content providers. This may also stretch to preparatory measures like preserving data and verifying the identity of new subscribers. However, most governments are still struggling to find a balance between this requirement and the resulting infringement of privacy regulations.

There is sufficient room for regulating provider liability within each national state. However, to prevent major differences between the national regulations (which could impede international e-commerce), international harmonisation is called for, hence the regulation in the European E-Commerce Directive.

As to the international problems of illegal content – addressing content that is illegal in a country but that is hosted abroad – the general position of governments is one of reserve. States do not view provider liability a good way to address this (it is interesting to note that Australia and Singapore are exceptions to this, with regulations that put obligations on national providers with respect to content hosted abroad). For the time being, states take recourse to stimulating international cooperation between private-sector hotlines.

Conclusions

The findings of the research suggest that several distinctions and trade-offs are relevant to creating ICT-law policies.

- **Offline – online**: the adage "what holds offline, should also hold online", a useful concept in the early days of ICT law, appears to be no longer generally applicable. It is still relevant in relation to the interests and the level of protection that underlie the regulatory systems of the offline and online worlds, but rather than focusing on transposing the offline rule system to the online world, governments should focus on the specificity of the problems in the online world.
- **Government regulation – self-regulation**: the general preference for self-regulation that until recently pervaded thinking about ICT law is generally giving way to a preference for co-regulation, since governments have come to the conclusion that safeguarding crucial interests and legal certainty calls for a more prominent role of governments. This new balance between government and market regulation is termed co-regulation everywhere, but the specific interpretation of this term varies per country. Some countries put more stress on the government side, and others on the market side, largely because of their cultural and legislative traditions. This influences, among others, the choice of a voluntary or an obligatory enforcement mechanism. From an international perspective, it is important to be aware of the variation in the views on co-regulation and in the underlying national values.
- **Overall principles – specific solutions**: governments had better concentrate on tailoring solutions to each specific issue that requires regulation rather than try to define general guidelines and principles for the broad field of ICT law. General principles (such as an overall preference for self-regulation and "offline = online") do injustice to the specific problems of all the various issues. In order to make clear the government position in international platforms, it may be useful to define certain general positions that mirror national interests and traditions, but this holds the risk that national governments stick to their general position as outlined, and thus hamper the search for a creative solution. It is more important in international platforms for governments to have an open attitude that is sympathetic to other valid approaches and principles.
- **Answering – steering:** conceptually, one can distinguish between regulations that primarily try to answer practical questions in order to create legal certainty (e.g., "can I use a digital signature to sign a contract?") and regulations that aim at influencing behaviour (e.g., "do not use encryption that hampers investigation"). With 'answering

issues', the addressees, in principle, care less about the particular outcome as long as a choice is made by the government, whereas with 'steering issues', addressees have a clear preference for a particular outcome. It is true that regulation is never completely answering or completely steering, but in most cases, there is an emphasis on one side or the other. This affects the likelihood of compliance, the enforcement options, and thus the effectiveness of the regulation. In the short term, primarily answering regulations are called for in order to establish legal certainty, whereas more steering regulation should only be undertaken once it has become sufficiently clear what 'steering goals' are envisioned and what are the best means to achieve those goals.

- **Top-down – bottom-up**: certain topics, such as Internet-provider liability and electronic signatures, are essentially national issues that can be addressed at a national level; given the fact of internationalisation, however, these national regulations must be made internationally consistent, which is done at an international level. The resulting interaction between national and international actions is not always optimal, because states sometimes at an early stage create national legislation that significantly diverges from solutions proposed internationally.

  Other topics call for an international approach by definition, such as private international law for online contracts and cross-border criminal investigation. In these areas, policies are made nearly only at the international level, which holds the risk that national governments do not publish their opinions and do not trigger a national debate on these topics. This can also hamper the interaction between national and international policy-making. Both the primarily bottom-up issues and the primarily top-down issues, then, call upon governments to be more aware of the international dimension of the policies under discussion, and to optimise the interaction between national and international policy-making.

What conclusions can be drawn from this analysis? We discern a desire for a uniform approach of the various problems, but at the same time a need to be aware of the specific dynamics of each issue, the range of interests involved, and the variety of cultural and legislative national traditions. In short, there must be variety in unity.

This means that in various areas, international agreement can be problematic. The creative approach that is needed implies in the first place a search for areas where the interests are mutual and where it is relatively easy to reach agreement. Once governments agree upon the major points in such areas, topics could be addressed where the positions diverge more. The broad field of ICT law must thus be addressed slowly, step by step.

It is of primary importance that each issue is indeed addressed from an *international* perspective. Our research indicates that the thinking about ICT law is still taking place to a large extent from a national perspective. This is not surprising in the light of the 'growing-up' of ICT law, but it is undesirable to keep the international perspective out of sight any longer. Questions of internationalisation are so intrinsic to policy-making in the area of ICT law, that the national and international perspectives cannot do without each other.

We think the time has come to take the next step in regulating the information society. Five years ago, policy concentrated on addressing national problems. Now that this approach is well on its way, it is time to include the international dimension of the problems. Although governments currently proclaim that policies must be made internationally consistent, our analysis shows that in reality, few things come off the ground, and that it is often noted that problems should first take shape at a national level. There are many initiatives by international organisations, but these have yielded few concrete results so far. In short, both at the national and at the international level, there is little effective progress in policy-making from the perspective of internationalisation.

Governments should therefore urge the international community to structurally pay attention to the perspective of internationalisation in all the platforms that discuss ICT-law issues. Also, governments should make a case for better fine-tuning the policy-making in all the various international bodies and platforms. In order to facilitate the international discussions in which they take part, the formulation of general principles that support the national positioning, such as the Dutch working principles of the ILIS Memorandum, may be useful, but these can be no more than starting points for discussion. First and foremost, and even more so than with traditional legal topics, governments should have a flexible and particularly open attitude that is sympathetic to all the subtleties of the issue at stake and to the variety of national positions that are intrinsic to the internationalisation problems in ICT law.

The final conclusion is that governments should incorporate the international dimension more explicitly in the national and international policy-making in the field of ICT law. ICT law has by now outgrown the infancy stage of general starting points and national interim solutions. A grown-up ICT law calls for structurally incorporating the perspective of internationalisation.

Foreword

This study was commissioned and financed by the Dutch Ministry of Justice (WODC Research and Documentation Center) and the National Programme for Information Technology and Law (*ITeR*). It is a comparative-law research that supported the Dutch Ministry of Justice in writing the memorandum *Internationalisation and Law in the Information Society* (hereafter: ILIS Memorandum), which was presented to the Dutch Parliament in May 2000 as a follow-up of the 1998 memorandum *Legislation for the Electronic Highways* (hereafter: LEH Memorandum). This research is a follow-up of the study *Netiquette of Wetiquette (Netiquette or Legiquette)*, which Tilburg University wrote in 1997 to support the LEH Memorandum.[75]

This research aims at presenting a bird's eye view of the opinions of foreign governments on the most important themes in the area of ICT law in the light of internationalisation. Given the brief period of executing the research (January through April 2000) and the broad field of research, we have in some ways restricted its scope.

First, after consulting the Ministry of Justice, we have restricted the research to the four countries the most relevant for the Netherlands in developing a national policy in line with international positions: Germany, France, the United Kingdom, and the United States. Yet in order to meet interesting developments in the area of ICT law in countries such as Sweden, Singapore, and Australia, which can be equally relevant for developing an internationally consistent ICT-law policy, with some subjects, we have paid attention to the positions and developments in these other countries, especially when these differ from the positions and developments found in the four countries of the research.

Second, the scope of the research has been restricted in terms of subject matter. By mutual agreement with the Ministry of Justice, we have chosen to research the three most important general themes of the LEH Memorandum: the adage 'online = offline', self-regulation, and enforcement. These general themes affect all the subjects in ICT law that call for policy-making. In order to see how these themes influence specific subjects, we have chosen to study four 'Selected Topics' that the Ministry of Justice found most interesting: double criminality, cooperation between criminal-law enforcement authorities, private international law for online contracts, and civil liability of Internet providers.

Third, the research is limited in depth: it has the character of a quick scan. We have restricted ourselves to the positions of governments in official policy documents and the main current or proposed legislation in the area of ICT law. For the countries with a federal structure (US, Germany), we have restricted ourselves to the federal government.

---

75 Van der Hof a.o. 1997.

As commissioned, this research emphasises the positions of *national* governments on ICT law. This is connected with the Ministry of Justice's desire to get to know the most important national positions on various issues, in order to enable Dutch representatives in international negotiations and meetings to gear their positioning towards these points of view. As a result, this research focuses on the positions of the governments of Germany, France, the United Kingdom, and the United States. In a way, that misrepresents reality, since much ICT law and policy are developed and harmonised in international platforms and by international organisations. Therefore, we start each subject by indicating the most important developments in international organisations, which provides a frame of reference for the positions of the national governments that follow.

The research was executed by analysing documentation and by means of an international workshop. The analysis was based on the official policy documents, legislation, and case-law, as they can be found at the various websites of the countries and bodies researched, as well as on articles and reports in the literature (including *Computer und Recht*, *The Computer Law & Security Report*, *Computer and Telecommunications Law Review*, and *Electronic Commerce and Law Report*). This research was supported by correspondents from France and the United Kingdom, who filled in a complete questionnaire about the research issues, and by correspondents from Germany and the United States, who provided further information on specific issues.

Preliminary research results were tested at an international workshop organised by the researchers on 29 March 2000 in Amsterdam. Twenty-one experts in the area of ICT law and ICT policy participated. During the workshop, the three general themes and selected topics in civil and criminal law were discussed. Subsequently, the workshop results were incorporated in this study. Also, where relevant, we have explicitly mentioned the results of the workshop as such in this report, because the participants' expertise warrants using the workshop conclusions as an independent source. The report and the list of participants of the workshop are included in Appendix IV.

We have been assisted by a monitoring committee, which discussed and commented on the research results in two meetings. We thank the members of this committee for their contributions, which were valuable and helpful for writing the final report. We also thank Simone van der Hof for her comments and help.

The original research was done from 1 January to 30 April 2000 for the report in Dutch.[76] For publication in this book, we have translated and updated the report, finalising the research in July 2000. All translations from non-English language documents are ours.

[76] The Dutch report is published in volume 39 of the *ITeR* series, Den Haag: Sdu. It is also available at <http://rechten.kub.nl/crbi/rapport.pdf>.

1. Introduction

1.1 The development of ICT law

In a short period, the electronic highway has conquered the (Western) world. While in the early 1990s, few people had heard of email or the Internet, hardly ten years later, these technologies have become institutionalised and common-place. It is hard yet to grasp the influence of this on society, but it is certain that the world with an electronic highway is, in various ways, functioning differently from the world of ten years ago. This affects the law.

Together with the rise of information and communications technologies (ICT) and the electronic highway, ICT law has also grown. While various areas of the law have tried to keep pace with the developments in ICT since the 1970s, in the 1990s, it was recognised that the rise of ICT and the electronic highway also have a more fundamental influence on the law as a whole. After all, ICT affects all aspects of social life, and thus, ICT cuts right through all the traditional branches of law. As a result, the question arose how the law as a whole should react to these developments. In 1998, the Dutch Cabinet tried to answer this question with the memorandum *Legislation for the Electronic Highways* (LEH Memorandum); this was followed up in May 2000 by a more specific memorandum on internationalisation, *Internationalisation and Law in the Information Society* (ILIS Memorandum). Other countries as well have extensively dwelt upon the problems that ICT developments pose for the law.

In answering ICT-law questions, one has to take into account the strong internationalising effects of ICT – the electronic highway is pre-eminently a cross-border affair. This directly results in jurisdiction questions: which law applies to acts that stretch across several jurisdictions at a time, without it being clear in advance on which territory 'Cyberspace acts' take place? And how is one to reconcile this with the fact that divergent national rules offer differing levels of legal protection? The aspects of internationalisation are therefore intrinsically related to ICT law, and governments that took it upon themselves to create ICT law have always realised this.

Nevertheless, in truly answering concrete ICT-law questions, governments have not always taken the aspect of internationalisation into account. Often, the problem was already sufficiently hard to solve in the national context of the national law, so that little room was left for developing ideas about the international dimension of the problem. For many issues in the area of ICT law, this has resulted in a primary focus of attention on the national context.

In the long term, that is not a practicable situation. ICT law that is formed primarily within the national context will meet with problems in the international ICT society. Diverging national rules result in differences in legal protection and in differing conditions for electronic commerce, which is at great odds with the broadly shared desire to develop an international market for electronic commerce.

Therefore, ICT law should not be shaped primarily within the national context, but within the international context. This does not mean that ICT law can only be formed at the international level, but rather, it means that governments, in making ICT law, must truly take into account the international context in which the object of the regulation will have to thrive.

1.2 Objective and structure

In this study, we look at how various governments adopt the perspective of internationalisation when they think about and shape ICT law. The objective of this study is to provide a bird's eye view of the positions of the governments of Germany, France, the United Kingdom, and the United States on the most important themes in the area of ICT law in the light of internationalisation.

As a framework for this study, in the remainder of this chapter, we indicate the main lines of the countries' government policies on ICT law, as they have been laid down in official policy documents and legislation.

Next, in the first part of this study, we outline ideas on three overall themes that affect the entire field of ICT law: the question whether the rules of the 'traditional' world or rather different ones should apply to the electronic highway (chapter 2), the shaping of these rules and the role of self-regulation (chapter 3), and the question how one can safeguard the enforcement of these rules (chapter 4). These general themes indicate what starting points or frameworks governments determine or envision for ICT law in general.

In the second part of this study, we follow some 'Selected Topics' of ICT law, both in criminal law and civil law: the requirement of double criminality (chapter 5) and the cooperation between criminal-law enforcement authorities (chapter 6), and, subsequently, private international law for online contracts (chapter 7) and civil liability of Internet providers (chapter 8). These specific subjects indicate how the envisioned general starting points and frameworks are satisfied in reality with concrete problems.

The study concludes with a summary and conclusions (chapter 9).

1.3 Germany on ICT law and ICT policy

In Germany, the first steps in developing a legislative policy on the electronic highway were taken in 1996 with the publication of the report *Info 2000: Deutschland's Weg in die Informationsgesellschaft* (*Info 2000: Germany's Way into the Information Society*; hereafter: Info 2000 report).[77] Already in this report, the German government pointed out the necessity of an international legal framework for the problems. Subsequently, the German government set forth policy plans regarding multimedia in the policy memorandum *Multimedia möglich machen. Deutschland's Weg in die Wissensgesellschaft* (*Enabling Multimedia. Germany's Way into the Knowledge Society*)[78] of February 1998, by the Federal Ministry of Education, Science, Research and Technology.

A direct consequence of the plans launched in the Info 2000 report was the federal government's Multimedia Act, *Gesetz zur Regelung der Rahmenbedingungen für Informations- und Kommunikationsdienste (IuKDG)* (*Law to Regulate the Framework Conditions for Information and Communications Services*),[79] that entered into force largely on 1 August 1997. This act regulates several issues as a framework act, including teleservices and ISP liability (*Teledienstegesetz* (*Teleservices Act*), art. 1), the protection of personal data in teleservices (*Teledienstedatenschutzgesetz* (*Teleservices Data Protection Act*), art. 2), and digital signatures (*Gesetz zur digitalen Signatur* (*Digital Signatures Act*), art. 3); also, it adapts existing legislation. Besides, the German *Länder* have concluded a *Mediendienste-Staatsvertrag* (*MDStV*) (*Interstate Media Services Treaty*), in force since 1 August 1997, that regulates the (broadcasting) media services.

Like the German government had already announced, the IuKDG was evaluated in 1999. It appeared that there was no reason to fundamentally adapt the IuKDG. Except for some points, the federal government was satisfied with the effect of the legislative policy regarding the electronic highway.

The next step was taken in the middle of 1999: the Action Programme *Innovation und Arbeitsplätze in der Informationsgesellschaft des 21. Jahrhunderts* (*Innovation and Job Opportunities in the 21st Century Information Society*).[80] In this programme, the federal government lays down the ambition to bring about a single legal regulatory framework for telecommunications means, media, and teleservices. Various current laws (besides the *IuKDG*, the *Interstate Media Services Treaty*, and the *Telekommunikationsgesetz* (*Telecommunications Act*)) will have to be included partially or entirely in this regulatory framework.

Specifically, in light of the central theme of this study, internationalisation, it is worth mentioning that on 31 May 2000, the German government approved an amendment of the Digital Signatures Act. One of the prime reasons for amending the Act was the desire to bring it more in line with the international dimension of the issue.[81]

77 BMWi 1996.

78 BMBF 1999.

79 See <http://www.iid.de/rahmen/iukdgebt.html>. An English version is available at <http://www.kuner.com/data/reg/multimd3.htm>.

80 Bundesregierung 1999.

81 See <http://www.iid.de/iukdg/gesetz/pressesigvo.html>.

1.4 France on ICT law and ICT policy

On 25 August 1997, Prime Minister Jospin announced a French government action plan on the information society,[82] which was published subsequently in January 1998: the *Programme d'Action Gouvernemental pour la Société de l'Information* (PAGSI) (*Government Program for the Information Society*).[83] The action programme intends, among other things, to promote an efficient regulation and development of a protective framework for the information society. A year later, the progress of the action programme was discussed in the *Comité Interministériel pour la Société de l'Information* (CISI, the Interministerial Committee for the Information Society), in which positions were taken or accentuated in various areas.[84] In the meantime, in July 1998, the Conseil d'Etat (State Council) had published an extensive opinion on regulation for electronic highways: *Internet et les résaux numériques* (*The Internet and Digital Networks*).[85] The Ministry of Economic Affairs paid specific attention to electronic commerce in the January 1998 Lorentz report,[86] in the addendum to this of March 1998,[87] and in its evaluation of a year later.[88] Also, it made proposals for a legal framework for e-commerce.

After formulating these policy starting points and policy intentions, the government published an overall consultation document in November 1999, which is to lead to a legislation proposal on the information society: *Une société de l'information pour tous. Adaptation du cadre législatif de la société de l'information. Document d'orientation soumis à consultation publique* (*Policy Paper on the Adaptation of the Legal Framework to the Information Society*).[89] The legislation proposal would have to have three pillars: clarifying everyone's rights and duties, democratising access to the information society, and ensuring security and trust in electronic transactions. The government intends to present the proposal to the Council of Ministers in the autumn of 2000 and to parliament in early 2001. Meanwhile, another important document has been published by MP Christian Paul as a result of the government's initiatives to establish a 'co-regulation organism' (*organisme de corégulation*).[90] In this report of June 2000, Christian Paul proposes to establish an Internet Rights Forum (*Forum des Droits sur l'internet*) in order to stimulate an open debate on how to regulate the Internet at a national and a global level.[91]

Finally, it is worth mentioning that the French government has established a website specifically for the action programme on the information society: <www.internet.gouv.fr>, which gives an overview of the various government actions in this area.

---

82 Jospin 1997.

83 PAGSI 1998.

84 CISI 1999.

85 Conseil d'Etat 1998.

86 Lorentz 1998a.

87 Lorentz 1998b.

88 Lorentz 1999.

89 Strauss Kahn a.o. 1999.

90 See <http://www.internet.gouv.fr/francais/textesref/pagsi2/lsi/rapportcpaul/rapcpaul2intro.htm>.

91 Paul 2000.

1.5 The United Kingdom on ICT law and ICT policy

The British government published their policy intentions on the information society and the Internet in 1998. The policy document *Our Information Age. The Government's Vision* sets forth the government's ideas on a coordinated strategy for the information age, in order to enhance the UK's competitive power and to ensure quality, among other things.[92] Subsequently, the Minister for Science, Energy and Industry John Battle explained once again the government's strategy on the Internet in a speech to the House of Commons of 18 March 1998.[93] He formulated four principles for regulating the Internet: law should apply online as it does offline, international cooperation is vital, businesses and consumers should have access to tools that enable them to protect themselves, and service providers should take voluntary action to uphold the law online. Following this, the government collected and summarised their policy for the information age on a website, *The Government's policy for the information age* <http://www.isi.gov.uk/isi/infosoc/govpolicy.htm>,[94] while an E-Minister, Patricia Hewitt,[95] and an E-Envoy, Alex Allan,[96] have been appointed as well.

Besides the overall policy for the information age, the British government has above all things stressed electronic commerce, particularly in the report *E-commerce@its.best.uk*, which provides a strategy to "make the UK the world's best environment for electronic commerce".[97] This resulted in the submission in late 1999 of a Bill with a legal framework for electronic commerce, the *Electronic Communications Bill*. The House of Commons passed the bill in amended form, and on 25 May 2000, it received Royal Assent as the Electronic Communications Act 2000.[98]

Besides, it is worth mentioning that already in July 1996, long before the government formulated its policy, the British House of Lords had drawn up an Agenda for Action on the information society, in which various policy proposals were made.[99] The British House of Commons examined information-society policy in 1999.[100]

1.6 The United States on ICT law and ICT policy

The United States government have not published policy documents on the electronic highway or the Internet; instead, they have concentrated on electronic-commerce policy.

92 Blair 1998.
93 Battle 1998.
94 ISI 1999.
95 See <http://www.e-envoy.gov.uk/2000/strategy/workstreams/programme_management/e-minister.htm>.
96 See <http://www.e-envoy.gov.uk>.
97 Cabinet Office 1999.
98 See <http://www.legislation.hmso.gov.uk/acts/acts2000/20000007.htm>.
99 House of Lords 1996.
100 House of Commons 1999.

On 1 July 1997, President Clinton and Vice-President Gore presented the policy memorandum *A Framework for Global Electronic Commerce*,[101] together with a *Presidential Directive*.[102] Both in this memorandum and in the FCC report *Digital Tornado: The Internet and Telecommunications Policy*,[103] which also appeared in 1997, the US government opts for a non-regulatory, market-oriented approach to electronic commerce that fosters a transparent and predictable legal environment. Important starting points for this are a leading role for the private sector and, in the words of the Framework, a "predictable, minimalist, consistent and simple legal environment for commerce".

As to the theme of internationalisation, the policy memorandum indicated that electronic commerce should be stimulated on a world-wide basis, while the legal framework must consist of principles that yield internationally predictable results, regardless of the jurisdiction to which parties belong.

In 1998, various government organisations published reports and plans on issues in the area of ICT law. For example, the Department of Commerce issued the report *The Emerging Digital Economy*,[104] and the National Science Foundation published the programme *Digital Government*.[105]

On 29 November 1999, over two years after publishing the *Framework*, President Clinton ordered setting up an Electronic Commerce Advisory Group, a sub-group of the US Government Working Group on Electronic Commerce. This advisory group has the task of identifying legal barriers that impede the further growth of electronic commerce. President Clinton emphasised the necessity of creating a uniform approach to legislative measures. Besides commissioning the advisory group "to discuss ways to ensure that public interest protections for online transactions will be equivalent to those now provided for off-line transactions", The president also provided the advisory group with three central starting points for making recommendations: "technological neutrality, minimise legal and regulatory barriers to electronic commerce; and take into account cross-border transactions that are now likely to occur electronically."[106]

Whereas these documents all concentrate on electronic-commerce policy, more recently, the concept of 'electronic government' has also gained attention. On 24 June 2000, President Clinton and Vice-President Gore unveiled a series of E-Government initiatives. One of these will make it possible for US people to go online and bid on, or apply for, the vast majority of the contracts that the government yearly awards.[107]

Although ICT law and ICT policy in the US are to a large extent left to the market, the regulatory framework is nonetheless also shaped by some important laws, such as the Telecommunications Act 1996, the Electronic Signatures in Global and National Commerce Act of 2000, and, not in the least, several Amendments of the Constitution.

---

101 Clinton & Gore 1997.
102 Clinton 1997.
103 FCC 1997.
104 Department of Commerce 1998.
105 See <http://www.nsf.gov/pubs/1998/nsf98121/nsf98121.htm>.
106 White House 1999.
107 See <http://www.whitehouse.gov/WH/New/html/e-government.html>.

1.7 Overview of governments on ICT law and ICT policy

From the policy documents indicated above, one can distil a rough picture of the overall view on ICT law and ICT policy in each country, and of the goals and the strategy of each government. In almost all the documents, electronic commerce is emphasised, for which a regulatory framework should be developed. In Appendix I, we indicate these aspects for each country.

Part I – General Themes

2. The Relationship between Offline and Online

2.1 Introduction

On several occasions, the Dutch government has stated that in discussions on how to regulate developments like electronic commerce, the Internet, and, more in general, the electronic highway, the leitmotiv should be: "what holds offline, should in principle also hold online." In the LEH Memorandum, the Cabinet puts it thus in relation to internationalisation: "In the first place, the Cabinet chooses as a starting point that the norms that hold for the electronic highway must be the same as the norms in the physical world."[108] In some situations, however, this starting point can not be met. For example, in situations in which the traditional legal provisions for the physical world result in problems when they are applied to an electronic environment, one will have to consider whether other rules have to apply. Besides, existing and future European and international agreements sometimes do not leave room for maintaining the adage.[109] Thus, the desire to create an international approach to certain ICT-related problems will result in different rules applying for the offline and the online worlds.[110]

Two years after the publication of the LEH Memorandum, the Dutch government appears to have developed a less stringent view on the leitmotiv. Various developments have shown that one should also look at the differences between the offline and online worlds.[111] In light of these developments, the Dutch government, in its most recent policy paper, recognises that applying the 'online = offline' approach is no longer a realistic way to go forward. Instead, the starting point should be that the same norms must apply in the online world as in the offline world.[112]

---

108 LEH Memorandum, p. 114.

109 See, for instance, the Minister of Justice's answer to questions by the standing committee on judicial affairs in TK 1999-2000, 26 538, no. 2, p. 5.

110 LEH Memorandum, p. 114.

111 ILIS Memorandum, section 2.3.

112 ILIS Memorandum, section 2.3.

2.2 International organisations

Insofar as international organisations and platforms pay attention to the relationship between offline and online, they generally have the position that the online world is not a new, separate world. Thus, in principle, the same norms apply in the online world as in the offline world. This finding is confirmed by the various policy plans at an international level: in formulating these plans, the rules that hold in the offline world are taken as the starting point.[113] It is only for the purpose of certain interests (such as legal certainty) that further rules may be made. A recent confirmation of this view can be found in the *Okinawa Charter on Global Information Society* issued by the Group of Eight (G8) at their Kyushu-Okinawa summit in July 2000. The charter expressly refers to the view when talking about consumer trust in the electronic marketplace. It is considered a key approach "to provide equivalent consumer protection in the online world as in the offline world".[114]

Nevertheless, practice shows that this approach is abandoned at an international level when it comes to shaping certain policy priorities. A clear example is the European Electronic Commerce Directive, which sets specific rules for the online world in order to promote the common market for electronic commerce (possibly even to the detriment of commerce in the offline world).

2.3 Germany

The initial position of the Dutch government can not be found in the German policy documents as such. Still, from the approach proposed in the various policy documents, one could infer that the adage is generally supported in Germany. An example is the recent, gigantic legislative project to adapt form requirements in private law, in order to facilitate modern business.[115] The project aims at adapting each and every form requirement through the 'functional approach': first analyse what is the function of the form requirement in traditional legal matters, and then look at how one can fulfil the same function with electronic means.

Looking at the IuKDG, however, one discovers that when it comes to the regulation of concrete topics, in the online world, other rules apply than in the traditional world. An example of this is section 5 Teleservices Act, which privileges certain Internet providers above traditional press intermediaries.

---

[113] See also Den Haan 1998, p. 30.

[114] G8 2000.

[115] *Gesetz zur Anpassung der Formvorschriften des Privatrechts und anderer Vorschriften an den modernen Rechtsgeschäftsverkehr. Referentenentwurf* (*Pre-draft Act on the Adaptation of Form Requirements in Private Law and Other Requirements to Modern Legal Business Matters*), 5 June 2000, <http://www.bmj.bund.de/ggv/ggv010.pdf>.

2.4 France

Even though the French government has never formulated the starting point "what holds offline, should also hold online" as such, it can actually be inferred from various remarks in the policy documents. For instance, the State Council observes the following in the report *The Internet and Digital Networks*, which dates from 2 July 1998: "First, contrary to what one hears sometimes, the total of existing legislation applies to Internet actors", continuing that this holds particularly for consumer protection and aspects of public interest. In short, "There does not exist and there is no need whatsoever for a law specific to the Internet and networks."[116]

Even so, the government also recognises that for the protection of certain interests (consumer interests and dealing with illegal and harmful content are mentioned), specific rules might have to be introduced.[117]

2.5 United Kingdom

The British government has explicitly expressed the position "what holds online, should also hold offline" in *Her Majesty's Government Strategy for the Internet* of 18 March 1998. It is mentioned as the first of the four starting points in the UK policy: "First, existing law should apply on-line as it does off-line. With very few exceptions where this is not possible, this is already the case in the UK."[118]

Likewise, the importance of this position in cross-border situations is pointed out: "Neutrality between trade carried out on-line and off-line should be the key principle underpinning any future consideration of the relationship between electronic commerce and international trade".[119]

In various documents, the general position is further accentuated in concrete topics. For example, the English Data Registrar indicated: "although the application of the technologies involved in e-commerce are new the data protection issues which arise are not. The provisions of the Data Protection Acts 1984 and 1998 apply to the processing of personal data on-line as much as off-line".[120]

Nonetheless, it also appears here that this starting point can not always be maintained. The Electronic Communications Act 2000, for instance, which implements elements of the European Directives on electronic signatures, distance selling, and e-commerce, shows that in-

116 "Tout d'abord, contrairement à ce que l'on entend parfois, l'ensemble de la législation existante s'applique aux acteurs d'Internet". "Il n'existe pas et il n'est nul besoin d'un droit spécifique de l'Internet et des réseaux." Conseil d'Etat 1998.

117 See, for instance, PAGSI 1998, p. 58, and Strauss Kahn a.o. 1999, p. 31.

118 Battle 1998.

119 House of Commons 1999, p. 7-8.

120 Quoted in House of Commons 1999, p. 9.

deed, differences arise between the rules in the online world and in the offline world. Likewise, the view that is developed at the moment in the United Kingdom on the theme of convergence shows that there are topics that call for a different approach in the online world.[121]

During the international workshop, an expert from the UK remarked that applying the 'online = offline' approach is a complete illusion. Propagating this adage really comes down to holding on to a romantic and outdated concept. Instead of doing this, one will have to analyse *why* certain rules exist in the offline world and *why* these rules should be maintained in the online world. While doing this, the legislature will have to pay marked attention to the underlying goals of the rules at issue. If the online world introduces specific differences with the offline world, one will have to analyse what effect these differences have on the existing rules, considering the rationale of these rules. Rather than automatically transpose the rules of the physical world to the online world, the legislature should creatively look for solutions to the specific problems of the online world.

The UK experts also remarked at the international workshop that the 'offline = online' approach can also work the other way around: "what holds online, must also hold offline". In short, the legislature will have to observe the interaction between the rules of the two worlds, and not merely argue within the framework of the offline-world rules.

2.6 United States

On 29 November 1999, President Clinton ordered setting up an Electronic Commerce Advisory Group, as a subgroup of the US Government Working Group on Electronic Commerce. This advisory group was given the task of identifying legal barriers that impede the further growth of electronic commerce. Relevant to the theme "what holds offline, should also hold online" is the message President Clinton gave the advisory group: its recommendations should "discuss ways to ensure that public interest protections for online transactions will be equivalent to those now provided for offline transactions". Concretely, the president posits that "it is critical that consumers and the public at large be assured of a level of protection in electronic commerce equivalent to that which they now enjoy in more traditional forms of commerce".[122] President Clinton once again drew attention to this position in his Statement of 30 June 2000, on the occasion of passing the Electronic Signatures in Global and National Commerce Act into law: "They need to know that the same 'rules of the road' apply to on-line business disputes as to those in the paper world. The Act will also ensure that on-line consumers will have legal protections equivalent to those in the off-line world." [123]

A few months earlier, the President's Working Group on Unlawful Conduct on the Internet, in the March 2000 report *The Electronic Frontier: the Challenge of Unlawful Conduct Involving the Use of the Internet* had noted that "substantive regulation of unlawful conduct

---

[121] See <http://www.culture.gov.uk/CONREP.htm>.

[122] White House 1999.

[123] White House 2000b.

(...) should as a rule apply in the same way to conduct in the cyberworld as it does to conduct in the physical world." Subsequently, the working group posed that the report's analysis shows that "existing substantive law is generally sufficient to cover unlawful conduct involving the use of the Internet".[124]

Nevertheless, it is also recognised that this starting point can not always be sustained: "At the same time, we must recognise that different media may require different approaches and that public interest protections designed for the physical world may not fit in the electronic commerce arena. We should attempt to develop an equivalent level of protection, recognising that different means may be necessary to accomplish that goal."[125]

The fact that the United States acknowledge that the adage "what holds offline, should also hold online" can not always be the starting point, also appears from a comment Department of Commerce Secretary W.M. Daley made on 1 February 2000: "Some laws and regulations designed for the 'physical world' may not always work in cyberspace." Mr. Daley pointed out that "many current laws pre-date the expansion of electronic commerce and some licensing requirements or technical standards may inadvertently serve to prevent online transactions, while others may continue to make sense."[126]

Finally, an expert from the US noticed at the internationalisation workshop that the issue of enforcement is of crucial importance to the discussion over the offline/online approach. In thinking about the part the adage 'online = offline' should play, one will have to pay express attention to its consequences for enforcing the law.

2.7 Comparison and conclusion

From the analysis in this chapter, it appears that the governments of France and the United Kingdom have formulated the adage "what holds offline, should also hold online" implicitly (France) or explicitly (UK)[127] as a starting point. Yet legislative initiatives on concrete topics show that the starting point is not always upheld.

The German documents do not mention the position as such, but they implicitly suggest it. Looking at the IuKDG, however, one also discovers that when it comes to the regulation of concrete topics, other rules can apply in the online world than in the physical world.

---

[124] President's Working Group 2000.

[125] White House 1999.

[126] Quoted in *Electronic Commerce & Law Report*, 9 February 2000, p. 138-139.

[127] Also Australia has explicitly mentioned in policy documents the position that "what holds offline, should also hold online". One of the principles for government policy is to "provide for functional equivalence, i.e. online transactions will be treated similarly to offline transactions". See <http://www.noie.gov.au/legreg/body_index.htm>. Likewise, the responsible Australian minister stated in a speech: "What is illegal offline should be illegal online". See <http://www.noie.gov.au/legreg.htm> at *speeches*.

Finally, recent developments in the United States show that, although equal starting points for the online and offline worlds are considered important, it is also expressly noted that this will not always be maintainable. It should be mentioned here that where the US government speaks of the relationship between the offline and online worlds, it is not so much asserted that concrete rules should be the same, but rather that the level of protection in both worlds must be equal.

None of the countries researched have taken an explicit position on a general Lex Internet, an overall Act that should regulate all aspects of the Internet. The Dutch government, in the LEH Memorandum, said that a Lex Internet is not expedient for the moment, but that it is an interesting option in the longer run.[128]

Concluding, we can say that the adage "what holds offline, should also hold online" has until recently been supported as a general starting point in the various countries. More recently, however, it has become clear that it is getting increasingly problematic to uphold this approach consistently when dealing with the various specific problems. The adage appears to have to taste defeat when concrete topics are worked out, because – given certain interests (such as consumer protection, legal certainty, promoting electronic commerce) – specific rules for the online world are being introduced nonetheless. One can also perceive this tendency at an international level (in any case, in the European Union).

During the international workshop, people confirmed that the adage proved useful in the early days of ICT regulation (the mid-1990s), since it established that the Internet was not a legal vacuum; however, by now, it has become merely a romantic and outdated concept. The complexity of the matter proves that the problems in the online world differ from those in the offline world. Therefore, it is unwise, when thinking about regulation, to hold on to the concrete rules of the offline world as a starting point. One should not so much equate in principle the concrete rules of the online world with those of the offline world, but rather, the level of protection in both worlds should be the same. Thus, the government should pay much more attention to the *interests and goals* that (ought to) underpin the rules of the offline and online worlds respectively. The question one is to pose oneself is *why* certain rules prevail in the offline world and *why* these rules should be maintained in the online world. If the online world introduces specific differences with the offline world, one will have to analyse the effect of these differences on the existing rules, considering the rationale of these rules. Rather than automatically transpose the rules of the physical world to the online world, the legislature should be creative in finding solutions to the specific problems of the online world.

Another point that comes up is the fact that the 'offline = online' approach can also work the other way around: "what holds online, must also hold offline". In short, the legislature will have to observe the interaction between the rules of the two worlds, and not merely argue within the framework of the offline-world rules.

---

[128] LEH Memorandum, p. 119.

It should also be stated that the issue of enforcement is of crucial importance to the discussion over the offline/online approach. The effectiveness of a policy choice depends upon the enforcement consequences of the prescribed rules. In thinking about the part the adage 'online = offline' should play, one will have to pay express attention to its consequences for enforcement.

3. Self-Regulation

3.1 Introduction

Self-regulation is a central theme in the various national and international policy documents. In the LEH Memorandum, the Dutch government shows itself a strong proponent of using self-regulatory mechanisms in solving legal uncertainty about the cross-border consequences of electronic communications. It is exactly by supporting the instrument of self-regulation that the government hopes to provide sufficient flexibility at a time when technological and societal turbulence prevail. An additional advantage is that self-regulation is, in principle, not bound by national frontiers, which is also an important advantage with a view to the borderless character of the Internet. Apart from that, in the Dutch government's view, the instrument of government regulation remains the starting point if fundamental norms and values of the rule of law are at stake.[129] The Cabinet mentions in this respect protecting the classic fundamental rights of citizens, preventing and investigating breaches of the rule of law, and state security. Later documents also mention, for example, the interest of consumer protection in relation to security and reliability (e.g., in electronic payments), privacy, and applicable law.[130]

The LEH Memorandum does bestow upon the government the task of supervising the preconditions that apply to self-regulation. These preconditions are: target groups must be sufficiently organised, societal interests must be promoted equitably, all parties must be sufficiently bound, and the enforcement of the agreements must be sufficiently guaranteed. The government's task consists of:[131]

- promoting – vulnerable – interests that are insufficiently represented;
- drafting supporting legislation;
- threatening to make laws;
- supervising;
- cooperating in enforcement (such as through hotlines).

In the ILIS Memorandum, the Dutch government appears no longer an explicit proponent of self-regulation. They recognise that the government also has an important role in establishing

[129] LEH Memorandum, p. 180-181.
[130] TK 1999-2000, 21 501-15 and 23 162, no. 45, p. 3.
[131] LEH Memorandum, p. 181.

a policy for ICT-related matters: regulation should be a joint enterprise of the government and the private sector.[132] As we will see below, this theme of co-regulation appears a popular scheme in several other countries as well.

When we talk about the specific part of the government in self-regulation, we can distinguish several schemes. The literature mentions pure self-regulation (in which the government does not have a steering or initiating part, and where the market parties take all initiatives), statutorily conditioned self-regulation (in which the government poses certain mandatory statutory preconditions), and co-regulation (in which the government and the private sector, as it were, join forces in order to shape policy). This third scheme is strongly gaining popularity when it comes to regulating ICT problems.[133] However, it will also appear that there is no unequivocal understanding of just what is meant by the concept of 'co-regulation'.

Given the Dutch government's initial wager on self-regulation in solving problems related to cross-border electronic communications and their recent remarks on the importance of co-regulation, the question arises to what extent these views are in line with the policy of the relevant international organisations and the countries studied in this research. In the following sections, we discuss the views laid down in the various policy documents. We not only deal with the conceptions of self-regulation as such, but we also indicate the domains and topics that can, that can not, or that can partially be left to self-regulation, according to the documents.

3.2 International organisations

The general position on self-regulation of the various international organisations and platforms (EU, Council of Europe, and OECD) is positive. Even so, it is striking that, while these organisations used to be proponents of pure self-regulation, more recently, a policy has been advocated that takes co-regulation as its starting point. Thus, the OECD showed themselves exponents of this form of regulation at a Paris conference in October 1999, expressly indicating that regulation must be a joint enterprise of government and private parties.[134] More recently, in the July 2000 *Okinawa Charter on Global Information Society*, the Group of Eight (G8) have recognised the need for a dialogue and cooperation between governments and industry in addressing the issues of the information society.[135] Especially with a view to the interest of, among other things, legal certainty and protecting vulnerable interests (e.g., of consumers), self-regulation must be supplemented with government regulation.

---

[132] ILIS Memorandum, section 2.2.1.

[133] We observe that, although this variant of co-regulation has only recently shown up in the various policy documents on ICT law, it has been propagated for a longer time in other policy areas, such as environment law. Compare the contributions in Eijlander a.o. 1993 and see Prins & Van Kralingen 1997, p. 121-122, who talk about 'coproduction'.

[134] OECD 1999, p. 11.

[135] G8 2000.

As to the role of self-regulation as a means to address jurisdiction problems, the major documents do not suggest a positioning. Neither do the documents remark the potential negative effects of self-regulation on international trade. After all, self-regulation may hold the danger that, unintentionally, trade barriers are raised. One can, for instance, think of the conditions that various countries stipulate for carrying a seal of approval for safe electronic commerce. Thus, some countries may impose upon companies a higher level of consumer protection than others.

Apart from this, we also note that some organisations do advocate government intervention with specific topics. Where fundamental rule-of-law principles are concerned (such as privacy protection), pure self-regulation and even co-regulation are not suitable policy instruments. A clear example of this is the Council of Europe's position on dealing with ICT-related crime (draft convention *Crime in Cyberspace*).[136]

3.3 Germany

The leitmotiv in the German approach is the motto "deregulation takes precedence over regulation": "At the basis of the German regulatory framework is the thought that private initiative should fundamentally be given precedence over sovereign or administrative measures respectively, in order to achieve a market-economic development of the information society."[137] From this point of departure, the IuKDG restricts itself to mentioning topics that clearly require further regulation in the very short term in order to achieve an adequate legal framework for developing the information society. Thus, the IuKDG tries to secure two interests: a) legal certainty and b) protecting public interests, such as consumer protection. In all this, it is considered greatly important that the legal framework stimulates and does not slow down technological developments.

Like the German government had already announced, the IuKDG was evaluated in 1999. The market was closely involved in this. The evaluation showed that there was no occasion to adapt the IuKDG radically. Apart from some isolated sectors, including protecting consumers and minors, there is no need for adapting the legal framework. It does appear necessary to better gear the various regulations in the area of privacy protection to one another, so that the applicable regime will be more transparent and streamlined. Apart from that, it is found that the IuKDG as well as the underlying regulations may have to be adapted as a

---

136 Council of Europe 2000, see section 6.2.

137 "Dem deutschen Regelungsrahmen liegt der Gedanke zugrunde, daß der privaten Initiative grundsätzlich Vorrang vor hoheitlichen bzw. administrativen Maßnahmen einzuräumen ist, um eine marktwirtschaftliche Entwicklung der Informationsgesellschaft zu gewährleisten." *Stellungnahme der Bundesrepublik Deutschland zum Grunbuch der EU-Kommission "Konvergenz der Branchen Telekommunikation Medien und Informationstechnologie und ihre ordnungspolitischen Auswirkungen"*; see also the report *Regulierung und Selbstregulierung* of 26 March 1996 by the project group *Rechtsprobleme des Internet.*

consequence of European regulations.[138] In any case, it could be determined that the aforementioned motto of the German approach does not have to be abandoned. All things considered, Minister Müller observed: "The Multimedia Act has provided an important basis for the development of e-commerce in Germany."[139]

These results of the evaluation were incorporated in the federal government's Action Programme *Innovation and Job Opportunities in the 21st Century Information Society*.[140] The German government proclaims the ambition to achieve a legal regulatory framework for telecommunications means, media, and teleservices. Various current laws (besides the IuKDG, the Interstate Media Services Treaty, and the Telecommunications Act) will have to be included wholly or partially in this regulatory framework.

The government also indicates that they set great store by attention for the interests of consumers and minors in the legislative policy, and they feel very strongly about the right of informational self-determination as well. With this perspective, the Action Programme announces legislation in the area of consumer protection (in which the European Distance-Selling Directive is central) and privacy protection (a new legislative concept will be developed that will incorporate the current Teleservices Data Protection Act rules in the Federal Data Protection Act (*Bundesdatenschutzgesetz*)). Besides, the campaign *Security in the Information Society* (*Sicherheit in der Informationsgesellschaft*[141] will be intensified in order to promote citizen trust in the Internet. Finally, the German government indicates they will continue to take an active stand in the various international platforms, having Internet tax and consumer protection as important points of interest.

It is striking that the general policy line of self-regulation can hardly be found as such in the Action Programme, but that the various action items announced manifest to a great extent the importance of self-regulation and a responsibility of their own for the market parties. One can hold that the Action Programme clearly shows how the general policy line of self-regulation can be developed in concrete legislative proposals. An example of this is the action items announced in the area of privacy protection. First, the system of different legal regimes, which is currently very complex, will be trimmed down and simplified. Also, the separate responsibility of processors of personal data will be shaped through a voluntary – but statutorily embedded – privacy audit.

A report that extensively discusses the relationship between self-regulation and government regulation in the area of illegal and harmful content is the report of the Bertelsmann Foundation of September 1999.[142] The following remarks in the report are relevant here:

---

138 An example is the *Fernabsatzgestz* (*Distance Marketing Act*) of 9 June 2000, *Bundestagsdrucksache* 14/3195, which implements the EC Distance-Selling Directive, available at <http://www.uni-muenster.de/Jura.itm/hoeren/mitarbeiter/unruh/FernAG_BTDrs_14-3195.doc>.

139 "Das Multimediagesetz hat eine wichtige Grundlage für die Entwicklung von E-Commerce in Deutschland gelegt." BMWi 1999.

140 Bundesregierung 1999.

141 See <http://www.sicherheit-im-internet.de>.

142 Bertelsmann 1999, p. 46.

- "Providers party to an enforceable and broadly representative self-regulatory regime, recognized by public authorities, should not be liable for third party content when complying with the requirements of that regime and the decisions of the relevant selfregulatory body."
- "Laws should recognise (self-)rating and filtering mechanisms as well as age verification systems to exclude responsibility of providers for content harmful for children."
- "It is essential to have adequate legislative powers with respect to computer-based investigations, in particular, adequate powers for search and seizure. It would be helpful to make available a preservation order, which could 'freeze' evidence in a fast procedure and thus leave the decision about its delivery to a court judgement. In addition, legislation should be clearer on the obligations of Internet providers with respect to collection, storage and transfer to law enforcement of data relevant to investigations."

This clearly shows that the government is expected to offer a certain protection to self-regulatory providers. In the meantime, this position has been criticised in the literature, because it would give the providers a lot of power to check.

Finally, we mention the association Voluntary Self-Control Multimedia Service Providers (*Freiwillige Selbstkontrolle Multimedia-Dienstenanbieter*) that operates in Germany. Besides, German companies are affiliated with the Internet Content Rating Association (ICRA).[143]

3.4 France

The French government, in the PAGSI report of January 1998, recognises that the development of Internet and electronic commerce calls into question traditional forms of government control. This does not mean that the government should become idle, according to the report. The starting point for French government policy on ICT regulation should be the distinction between, on the one hand, areas where government intervention is necessary, because statutory regulations need to be adapted to facilitate electronic commerce, and, on the other hand, areas in which the government should merely set an example, for instance, by stimulating developments. Focusing on regulation, the government is charged with the task of:

- setting the necessary preconditions for promoting trust between service providers and consumers in electronic commerce;
- removing barriers resulting from applicable law and custom because these are not tailored to electronic commerce;
- supervising the enforcement of the various legal requirements.

Given these three tasks, the government, in 1998, set themselves the goal of promoting consumer and market trust through certain facilities in at least the following areas:

- evidence, in particular electronic signatures;
- encryption and reliability of communications;

---

143 See <http://www.icra.org>.

- data protection;
- payment systems that are compatible with European and international standards;
- applicable law, particularly in relation to consumer issues.

As to the role of self-regulation in these plans, both the French government, in the Action Programme, and the State Council, in *The Internet and Digital Networks*,[144] note that this form of control must be considered in all those situations where the current legal regime does not provide for a solution to certain behaviour. To put it briefly, France takes the view that the current legislative regime applies to the Internet and electronic commerce. Self-regulation is accorded a supplementary role. In this context, the development of the Netiquette[145] is warmly welcomed. Likewise, other forms of self-regulation that contribute in a realistic and effective way to regulating the Internet will be supported by the French government, according to the Action Programme.

Nonetheless, the role of self-regulation is a supplementary one, and it is restrained by preconditions. An important reason for setting preconditions is the view that the information society is about more than only electronic commerce. Cultural values and employment must also be taken into account, namely through statutory preconditions.

The Action Programme has meanwhile been followed up by various other documents and reports published on behalf of the government. For example, on 19 January 1999, a progress report appeared, which was discussed in the Interministerial Committee for the Information Society (CISI).[146] The French government was clearly satisfied with the progress of the lines set out in the Action Programme.[147] Half a year later, prime minister Jospin again announced concrete government action. This time, he indicated that the government intended to present a bill on the information society to parliament in early 2000.[148] The first outlines of this bill emerged when the consultation document *Policy Paper on the Adaptation of the Legal Framework to the Information Society* was published on 5 October 1999:[149]

- clarifying the rights and responsibilities of everyone in order to safeguard free online communications;
- democratising access to ICT;
- security and reliability in electronic transactions.

On 1 December 1999, prime minister Jospin again lectured about the importance of a good French Internet policy. He indicated that self-regulation can play a part in this policy, but from the perspective of co-regulation: "Co-regulation in effect necessitates a constant dia-

---

144 Conseil d'Etat 1998.

145 The rules drafted by the Internet community for proper Internet use, see <http://www.ietf.org/rfc/rfc1855.txt>.

146 CISI 1999.

147 See also Lorentz 1999.

148 Jospin 1999a. The Bill is now planned for presentation to parliament in 2001.

149 Strauss Kahn a.o. 1999.

logue between all its participants."[150] Now, the government has initiated the establishment of a 'co-regulation organism' (*organisme de corégulation*), chaired by MP Christian Paul.[151] On 29 June 2000, Mr. Paul published his first report *On Internet Rights and Liberties. Co-regulation, a French Contribution to a Global Regulation* (*Du droit et des libertés sur l'internet. La corégulation, contribution française pour une régulation mondiale*). In the report, it is proposed to establish an Internet Rights Forum (*Forum des Droits sur l'internet*), which will be, "above all, a meeting place between public regulation and self-regulation, between the expectations of economic actors and those of network users".[152] According to Christian Paul, it is of particular importance that the international dimension of Internet developments is taken into consideration when discussing a regulatory policy. Specifically with respect to the concept of co-regulation, he notes that "co-regulation is, in the first place, a method. Taking into account the novelty of the issues to be dealt with and their international dimension, as well as the variety of the players involved, it is important to ensure the encounter of points of view, and even, if possible, to foster consensus".[153]

As to France's involvement in the various international platforms, we find that the country – like most countries – wants to play an active part in shaping international electronic-commerce and Internet policy. More specifically, in the 1998 Action Programme, the French government recognised the necessity of playing a more active part in the international organisations that are involved in developing technical standards relevant to the Internet.[154]

3.5 United Kingdom

The British government thinks that self-regulation should be strongly emphasised. This position has been made explicit in, among others, Minister Battle's 1998 speech on *Her Majesty's Government Strategy for the Internet* and the Electronic Communications Act 2000.

In principle, pure self-regulation is the starting point: the government's task lies mainly in what is indicated with the catchwords: stimulate, invest, and inform. As to 'informing', the British government considers it highly important for the development and shaping of national self-regulation initiatives, that European Union member states share their self-regulation experiences with each other.

---

150 "La corégulation nécessite en effet un dialogue contstant entre tous ses participants". Jospin 1999b.

151 See <http://www.internet.gouv.fr/francais/textesref/pagsi2/lsi/coregulation.htm>.

152 "Pensé avant tout comme un espace de rencontre entre la régulation publique et l'autorégulation, entre les attentes des acteurs économiques et celles des utilisateurs du réseau". Paul 2000.

153 "La corégulation est d'abord une méthode. Compte tenu de la nouveauté des sujets à traiter et de leur dimension internationale ainsi que de la diversité des acteurs concernés, il importe d'assurer la rencontre entre les points de vue, voire, quand c'est possible, de faire murir des consensus". Paul 2000.

154 Conseil d'Etat 1998.

Nevertheless, also the British government recognises that pure self-regulation can not always be the starting point. The main reason to choose to regulate certain topics after all are European obligations (primarily in the area of electronic commerce). Besides, the government thinks it desirable to develop legislative initiatives in the areas of illegal and harmful content, combating fraud, and education. Especially this third issue appears high on the government's agenda. After all, "it is vital to have an ICT literate business and workforce".[155] By now, the Cabinet Office, the Department of Trade and Industry (DTI), and the Department for Education and Employment are actively developing educational initiatives and programmes.[156]

These topics had already been identified as topics for the regulation agenda by the British government in *Our Information Age*, published by prime minister Blair in 1998.[157] Concretely, this states: "The Government will not attempt to replace the private sector – competitive markets will bring the greatest benefits to the economy and consumers alike. But the Government does have an important role to play in five key areas:

- transforming education – to harness new technology so that all can gain knowledge and skills they need for the information age;
- widening access – to ensure that the benefits of the information age are open to all, with no split between information haves and have nots;
- promoting competition and competitiveness – to help harness change and prosper, for the benefit of customers, jobs and the wider economy;
- fostering quality – to ensure that the content of new services matches and exceeds the best available today;
- modernising government – to ensure the Government uses new technology to deliver better, more convenient, services."

But also when the British government indicates that government intervention is necessary, there remains room for self-regulation initiatives. We can hold that in these areas, the British government's position is one of conditioned self-regulation. A good example is dealing with illegal and harmful content. Apart from concrete statutory measures, the government stimulates the drafting of codes of conduct by the trade. In addition, other forms of co-regulation are also considered necessary, for example, where the ICT industry, enforcement authorities, and representatives of parents and teachers cooperate in developing measures that protect minors.

The concept of co-regulation as a form of self-regulation is a central theme in the September 1999 report *E-commerce@its.best.uk*.[158] The report discusses extensively the pros and cons of this mechanism for regulating electronic commerce. The main motive for co-regulation is the feeling that the government has the task of providing a certain level of legal certainty and trust to both consumers and business: "To give consumers and business this trust and thus to

---

155 S. Saxby, interview.
156 ISI 1999.
157 Blair 1998.
158 Cabinet Office 1999.

facilitate the growth of e-business, an underpinning legal and regulatory framework is essential." However, the report continues, implementing legislation is too slow for the fast changes in an e-commerce market. So, co-regulation provides an alternative: "Co-regulation is a partnership between government and business designed to put in place an overall framework for e-commerce. Government defines the public policy objectives that need to be secured, but tasks industry to design and operate self-regulatory solutions and stands behind industry ready to take statutory action if necessary".

The report mentions the following advantages of co-regulation:

- flexibility and adaptability;
- timeliness;
- appropriateness; and
- "it will help create a distinctive 'Based in the UK' brand for UK e-business by giving consumers here and overseas trust in e-businesses based in the UK and enhancing the attractiveness of the UK as a location for e-businesses."

The report also goes into a major disadvantage: market parties will use the results of co-regulation as an instrument in creating barriers to market newcomers. However, competition law is sufficiently trusted to handle such problems.

As a result, the report concludes that the advantages of co-regulation far outweigh its drawbacks, and it calls upon the government to explicitly take co-regulation as the starting point: it "should therefore be the first option for addressing regulatory issues concerning e-commerce." Thus, the report presents the following position on regulating e-commerce: "A recognition of a unique balance between 'light touch' regulation and freedom to innovation expressed through a 'based in the UK' brand, such that:

- Government intervention is only used as a last resort;
- co-regulation is the norm, with a presumption for industry self regulation within a Government backed framework of codes of good practices in the first choice;[159]
- disincentives to the use of electronic commerce no longer exist (...); and
- Government is truly 'joined up', with close co-ordination of both policy and its delivery."

The 30 June 2000 progress report of the E-Minister and the E-Envoy mentions the proposals forwarded by OFTEL to encourage greater involvement by consumer groups and the telecoms industry in protecting consumer interests.[160] The report states that the proposals published by OFTEL are in line with the commitment of the UK government to a co-regulatory approach. Such a co-regulatory role would be effected on issues such as information on pricing, contract terms, complaint handling, and dispute resolution. It

---

159 Australia applies this starting point as well. An interesting Australian example of statutorily conditioned self-regulation is the draft *Code of Practice for Internet Business* (see <http://www.iia.net.au>) that the Internet Industry Association (IIA) presented on 30 August 1999. The Code contains a set of best practices in many areas: privacy, e-commerce transactions, spamming, illegal and harmful content, copyright, and fair business competition. Enterprises complying with the best practices can show a seal of approval on their websites. The IIA considers it greatly important that an independent enforcement system is provided.

160 <http://www.cabinet-office.gov.uk/e-envoy/2000/progress/pmreports/pmreport30jun00.htm>.

should also be mentioned that the E-Minister and the E-Envoy referred in this report to the upcoming G8 summit in Kyushu-Okinawa (held in late July 2000), stating that the UK government will ensure that this summit gives "a political push to e-commerce international issues, including the digital divide and co-operation on co-regulatory schemes to strengthen consumer confidence".

Looking at concrete results of self-regulation in the United Kingdom, we should first of all mention the hotline system. On various occasions, the British government has voiced its great appreciation of the Internet Watch Foundation.[161] It is stressed that good experiences are gained in increasing consumer trust.

When various self-regulation initiatives were set up, the British government acted as a direct stimulator. We can also mention the establishment of the British Internet Service Providers Association and the TrustUK initiative (a seal of approval for online consumer services on the basis of a code of conduct). Since March 2000, this latter organisation offers a seal of approval to e-commerce businesses that comply with certain conditions in the area of consumer protection and privacy.[162]

An example of a self-regulatory scheme with a regulatory 'back-up' provision is the industry approval scheme for cryptography service providers, which is being prepared by the Alliance for Electronic Business (known as the 'T-Scheme'). This voluntary approval system is expressly adopted under the Electronic Communications Act, which received Royal Assent on 25 May 2000.[163] In case the self-regulatory scheme turns out unsuccessful, the Act provides the government with the power to introduce a statutory approval system.

Also, the British government has called for using certain technical protection measures, such as PICS.[164] Finally, one can point out the government's involvement in setting up The Information Society Initiative (by DTI) in February 1996, in order to stimulate ICT applications in small and medium-sized enterprises.[165]

In the meantime, in early 2000, Alex Allan was appointed as the government's E-Envoy. When he presented his plans, Mr. Allan also mentioned the private sector's important role in shaping e-commerce policy.[166]

Experts from the United Kingdom at the international workshop observed that when one considers the government's role, particular attention has to be paid to the enforcement consequences of the chosen approach. UK experiences with certification services show that a government policy working with a system of voluntary private-sector cooperation can be very effective: business and organisations appear to want to comply with this policy, because it can offer a competitive advantage.

---

161 Battle 1998 and Blair 1998.

162 See <http://www.trustuk.org.uk>.

163 See <http://www.legislation.hmso.gov.uk/acts/acts2000/20000007.htm>.

164 See <http://www.dti.gov.uk/CPORN/r3.htm>.

165 See <http://www.isi.gov.uk/isi>.

166 See *World Internet Law Report*, 2000 no. 2, p. 6-7. See House of Commons 1999 for a description of the E-Envoy task.

We conclude that there is distinctly room for self-regulation in the United Kingdom, while the starting point of self-regulation seems to have given way to co-regulation. In this view, the government's role consists of more than merely stimulating. Government have a steering role in the interest of legal certainty and trust, and they set minimum requirements to that end. Together with this, there is a marked attention for a government policy working with a system of voluntary private-sector cooperation. The result of this is co-regulation, in which self-regulation is combined with "a light touch regulation".[167]

Finally, with respect to the United Kingdom's position in relation to international platforms, we note that the UK is a prominent advocate of cooperation between the OECD and the Global Business Dialogue on electronic commerce (GBDe)[168]. They declare that the European Commission should participate more actively in the GBDe, to prevent this body from being directed too much by companies from outside the European Union.

3.6 United States

In the mid-1990s, the United States published various policy documents that presented an overall view of the development of electronic commerce. The 1996 Telecommunications Act was the first clear demonstration of the US government's policy, followed in 1997 by the reports *Digital Tornado: The Internet and Telecommunications Policy*[169] and *A Framework for Global Electronic Commerce*.[170]

The great importance of self-regulation is evident from both policy documents. The starting point of the US policy was the proposition: primarily aim for self-regulation, with government regulation to fall back on. "The success of electronic commerce will require an effective partnership between the private and public sectors, with the private sector in the lead." In short, pure self-regulation is the starting point,[171] with the government also stimulating the use of filtering, labelling, and other techniques.

Looking at actual practice, many initiatives have been established from this self-regulation perspective, such as BBBOnline, the e-mail preference service of the Direct Marketing trade,[172] and, recently, the Network Advertising Initiative Guidelines established by the Federal Trade Commission (FTC) and the Network Advertising Initiative (NAI)[173]. The US government is warmly advocating these initiatives. Others, however, warn against these self-regulatory schemes, arguing that without significant involvement

---

167 See Cabinet Office 1999.

168 See <http://www.gbd.org>.

169 FCC 1997.

170 Clinton & Gore 1997.

171 See also Department of Commerce 1997.

172 See <http://www.the-dma.org>.

173 See <http://www.ftc.gov/opa/2000/07/onlineprofiling.htm>.

from consumer and privacy groups, these initiatives do not provide an adequate level of privacy and consumer protection.[174]

The government's preference for self-regulation is also used in the negotiations in the various international platforms. A good example are the Safe Harbor Principles promoted in the negotiations with the European Union on data protection.[175] This position is also apparent in the appreciation for the Global Business Dialogue's work voiced during various meetings by international organisations.

Three years after both documents were published, however, it appears that there is increasing pressure to introduce government intervention in certain areas. In the past, legislation has been proposed (be it successfully or not),[176] bills on diverse topics (online gambling, databases) are being discussed in Congress, and various Congress members are notably interested in other issues (consumer protection and privacy). An illustration of the regulatory zeal at both the federal and the state level are the no less than 252 electronic-signature acts currently proposed or in force in fifty states in the area of electronic signatures, as was mentioned at the international workshop. It is, however, expected that many legislation initiatives will suffer from the election fever next year.[177]

The inclination to a somewhat more steering government role is connected with another important starting point present in both policy documents from 1997. This is the ambition to develop an overall and consistent framework for the further growth of electronic commerce: "Government participation must be coherent and cautious" and "The variety of issues being raised, the interaction among them, and the disparate fora in which they are being addressed will necessitate a coordinated, targeted governmental approach".[178]

It is the realisation of this starting point that has recently been criticised from various sides. It is noted that the government is indeed active in stimulating and developing a variety of initiatives, but that these initiatives lack a uniform approach. The government runs the risk of stepping in precisely that pitfall for which they warn in their policy documents, according to various experts. Or, as Michael Froomkin worded it at a University of California, Berkeley conference that 'evaluated' the 1997 policy documents: "The White Paper is a fundamentally political document consumed by short-term policies and fails to grasp the consequences for governance."[179] A long-term view is lacking, which results in a policy of "loose ends and unanswered questions". Increasingly, the government is called upon to take a more steering role, in order to safeguard a coherent approach. Also, the issue of legal certainty

---

174 See, for example, the EPIC report *Network Advertising Initiative: Principles not Privacy* <http://www.epic.org/privacy/internet/NAI_analysis.html>.

175 See <http://www.ita.doc.gov/td/ecom/menu.html> for information on the Safe Harbor Principles.

176 Compare the Communications Decency Act, the Child Online Protection Act, and the Child Pornography Prevention Act.

177 See 'Federal Legislative Outlook', *Electronic Commerce & Law Report*, 26 January 2000, p. 82-83.

178 Clinton & Gore 1997, p. 30.

179 *Electronic Commerce & Law Report*, 17 March 1999, p. 241-243.

plays an important part in that respect. Moreover, people call attention to the necessity of involving the various individual states much more closely in electronic-commerce policy.

The role of consumer organisations was also referred to at the international workshop. These make themselves increasingly heard as of lately, and they call upon the government to make statutory rules that safeguard consumer interests.

The US literature discerns three important problems with self-regulation specifically with respect to consumer protection:

- self-regulation is insufficiently effective in a market with many small enterprises and minor conditions for market access;
- foreign businesses are not covered by the enforcement measures of the Federal Trade Commission;
- self-regulation does not solve non-compliance with Internet-market agreements.

It is not clear whether it is a direct result of this criticism, but in his Memorandum of 29 November 1999, President Clinton refers explicitly to the necessity of a uniform approach in legislative measures. In the debate that is to be started on possible legal barriers to the further growth of electronic commerce, it is necessary "to discuss the potential for consistent approaches to these issues".[180]

A concrete example of this tendency is the establishment of an advisory body with the Federal Trade Commission that will have a pronounced role in implementing the 'privacy principles' of commercial websites.[181]

A recent illustration of the fact that consumer protection requires the government to play an active role is the Electronic Signatures in Global and National Commerce Act, which was signed into law on 30 June 2000. In his statement on this occasion, President Clinton referred to the 1997 *Framework for Global Electronic Commerce*; he remembered that this Framework also noted that government action "may prove necessary to (...) protect consumers." According to President Clinton, the Electronic Signatures in Global and National Commerce Act accomplishes both goals by providing business with a predictable, technology-neutral, legal environment while at the same time protecting consumers. "It shows what we can do when we work together – business and consumer and government, State and Federal, Republican and Democrat – in the public interest".[182]

Another example of the recent view that the government should play a more active role to protect certain interests on the Internet is the FTC report on online privacy, which was submitted to Congress on 22 May 2000. The FTC concludes that "ongoing consumer concerns regarding privacy online and the limited success of self-regulatory efforts to date make it time for government to act to protect consumers' privacy on the Internet."[183]

---

[180] White House 1999.

[181] See <http://www.ftc.gov>.

[182] White House 2000b.

[183] FTC 2000. The report eminently illustrates the shift in preference from self-regulation to co-regulation, since the recommendation was a 3:2 decision. The majority opinion considered self-

The FTC, however, acknowledges that industry self-regulation should still play an important role in any legislative framework.

We conclude that, while the US government are still using pure self-regulation as a starting point, they are by now also convinced that government guidance must play a more prominent part in order to realise a uniform and consistent policy, which can at the same time safeguard certain interests (consumer protection, privacy, and legal certainty). The international workshop confirmed this tendency towards 'co-regulation'.

3.7 Comparison and conclusion

The analysis of the situation in the various countries shows that the Dutch preference for self-regulation is broadly shared in these countries. Looking in more detail at the specific interpretation of the concept of self-regulation in the European countries that were studied, we note that the Dutch position is more in line with the German and UK views of self-regulation than with the French government's view. France considers it greatly important that the government sets specific preconditions for market regulation.

Nevertheless, one can observe a striking tendency in the countries researched, which originally took the position that government guidance is, in principle, undesirable and that the market should take the lead. We note that all these countries increasingly realise that the government cannot confine itself to merely stimulate, but that shaping electronic-commerce and Internet policy is a task for the government and the market together. 'Co-regulation' is the word that shows up conspicuously in many recent policy documents. Even in the US, one can perceive a tendency that indicates the view that the government must play a more steering part in shaping the policy. The starting point is the joining forces of government and market in developing policies. Finally, we have noted that the French government has now also mentioned the word co-regulation.

In noting this, however, one must keep in mind that the term 'co-regulation' is not interpreted the same way in the various countries. Likewise, at the international workshop it was clear that the exact interpretation of this concept is influenced to a large extent by the legislative tradition and the cultural background. In short, we must realise that the same term may have different meanings.

Looking at the various international policy-making bodies, we see that also there, the starting point of co-regulation is increasingly being advocated. For example, the OECD and the G8 have welcomed the concept of co-regulation. Although the past has shown that individual member states have insisted – where possible – upon maintaining their national regulation-policy lines in the international organisations, they have not yet explicitly placed the starting point of co-regulation on the international agenda. The reason

regulation inadequate, whereas the dissenting opinion argued that self-regulation is still the appropriate instrument.

may be that the starting point has only been put on the national agenda very recently and that it has not yet sufficiently matured for international consideration. Once it is placed on the international agenda, one will have to pay express attention to the fact that, as we have indicated, the concept of co-regulation is being interpreted differently by each country.

Finally, various governments mention the important part the Global Business Dialogue may play in further shaping international (more specifically, transatlantic) electronic-commerce policy. European countries do remark, however, that one has to prevent the GBDe's view from being totally controlled by US thinking.

The overview leads to the conclusion that the Dutch position on self-regulation is supported abroad, while its recent attention for co-regulation is likewise mirrored in the various countries and organisations. Thus, governments have to play a more steering part in shaping the policy than they have done so far. The starting point is the joint action of government and market in developing policies. Governments must nevertheless be aware that the same term may be interpreted differently in various countries. The exact interpretation of the concept of co-regulation depends to a great extent on legislative traditions and cultural backgrounds.

At the international workshop, a useful distinction was suggested for states when considering the necessity of government intervention: on the one hand, regulation that tries to answer practical questions in order to achieve, for instance, legal certainty (e.g., "can people use an electronic signature to perform a legal act?") and, on the other hand, regulation that aims at influencing behaviour (e.g., "do not use encryption that hampers criminal-investigation interests"). With the former, the market will have a positive attitude towards government intervention, while with the latter, it will often not agree with the necessity of regulation.

Finally, the aspect of enforcement proves to be eminently important when discussing (self-)regulation. The success of (self-)regulation initiatives ultimately depends on the effectiveness of enforcing the created rules. In thinking about the role of the government, primary attention will have to be paid to the enforcement consequences of the approach one chooses. Experiences in the United States and the United Kingdom show that a government policy working with a voluntary private-sector cooperation system can be effective: businesses and organisations seem to want to comply with this policy because it can offer competitive advantages.

4. Enforcement

4.1 Introduction

ICT-related internationalisation challenges the law in two ways. The first issue is how one must deal with the fact that more than one jurisdiction can apply to a single act, like in cross-border crime and electronic contracts. This issue is relatively straightforward to address through international treaties on jurisdiction and international cooperation. The second issue, however, is more problematic: if we hold on to national sovereignty, how can states enforce their (national) laws and regulations in the international information society?

The Dutch government thinks the electronic highway must not become a legal vacuum: in principle, existing law simply applies to the Internet (see chapter 2). This implies that these laws will have to be enforced there as well.[184]

Given the problem of enforceability in the international context, agreements must be made at an international level. These can take the form of (stimulating or waiting for) international self-regulation, international treaties, harmonisation of substantive legal norms, or agreements on procedural rules (such as mutual assistance in criminal matters). Such agreements can be made at various levels, internationally (UN, OECD) and regionally (EU, Council of Europe) as well as bilaterally. The Dutch government takes a pragmatic approach here: depending on the enforcement problem and on the legal area, one can analyse what is the most feasible and effective way to ensure (international) enforcement.

In *criminal law*, the Dutch government takes the following starting points.[185]

- The electronic highway must not become a legal vacuum.
- Privacy violations caused by enforcement must always be balanced and should be as limited as possible[186].

---

[184] "Effective enforcement on the electronic highway is essential: the electronic highway must not become a legal vacuum." LEH Memorandum, p. 10. Likewise, where the Netherlands opt for self-regulation, the condition must be met that the enforcement of agreements is sufficiently ensured. LEH Memorandum, p. 13.

[185] LEH Memorandum, p. 168.

- Market development should be restricted as little as is possible.
- The enforcement-related costs for electronic-highway users must not be disproportionately high.

The problem areas in criminal enforcement that the Dutch government discerns in the LEH Memorandum are, above all, the adequacy of the repertory of investigation powers in an electronic environment, safeguarding the possibility of intercepting telecommunications, applying investigation powers on the Internet, data mining as an investigation means, cooperation duties for Internet providers and TTPs, and organising and educating the police and the judiciary.[187] The ILIS Memorandum adds that when it comes to cross-border investigation powers, in particular gathering data abroad, the Netherlands take a strict, rule-of-law position: in such cases, the other state must be notified and be able to prohibit the cross-border investigation or use of the resulting data.[188]

In the area of enforcement of *civil law*, the government notices the following points of interest: the evidentiary value of electronic information recorded by TTPs, digital signatures, evidence clauses (*bewijsovereenkomsten*) for closed networks, alternative dispute resolution,[189] and 'seizure' on the electronic highway.[190] The ILIS Memorandum particularly stresses the possibilities of alternative dispute resolution and technical measures (e.g., copyright-protection mechanisms) to supplement the traditional ways of enforcement.[191]

This chapter presents the positions of other countries on enforcement in general. The enforcement issues in specific areas will partly be dealt with in part II. By way of illustration, this chapter will provide an overview (which is not exhaustive) of the major areas and topics for which foreign governments discern potential enforcement problems, with a rough indication of the direction they choose to solve these problems.

4.2 International organisations

No overall initiatives are known within international organisations that aim at safeguarding enforcement of ICT law in general. Several initiatives do exist to ensure enforcement in specific areas.

One example is the protracted talks of the European Union and the United States on the Safe Harbor Principles – principles that should secure privacy, especially the safeguards of the European privacy directive, in the EU and the US. The talks proceeded far

---

186 LEH Memorandum, p. 10. Compare ILIS Memorandum, section 3.2, working principle no. 9.
187 LEH Memorandum, p. 168-169.
188 ILIS Memorandum, section 2.4.
189 See TK 1999-2000, 26 352, no. 19 (*Beleidsbrief ADR*) (*Policy letter ADR*).
190 LEH Memorandum, p. 169.
191 ILIS Memorandum, section 2.4.

from smoothly, given the different opinions in the US and the EU on the role of self-regulation in protecting privacy. The final US version of the principles was approved by the European Commission on 26 July 2000, despite a negative European Parliament resolution of 5 July 2000 that argued that the principles did not provide adequate protection. The Commission promised to re-open negotiations on the principles if the remedies available to European citizens would eventually prove inadequate.[192] The OECD have also been involved intensively with privacy, among others in the OECD Privacy Guidelines of 1981. The ministerial declaration on privacy of the OECD Ottawa conference of December 1998 states that countries must take the necessary steps to effectively implement the OECD Privacy Guidelines, among others by ensuring "that effective enforcement mechanisms are available both to address non-compliance with privacy principles and policies and to ensure access to redress".[193] According to the Council of Europe, feedback mechanisms offered by Internet user groups, Internet service provider associations, data protection authorities, or other bodies are important ways of ensuring that the Council's 1981 guidelines for protecting individuals' privacy are respected.[194] However, mere self-regulation is not sufficient for enforcing privacy: the Council of Europe intends to extend the Guidelines with an Addendum on supervisory authorities that have powers of investigation, intervention, and engaging in legal proceedings.[195] Industry has seized up on these developments. For instance, the International Chamber of Commerce has drafted model clauses for use in contracts involving transborder data flows.[196]

Another example is the area of consumer protection. An OECD declaration states that enforcement in this area must be ensured through "increasing awareness among judicial and law enforcement officials of the need for international co-operation to protect consumers and combat cross-border fraudulent, misleading and unfair commercial conduct".[197] Partly with a view to this, the OECD have drafted guidelines for consumer protection in e-commerce in late 1999.[198]

For enforcing the regulatory e-commerce framework, alternative dispute resolution can be an important mechanism, especially in online variants. The European Electronic Commerce Directive requires member states to remove statutory barriers to online out-of-court dispute resolution (art. 17). The result of this "must be to make the functioning of such schemes genuinely and effectively possible in law and in practice, even across borders" (consideration 51).[199] The European Commission intends to establish minimum

---

[192] See <http://www.ita.doc.gov/td/ecom/menu.html> on the Safe Harbor Principles.

[193] OECD 1998a.

[194] Council of Europe 1999.

[195] Council of Europe, Draft additional protocol to Convention for the Protection of Individuals with regard to Automatic Processing of Personal Data (ETS No 108) regarding supervisory authorities and transborder data flows, <http://www.coe.fr/dataprotection/Treaties/projet%20de%20protocole%20E.htm>.

[196] See <http://www.iccwbo.org/home/statements_rules/rules/1998/model_clauses.asp>.

[197] OECD 1998b.

[198] See <http://www.oecd.org/dsti/sti/it/consumer/prod/guidelines.htm>.

[199] Directive 2000/31/EC ("Directive on electronic commerce"), *OJ* L 178/1, 17 June 2000, <http://europa.eu.int/eur-lex/en/dat/2000/l_178/l_17820000717en00010016.pdf>. In the same

quality standards for the extrajudicial settlement of disputes and an ADR working method on a European scale.[200] Besides, a European extrajudicial network will be set up by June 2001, which will consist of clearing houses in each member state to gather information and pass on complaints to sectorial regulators; eventually, the network will also offer online dispute settlement.[201]

On a more global scale, the G8 likewise underline the necessity of developing ADR mechanisms to "alleviate the difficulties faced by consumers in cross-border disputes".[202] In this respect, it is interesting to note the alternative dispute-resolution procedure developed within the ICANN (Internet Corporation for Assignment of Names and Numbers), the organisation that is responsible world-wide for supervising the issuing of domain names. The ICANN has accredited four bodies to provide online arbitration in domain-name disputes: the WIPO Arbitration and Mediation Center, the National Arbitration Forum, eResolution, and the CPR Institute for Dispute Resolution.[203]

Also in the area of criminal law, various platforms discuss enforcement. For instance, in 1997, the OECD have developed 'guidelines' for crypto policy, which, however, provide little guidance because of their compromise between e-commerce promotion and investigation.[204] In 1995, the Council of Europe made recommendations for computer-related investigation,[205] which recommend, among other things, enabling cross-border network searches. In order not to violate state sovereignty, there does have to be an unequivocal legal basis for this, which at the moment does not yet exist. The recommendations therefore express an urgent need for international negotiations to enable cross-border network searches. These negotiations are currently being conducted within the Council of Europe, in the preparations for the *Crime in Cyberspace* Convention. This convention will have to provide, among other things, a legal basis for cross-border network searches and satellite wiretaps, and it intends to set up a network of central authorities for promptly dealing with criminal-assistance requests (see further chapter 6). The G8 have also launched principles for cross-border access to computer data (which are still based on mutual assistance and therefore do not allow directly contacting foreign Internet providers), and

---

vein, the Conclusions of the European Council in Lisbon, 23 and 24 March 2000, at 11, <http://europa.eu.int/council/off/conclu/mar2000/mar2000_en.pdf>. The bodies for alternative dispute resolution do have to adhere to the principles of the *Commission Recommendation on the principles applicable to the bodies responsible for out-of-court settlement of consumer disputes* (98/257/CE), <http://europa.eu.int/comm/consumers/policy/developments/acce_just/acce_just02_en.html>. See also the exploratory study of 20 April 2000 by the EC Joint Research Centre, JRC 2000.

200 See the minutes of the meeting of Ministers of Justice and Home Affairs of 29 May 2000, available at <http://ue.eu.int/Newsroom/>.

201 See <http://www.ebusinesseurope.com/nletter/wk208.htm>.

202 G8 2000.

203 See <http://www.icann.org/udrp/approved-providers.htm>. Compare ICANN 1999.

204 OECD 1997.

205 Council of Europe 1995.

they have established an international network of contact points that can provide information 24 hours a day.[206] Likewise, the new European Convention on Mutual Assistance in Criminal Matters between the member states of the European Union deals with cross-border investigation.[207] The convention deals with, among other things, joint investigation teams (art. 13) and cross-border interception of telecommunications (art. 17-22). The convention includes a provision on intercepting telecommunications in another state through service providers who operate a gateway that is not directly accessible for the intercepting state (art. 19). Moreover, if a state taps a telecommunications address that is used in the territory of another state, and if the intercepting state does not need technical assistance from the other state, the intercepting state need only notify that other state (art. 20). The convention was adopted by the European Council on 29 May 2000; it will enter into force when at least eight EU member states have adopted it in accordance with their constitutional requirements.

For enforcement of criminal law in an ICT environment, intercepting telecommunications is eminently important.[208] Various initiatives have been taken to ensure the tappability of telecommunications networks. ILETS (International Law Enforcement on Telecommunications Seminar) is an informal discussion platform of, among other countries, the EU member states, the US, Canada, and Australia, which aims at enhancing cooperation between enforcement authorities and at tuning interception laws. A European Council decision of 1995 lists requirements member states should apply when defining and implementing measures that influence the lawful interception of telecommunications.[209] These are requirements made by investigation services to enable efficient and effective telecommunications interceptions. The requirements are remarkably similar to the requirements of the US CALEA Act[210] (see section 4.6). In this respect, also the predicaments involving Echelon deserve mention; this is a world-wide interception network of the intelligence services of the US, UK, Canada, Australia, and New Zealand. This network is suspected to intercept international telecommunications on a gigantic scale and to filter these on key words, after which, presumably, relevant data are passed to the security services of the participating countries (and possibly also to enterprises). The European Parliament commissioned two reports on Echelon, which they discussed in 1998 and in March 2000.[211]

Furthermore, especially important for this research are the many European Union initiatives to improve criminal-law enforcement. In countless formal and informal rela-

---

206 G8 1999, at 17 and 19. Compare the EU Common position 99/364/JAI of 27 May 1999.

207 Council Act of 29 May 2000 establishing (...) the Convention on Mutual Assistance in Criminal Matters between the Member States of the European Union (2000/C197/01), *OJ* 12 July 2000.

208 See for an overview of international initiatives in this area, Jansen & Janssen 1999.

209 European Council Resolution of 17 January 1995 on the lawful interception of telecommunications (96/C329/01), <http://www.privacy.org/pi/activities/tapping/eu_tap_resolution_1995.html>. See for a critical view of the legitimacy of this resolution, DPWP 1999.

210 A later, unpublished version, entitled 'Declaration of intent', requires parties to contact the director of the US FBI on the interception requirements. DPWP 1999, section A.2.

211 STOA 1998 and STOA 1999.

tionships and bodies, people work and cooperate on supervisory and criminal-law enforcement,[212] such as Schengen and Europol. In late 1999, the Tampere European Council triggered the establishment of a judicial equivalent of Europol, Eurojust. They also stated that the principle of mutual recognition should also apply to court orders preceding trial, in particular, those meant to promptly secure evidence. This may help to legitimate the powers of cross-border network searches and the 'preservation order' for foreign Internet providers that the draft *Crime in Cyberspace* Convention intends to introduce. It is striking, however, that the Tampere conclusions and recommendations emphasise trafficking in human beings, organised crime, and money laundering, whereas computer and Internet crime are only mentioned in the recommendations on harmonising substantive criminal law.[213] Neither are ICT-related investigation powers referred to as such. To make things worse, the eminently ICT-related EU Lisbon summit (on the knowledge economy and the information society) did not deal with investigation and enforcement.[214] ICT-related criminal-law enforcement therefore somewhat falls by the wayside of the European Council.

Finally, of a completely different order but nonetheless important for enforcement, is the international cooperation of the hotlines that have been established through self-regulatory initiatives in many countries. The Internet Hotline Providers in Europe Association is a cooperation between hotlines for illegal and harmful content in the Netherlands, Germany, France, Ireland, Austria, and the United Kingdom, with partners in the United States and Norway. They fight in particular child pornography on the Internet by setting up a network of effective national hotlines, training new hotlines, stimulating the awareness of Internet security with European Internet users, and drafting common procedures for notifying and reporting illegal and harmful content.[215]

4.3 Germany

The German government has not made statements or taken positions on enforcing ICT law in general. In specific areas, various proposals that should secure enforcement do avail, strongly supporting the necessity of international cooperation.

One area that is worrying Germany in particular when it comes to enforcement is consumer protection. Self-regulation of providers is, in an international context, only partially suitable for safeguarding consumer protection; the options for users to seek

---

212 See, for example, Den Boer 1999 for an overview of the many forms of police cooperation, and see the appendix of TK 1998-1999, 26 656, no. 1 (*Eurostrafrecht*) for an overview of legal instruments in the area of judicial and police cooperation.

213 Presidency conclusions, European Council of Tampere, 15 and 16 October 1999, <http://europa.eu.int/council/off/conclu/oct99/oct99_en.htm>.

214 Presidency conclusions, Extraordinary European Council of Lisbon, 23 and 24 March 2000, <http://europa.eu.int/council/off/conclu/mar2000/mar2000_en.pdf>.

215 See <http://www.inhope.org/>.

judgement abroad are usually limited and too expensive. Therefore, the options for consumers to choose their own national law and a national forum should be broadened.[216]

Other topics for which Germany considers international cooperation or harmonisation necessary in order to secure enforcement are, for example, alternative dispute resolution[217] and privacy[218]. Other than France, the UK, and the US, Germany does not so much see cryptography as a problem for criminal investigation. It is true that in Germany, and also in the German government, options for restricting cryptography have been extensively discussed, but concrete proposals never emerged. Since 1999, the German government has been an outspoken proponent of the free spread and stimulation of cryptography; the government emphasises much less than France and the UK the problems that this might cause for investigation and national security.[219]

4.4 France

One of the general French starting points for developing an electronic-commerce environment is that legislation must be adapted where necessary in order to create a framework for electronic commerce that generates trust of both buyers and vendors. These amendments must ensure that the new laws and regulations are limited and that they enhance international cooperation, in order to safeguard the enforcement of laws and regulations.[220] France therefore emphasises the necessity of international cooperation for enforcing ICT law in general.

This was also indicated by prime minister Jospin at the final meeting of a world conference of regulators (*régulateurs*) on the Internet: "Above all, closer cooperation is in the interest of us all, especially in order to gradually overcome the difficulties that the application of judicial decisions is currently meeting."[221] Moreover, this does not hold only for international cooperation: national supervisors must cooperate as well, since no single regulatory authority can by itself secure enforcement. This does not mean that a

[216] Enquete-Kommission 1998, p. 23. See also Bundesregierung 1999, p. 74-76.

[217] Enquete-Kommission 1998, p. 23. See also Bundesregierung 1999, p. 74-76.

[218] "Data protection is an international task given the global character of networks. The goal is to safeguard a level of data protection that is comparable world-wide." ("Der Datenschutz ist angesichts des globalen Charakters der Netze eine internationale Aufgabe. Ziel ist die Gewährleistung eines weltweit angemessenen Datenschutzniveaus.") Bundesregierung 1999, p. 74.

[219] See Koops 2000.

[220] "Any new legislation or regulation must be of a limited nature and favour an international cooperation in order to foster enforcement of existing laws." Lorentz 1998b, at II-1.2.

[221] "Surtout, une coopération plus étroite est de l'intérêt de tous, en particulier pour surmonter progressivement les difficultés que rencontre aujourd'hui l'application des décisions de justice." Jospin 1999b.

new supervisor specifically for the Internet should be established; rather, all existing authorities must better cooperate and exchange information.[222]

Apart from the starting point mentioned, France does not have specific positions or starting points on enforcing ICT law in general. The issue of enforcement only turns up in specific topics, such as the adequacy of the repertory of investigation powers on networks[223] and the enforceability of tax law[224].

The enforcement problem with which France has struggled most of all, is the use of cryptography hampering investigation and national-security protection.[225] France used to be the only EU country that strongly restricted crypto use through a licensing system. In the second half of the 1990s, France tried to ensure the effectiveness of wiretaps and computer searches through a key-escrow system, but this system never got off the ground. Confronted with the increasing importance of cryptography for electronic commerce and with its isolated position within the EU, France was forced to radically relax the crypto policy and to allow free use of cryptography, which they initiated to an important extent in 1999. This relaxation does not, however, particularly ease the problems for the law-enforcement authorities. The French government now intends to address this problem by creating a duty to decrypt or to provide plaintext.

4.5 United Kingdom

The British government has not published statements or positions on enforcing ICT law in general. Like in France, the question has emerged in the United Kingdom whether regulatory bodies should converge (in particular, OFTEL and the Independent Television Commission into a new communications regulator OFCOM). In the short term, the gov-

---

222 Jospin 1999b. An example of this is the establishment of a Central Office for the fight against ICT crime (*Office central de lutte contra la criminalité liée aux technologies de l'information et de la communication*), which became operational in May 2000.

223 "The judicial authorities and the police, in the case of criminal proceedings, will have to have the legal means to effect network investigations. This is an indispensable condition for effectively fighting illegal content. (...) A legislative provision has to be envisioned in order to permit the execution of this type of investigations on networks." ("Les autorités judiciaires et de police doivent, dans le cadre des procédures pénales, disposer des moyens juridiques pour effectuer des investigations sur les réseaux. C'est une condition indispensable pour lutter efficacement les contenus illicites. (...) une disposition legislative doit être envisagée pour permettre d'effectuer ce type d'investigations sur les réseaux.") Strauss Kahn a.o. 1999, p. 37-38.

224 "The speed and potential anonymity which are a feature of electronic transactions offer new possibilities for delocalization of taxable items, and even the non-taxation of certain transactions, which are the basic result of the practical difficulty of applying national taxation law over a worldwide network. There is therefore a need to find solutions to these problems so as to protect the interest of countries in terms of income from taxation and to prevent distortions of the marketplace." Lorentz 1998b, at II-2.1.

225 See Koops 2000 for an overview of French legislation and policy in this area.

ernment prefers closer cooperation between current supervisors to establishing a new supervisor.[226]

The government thinks that the electronic highway should not become a legal vacuum. In certain areas, this results in proposals to secure enforcement, while in other areas, enforcement is considered problematic, particularly with a view to the international context. Therefore, the necessity of international cooperation is recognised,[227] as is the necessity of voluntary market initiatives.[228]

It should, however, be noted that the United Kingdom has in the offline world already claimed extraterritoriality for the criminal regulation of sex tourism (Sexual Offences (Conspiracy and Incitement) Act 1996), which substantially eases enforcement in an international context. Following an evaluation of this Act, requirements were drafted for creating extraterritorial effect:[229]

a. it concerns serious offences;
b. evidence and witnesses must be likely to be available in the UK;
c. there is international agreement that the conduct in question is reprehensible;
d. action is needed because of the vulnerability of the victims;
e. action is in the interest of the standing and reputation of the UK; and
f. there is a risk that if the UK does not prosecute, the offenders will not be brought to justice.

These requirements are so strong (particularly the 3rd and 4th requirements restrict the potential scope) that one should not expect the UK to resort to extraterritoriality for internationally enforcing (criminal) ICT law in the Internet context.

The UK government is particularly worried about the enforceability of tax law. "E-commerce poses a number of challenges for tax policy and administration: (...) designing a tax regime for e-commerce that minimises losses of tax revenues whether because transactions are more difficult to trace (...) or because it is difficult to determine the country in which income or profit has been earned and thus to assess which country should get the tax".[230] The government considers the main conditions for ensuring tax-law enforcement to be, among other things, "international agreement to the implementation of [a clear set of principles to underpin the taxation of e-commerce]" and "putting in place new arrangements for collecting and enforcing taxes that keep pace with the change in technology."[231]

---

[226] House of Commons 1999.

[227] For example, in combating Internet fraud: "International collaboration between regulatory authorities is essential to search out the perpetrators of scams and sharp practices." House of Commons 1999.

[228] See the fourth principle for Internet regulation: "Service Providers should take voluntary action to uphold the law on-line. This works, and has real teeth because the first principle applies [*on-line = offline, editors*] and the voluntary action is backed up by the full force of existing law." Battle 1998.

[229] See the report of the international workshop in Appendix IV.

[230] Cabinet Office 1999, section 7.7.

[231] Cabinet Office 1999, section 7.8. Likewise, House of Commons 1999.

The Select Committee on Trade and Industry, however, is sceptical about the feasibility of such international agreements: "Rapid progress in reaching agreement on how the international tax system should be adjusted to take account of electronic commerce is unlikely, however. The issues are not only complicated but, especially in relation to sales taxes, solutions are hoped for rather than expected to be found."[232]

Like France, the British government is concerned about the crypto problems for enforcing investigation and national-security laws.[233] After repeated but unsuccessful proposals for key-escrow systems, the government finally, in the *Electronic Communications Bill*, proposed a power to command anyone (including suspects) to deliver a crypto key or plaintext. This proposal was exceedingly controversial in the UK, because of, among other things, a possible violation of the privilege against self-incrimination and the proposed reversal of the burden of proof (addressees who refuse would have to prove that they are unable to decrypt, under threat of two years' imprisonment). Because of this controversy, the decryption part was removed from the Electronic Communications Bill and transferred to the Regulation of Investigatory Powers Bill, which was submitted to the House of Commons in February 2000. Parliament passed the bill with several amendments to alleviate various criticisms. The alleged burden-of-proof reversal was somewhat mitigated, but may effectively continue to exist in the final version, depending on how the courts will interpret it (art. 53 para. 2-3). On 28 July 2000, the RIP Bill received Royal Assent as the Regulation of Investigatory Powers Act 2000 (RIPA).[234]

For enforcing the fight against illegal and harmful content, the British government expects much from the market initiative of hotlines. The Internet Watch Foundation (IWF) is an independent organisation that has been combating illegal content, particularly child porn, on the Internet since 1996. Apart from being a hotline for illegal content, the IWF also aims at promoting a classification system for Internet content to enable Internet users to surf along tailor-made websites.[235] The British government supports the IWF initiative as being a good example of market-government cooperation to enforce the law on the Internet.[236]

4.6 United States

The official policy documents of the United States do not offer general starting points or solutions for the problem of enforcing ICT law in an international context. However, in specific areas, a host of initiatives aim at effecting enforcement.

---

232 House of Commons 1999, at 106.

233 See Koops 2000.

234 See <http://www.homeoffice.gov.uk/ripa/ripact.htm>. Compare <http://www.fipr.org/rip/index.html>.

235 See <http://www.iwf.org.uk/>.

236 See Battle 1998 and Blair 1998. See also the remarks by various ministers at the relaunching of the IWF in January 2000, <http://www.iwf.org.uk/news/news.html>.

In criminal law, it must be put first that the US have traditionally not adhered to the principle of territoriality in a particularly strict way. Apart from using bilateral mutual-assistance treaties (Multi Lateral Assistance Treaties, MLAT's, to 13 of which the US are a party), investigation services often appear to engage in investigation activities abroad, in a mixture of extraterritorial prosecution and mutual assistance.[237] This implies that there may be a less urgent need in the US to establish overall, global agreements on mutual assistance and cross-border ICT investigation powers.

In the area of criminal law, the US are particularly disquieted by terrorist activities, given the international dimension of ICT developments. This shows most pressingly in the US crypto policy,[238] that is fuelled by the fear that foreign terrorist will use cryptography to escape the intercepting capabilities of the National Security Agency and the Central Intelligence Agency. As a result, the US have exerted great international pressure ever since the Cold War to restrict the export of cryptography, first within COCOM and subsequently within the Wassenaar Arrangement meetings. In doing so, the US have exported their crypto policy to the major developed countries. The international crypto export policy is, however, under increasing pressure, and it is being relaxed step by step.

Apart from crypto export legislation, the US government has also often tried to regulate cryptography domestically, out of fear for investigation blockades. So far, these efforts have come to nothing, resulting in domestic crypto use continuing to be free. Neither is it to be expected that a domestic crypto regulation will be effected in the short or medium term.

In the area of intercepting telecommunications, the US have initiated and guided international policy. The desire to maintain tappability of all telecommunications has resulted in requirements laid down in the Communications Assistance for Law Enforcement Act (CALEA) of 1995, which was a model for the tappability laws in other countries, including the European Council decision (see section 4.2). In CALEA's implementation course, the package of requirements for telecommunications providers is extensively discussed, for example, whether providers should also enable the provision of location data. Besides, wiretap laws, which to a considerable extent date from the 'telephone era', will be updated shortly for the Internet age, among other things, by harmonising the divergent standards that currently apply to intercepting wire, electronic, and cable communications.[239]

More in general, there is a broad programme for the prevention and investigation of cybercrime. This aims at protecting the critical infrastructure by establishing, among other things, a (controversial) Federal Intrusion Detection Network (FIDNET), a system that triggers a 'cyber alarm' when computer systems are attacked.[240] A similar controversial system has emerged in the FBI's plan to use a program called Carnivore to collect traffic data at Internet providers; the program can allegedly record much more information than the mere traffic data it should collect – as its name suggests.[241] These develop-

---

237 Van der Wilt 2000, p. 176.

238 See Koops 2000 for an overview of US crypto policy and laws.

239 White House 2000c.

240 White House 2000a.

241 See <http://www.house.gov/judiciary/corn0406.htm> and <http://stopcarnivore.org>.

ments illustrate the ongoing struggle between US law-enforcement authorities and civil-liberties groups over the extent to which enforcement should supersede privacy.

Another area in which the US take the lead in ensuring enforcement is online fraud. The Security Exchange Commission has set up an Office of Internet Enforcement (OIE), which coordinates the activities of a 'CyberForce' of 200 Internet patrolling guards looking for (securities) fraud on the Internet.[242] The OIE also functions as contact point for national and international enforcement authorities in Internet cases. Another initiative against online fraud is the Internet Fraud Complaint Center, a partnership between the FBI and the National White Collar Crime Center, which was established on 8 May 2000.[243]

In the area of private law, especially enforcing copyright law and developing alternative dispute-resolution mechanisms are considered important. For enforcing copyright law, technical protection measures, such as Electronic Copyright Management Systems and digital watermarks, are seen as essential. Such technical measures can, however, also be circumvented technically. The US, following the WIPO and to implement the WIPO treaties of 1996, have therefore chosen to additionally protect the technical measures with legal protection in the Digital Millennium Copyright Act, which was enacted on 12 October 1998.[244] This act penalises the circumvention of copyright-protection systems, as well as the manufacture, import, offering to the public, provision or trafficking of technology that is primarily designed or produced for the purpose of circumventing a technological measure that protects copyrighted works. The act was preceded by a fierce public debate, in which earlier bills bit the dust. In order to meet protests raised in this debate that the penalisations were going too far, in the end, an exception was included in the act for anti-anti-copying-system-actions in the interest of cryptographic research, reverse engineering in order to achieve product interoperability, and testing computer protection systems. Also, under certain conditions, there are exceptions for libraries, archives, and educational institutions.

For enforcing civil law, Alternative Dispute Resolution (ADR), particularly mediation and arbitration, is considered very valuable.[245] They are effective methods to solve conflicts, which can better satisfy both parties and which can be more efficient than settlement in court. The government policy therefore aims at stimulating ADR. The business sector is altogether actively developing proposals for ADR mechanisms.[246] Given the preference for self-regulation, so far, only a legal framework for ADR in government matters has been set up. The Administrative Dispute Resolution Act of 1996[247] authorises and stimulates ministries and government bodies to use ADR. A Presidential Memoran-

---

242 See <http://www.sec.gov/enforce/intrela.htm>.

243 See <http://www.ifccfbi.gov>.

244 See <http://www.gseis.ucla.edu/iclp/dmca1.htm> and <http://www.educause.edu/issues/dmca.html>.

245 See for an overview <http://www.hg.org/adr.html> and <http://www.usdoj.gov/odr/index.html>.

246 See, for instance, the proposals of the United States Council for International Business on online ADR of 17 April 2000, <http://www.uscib.org/policy/adrusgfl.htm>.

247 See <http://www.adr.org/law/federal/adminlaw.html>.

dum of 1998[248] established an Interagency Alternative Dispute Resolution Working Group (IADRWG), which coordinates, stimulates, and facilitates the use of ADR within the federal government.[249] Besides, the Alternative Dispute Resolution Act of 1998 requires courts to develop and implement an ADR programme.[250]

4.7 Comparison and conclusion

In the four countries we researched, no precise ideas were found on enforcing ICT law in general. Excepting France, which mentions international cooperation as necessary for enforcement, the governments have not formulated general starting points for enforcement like the Dutch government has done. Nonetheless, the four Dutch starting points are roughly similar to the policy initiatives in the four countries. There is agreement *that* the electronic highway must not become a legal vacuum, and there is agreement that the question of *how* that should be ensured is generally problematic. The official policy documents do not suggest a view that enforcement must or may be addressed in a general, overall way. The Dutch pragmatic approach, to decide on a case-by-case basis what is the best way in an international context to ensure enforcement, therefore turns up in all countries we researched.

The areas that cause particular enforcement concerns differ per country. There are nevertheless topics that are high on every country's list of enforcement problems to be addressed (often at the international level). Particular topics are tax law, privacy, intellectual property, the investigation repertory on the Internet, wiretapping and cryptography, and alternative dispute resolution. In all these areas, the necessity of international tuning and cooperation is acknowledged, but in many cases, no detailed ideas avail on what this tuning or cooperation should look like, or at what level a mutual solution to the enforcement problems can be found.

The overview leads to the conclusion that the Dutch government's ideas on enforcing ICT law in general are shared abroad. All governments realise that enforcement can be problematic in today's international context and that an international approach is required to ensure enforcement. In the general sense, that is as far as it gets: there are no ideas on how enforcement can be safeguarded on the Internet in general. One must analyse on a case-by-case basis at what level in which international platform which approach will be most promising and effective to ensure enforcement. This research finding has led the Dutch government to propose in the ILIS Memorandum to stimulate the international academic debate on enforcement, because "international legal developments could use an added boost when it comes to enforceability".[251]

---

248 White House 1998.

249 See <http://www.financenet.gov/iadrwg.htm>.

250 See <http://www.usdoj.gov/crt/adr/pl105-315.txt>.

251 ILIS Memorandum, sections 2.4 and 3.3.

The international workshop concluded that enforcement initiatives in an international context are most likely to be successful if the interests to be safeguarded are broadly shared, such as in the financial sector. In areas where the interests diverge more, in particular in criminal law, the international cooperation necessary for enforcement will be decidedly more difficult and slower to establish. So, it is advisable to start here as well in small areas where there is more agreement, such as in fighting child pornography, for which an international network of hotlines is already active.

Besides, according to the experts at the international workshop, constructions using national contact points are most promising to address enforcement internationally. In civil law, one can think of an international network of ombudspersons or Chambers of Commerce to function as intermediaries in solving cross-border conflicts. They could play a central part in international alternative dispute resolution. Also in the area of criminal law, an international network of contact points appears to be the construction that is currently most feasible and effective to secure enforcement. A network of contact points available 24 hours a day to directly deal with and coordinate mutual-assistance requests is a solution that can be realised in the short term and that can function as a basis for further-reaching forms of cross-border cooperation.

Part II – Specific Topics

5. Double Criminality

5.1 Introduction

Also on the Internet, crimes are committed. Examples are content-related offences: child pornography, defamation and slander, seditious publications, discrimination, and racist utterances.

These utterances are not – or not uniformly – criminalised in all countries, in particular due to cultural differences. One can aspire to harmonise criminalisations, but for many offences, this does not seem possible in the short term, if at all. Therefore, one could think of abandoning, under certain conditions, the requirement of double criminality for offences committed on the Internet.

This principle of double criminality is related to idea of state sovereignty, and it generally has an important territorial component. The characteristics of the Internet, such as dematerialisation, deterritorialisation, and globalisation, have led the Dutch government to suggest possibly abandoning the requirement of double criminality for fighting certain offences on the Internet. This discarding of the principle of double criminality would, in that case, introduce an exception to the adage that what holds offline, should also hold online.

The principle of double criminality holds that only international mutual assistance in criminal matters is provided if the fact for which assistance is sought is punishable in both the requesting and the requested state. Mutual assistance consists of (a) requests for assistance / letters rogatory, (b) extradition, (c) transfer of proceedings, and (d) transfer of execution of criminal judgements.

The position of the Dutch government

The Dutch government's commitment is to not reject harmonising criminalisations where possible. However, uniform criminalisations do not seem to be promptly and easily realisable. Currently, only for criminalising child pornography does such a 'universal' criminalisation seem feasible.[252]

---

[252] See TK, 1999-2000, 23 530, no. 49, p. 4-5, Letter from the Minister of Justice of 23 December 1999 on the preparation within the Council of Europe of the *Crime in Cyberspace* Convention. See on this convention in particular chapter 6.

Given the fact that harmonising criminalisations is not possible, for other content-related offences committed on the Internet one can think of abandoning the requirement of double criminality. In the view of the Dutch government as presented in the LEH Memorandum, that can be done if five cumulative conditions are met. The requirement of double criminality can be abandoned[253] for (1) providing information for the sake of enabling the tracing of an electronic trail of (2) serious offences that are determined in advance, while (3) the offence must be targeted at the rule of law of the requesting country. Furthermore, there is a requirement of (4) reciprocity, and (5) extradition is excluded.[254]

5.2 International organisations

In drafting a *Crime in Cyberspace* Convention, the Council of Europe discussed abandoning the requirement of double criminality, but this has not resulted in direct proposals to that effect.[255] As one of the general starting points for international cooperation (art. 20 of the draft text), a basis of uniform or reciprocal law is required, which does not suggest that double criminality can or should be discarded.

On the other hand, the wording of article 22, on mutual assistance, does suggest that double criminality need not be a requirement for assistance: "Where, in accordance with the provisions of the chapter, the requested Party is *permitted* to make mutual assistance conditional upon the existence of dual criminality (...)" (our italics). For one specific goal, the draft text even proposes *not* to make the requirement, in article 24 section 3, on requesting expedited preservation of stored computer data in another state: "For the purposes of responding to a request, dual criminality shall not be required as a condition to providing such preservation, but may be required for the disclosure of the data to the requesting Party." However, a note to this reads: "The Plenary agreed at its 7th meeting (March 2000) that further consideration was necessary on this matter, given that certain delegations expressed their reservation as to the possibility of giving up the requirement of dual criminality." So, for the time being, there is no agreement on abandoning the requirement in this specific case, and certain countries have reserved the right to maintain the requirement here. Moreover, abandoning the requirement only for *preserving* data will not help the requesting state if the requirement is subsequently upheld for being able to *obtain* the data. The draft text does not call into question the authority of states to require double criminality for the latter. Therefore, the requesting state will not find an effective means in the treaty to obtain data (e.g., to trace a digital trail) if the fact at issue is not punishable in the other state.

---

[253] LEH Memorandum, p. 8, 116-117, 121 en 205.

[254] The five conditions the Dutch government poses for abandoning the requirement of double criminality are not always quite clear. For instance, one can not exactly determine what is the scope of the condition that only information is concerned that enables the tracing of the electronic trail.

[255] Council of Europe 2000.

Overall, then the draft *Crime in Cyberspace* convention does not provide an opening to abandoning the requirement of double criminality. Even though the text seems to suggest that the requirement need or should not be absolute, there is no agreement on this among the participating states.

5.3 Germany

There is no indication that abandoning the requirement of double criminality for content-related offences is an issue in German government policy or policy preparation. No position, be it approving or opposing, is available.

5.4 France

There is no indication that abandoning the requirement of double criminality for content-related offences is an issue in French government policy or policy preparation. No position, be it approving or opposing, is available. The *Policy Paper on the Adaptation of the Legal Framework to the Information Society* simply refers to the current procedures in criminal investigations.[256]

5.5 United Kingdom

There is no indication either in the United Kingdom that abandoning the requirement of double criminality for content-related offences is an issue in government policy or policy preparation. No position, be it approving or opposing, is available. The government does support the Internet Watch Foundation (IWF) to fight content-related offences (see section 4.5).

5.6 United States

There is no indication that abandoning the requirement of double criminality for content-related offences is an issue in US government policy or policy preparation. No position, be it approving or opposing, is available.

---

256 Strauss Kahn a.o. 1999, p. 37.

5.7 Comparison and conclusion

We have not found an indication that other countries think of the option of abandoning the requirement of double criminality. Within the Council of Europe, discussions have taken place on this issue, but overall, the draft *Crime in Cyberspace* Convention does not open up the way for relinquishing the requirement of double criminality. Even though the text seems to suggest that the requirement need or should not be absolute, there is no agreement on this among the participating states. Moreover, abandoning the requirement as discussed is restricted to *preserving* data in another country and does not extend to *obtaining* the data; as a result, the requirement will at least effectively continue to exist.

The discussion at the international workshop did not support abandoning the requirement of double criminality either. The foreign experts appeared astonished rather than provoked to think along with the idea. The requirement of double criminality appeared so fundamental to them that, in fact, there is or should not be any room to impair this.[257]

As a result of this research finding, the Dutch government has now discarded the idea of abandoning double criminality for certain cases, since "this aim from the LEH Memorandum has met with a great deal of international resistance".[258]

Given the fact that abandoning the requirement of double criminality is internationally infeasible, together with the finding that harmonising criminalisations is hardly realistic in many cases, we come to the conclusion that the international fight against ICT crime will have to resort to cooperation between enforcement authorities.

---

[257] One may also remark here that, particularly with a view to the goal of enabling tracing, the question of abandoning the requirement of double criminality will probably not or less easily emerge in countries such as the United States and the United Kingdom, where it is possible, contrary to the Netherlands, to search a computer outside of the own territory with a court order.

[258] ILIS Memorandum, 11th working principle, section 3.2.

6. Cooperation between Enforcement Authorities

6.1 Introduction

The cross-border character of electronic highways implies that persons physically outside of one jurisdiction can relatively easily commit crimes with effects within – or even specifically targeted at – another jurisdiction. Enforcing national criminal law in such situations requires cooperation between enforcement authorities. With 'enforcement authorities', we indicate the various national and international investigation bodies.

Cooperating with foreign authorities is, of course, nothing new. The rules on cooperation between enforcement authorities are laid down in international treaties, of which at least the European Convention on Mutual Assistance in Criminal Matters and the Benelux Mutual Assistance Convention deserve mention.[259] Mutual assistance is traditionally provided through letters rogatory: the requesting state asks the requested state to use certain powers for the sake of criminal proceedings in the requesting state. The traditional ways of obtaining mutual assistance, however, do not suffice on the electronic highway in all respects. Particularly the lack of promptness is playing tricks on investigation bodies on the electronic highway. The LEH Memorandum draws attention to the difficulties in obtaining information from network operators abroad. For tracing hackers, one needs, for example, to obtain data at the moment the hacker is still 'there' in the system. Network operators play a key part in this: they have the required data at their disposal (loggings, subscriber data, and so on). However, by the time they are reached through the traditional mutual-assistance instruments, often, important logging data have been deleted, leaving enforcement authorities empty-handed. The LEH Memorandum views the quickness of acts in cyberspace and the volatility of the trail they leave as *the* problem in the cooperation between enforcement authorities. The question is whether this problem can be solved by better using current mutual-assistance instruments, or whether new solutions will have to be looked for. Given this problem area, we restrict ourselves here to 'simple' mutual assistance; we do not address extradition, transfer of proceedings, or transfer of execution of judgements.

---

[259] European Convention on Mutual Assistance in Criminal Matters of 20 April 1959, *Trb.* 1965, 10, and the Benelux Convention on Extradition and Assistance in Criminal Matters of 27 June 1962, *Trb.* 1962, 97.

The position of the Dutch government
The Dutch government considers it desirable to make rules on cooperation between enforcement authorities.[260] This is needed in particular to regulate investigation powers that address foreign Internet providers, and to ensure the cooperation of other countries in investigation.

In particular, the *Crime in Cyberspace* Convention must provide options to immediately obtain information from foreign network providers, according to the LEH Memorandum.[261] That is to say, investigation authorities must be able, under certain conditions, to address foreign network providers directly, without prior intervention of investigation authorities in the country of the network provider. Court review can then take place afterwards. However, in their most recent internationalisation document, the ILIS Memorandum, the Dutch government have not reiterated this view.

6.2 International organisations

On 10 December 1997, the G8 Ministers have specified ten principles and a ten-point action plan for combating high-tech crime.[262] Three of the ten principles are especially relevant for the cooperation between enforcement authorities. First, legislation must enable the preservation and prompt access to electronic data, because these data are critically important for successfully investigating crime (principle V). Second, mutual-assistance regimes must provide for powers to promptly collect and exchange evidence in cases involving international high-tech crime (principle VI). Finally, cross-border access of enforcement authorities to open-source information does not require the consent of the state in which the data are stored (principle VII).

In order to realise the aspirations laid down in the principles, an action plan was formulated. Worth mentioning are at least a network of expert enforcers that has been set up to safeguard prompt and effective addressing of cross-border high-tech cases. Moreover, contact points are being established that are available 24 hours a day. The G8 principles and action items are generally very important, because they (informally) influence the agenda of other international platforms.

Within the Council of Europe, since 1997, a group of experts – PC-CY – have been working on a draft convention that, for the time being, is called *Convention on Cyber-Crime* or also *Crime in Cyberspace*. Not until April 2000 was a first draft text published for consultation of public and private interested parties, the *Draft Convention on Cyber-Crime* (hereafter in this section: Draft Convention).[263] The Draft Convention regulates a large number of substantive and procedural topics, such as intercepting data transfers, searching computers and seizing computer data, preserving data, jurisdiction, mutual assistance, and access to public-domain data.

---

260 LEH Memorandum, p. 8.
261 LEH Memorandum, p. 116-117.
262 Sieber 1998, p. 183-185.
263 Council of Europe 2000.

One of the convention's starting points is that, in principle, investigation powers can not be applied across borders.[264] This implies that at all times, the authorities of the state at issue must be solicited. Since mutual assistance in cyberspace requires the utmost expediency, the convention arranges the setting up of national central authorities (art. 23 Draft Convention). These central authorities are staffed with expert personnel 24 hours a day and seven days a week. They are able to promptly reach the judicial authorities required for authorising and applying the requested powers. The Dutch government considers the central authorities – essentially no more than optimally using current mutual-assistance instruments – a step in the right direction.

The Draft Convention furthermore includes an investigation power particularly important for Internet providers: the preservation order (art. 16-17). This is a judicial power to order or otherwise ensure, during an investigation, the preservation of data stored in a computer system. This power can be applied only if there are grounds to believe that the data will be preserved for only a brief period or if they are otherwise particularly vulnerable to loss or modification. This is the case, for example, with telecommunications service providers who for reasons of privacy, in principle, have to delete (or anonymise) certain traffic data after a communication has ended.[265] For the sake of collecting traffic data about a communication, the party states will moreover have to provide for the necessary (statutory) measures to ensure the prompt disclosure to authorities of data that are sufficient to identify the service providers and the path along which the communication took place.

A preservation order can only be given for data stored within the territory of the own state or in another place where the own state has sovereignty. If the authorities of one party state wish to preserve data stored in another state, they will have to request the other state for mutual assistance. During the preparation of the Draft Convention, the idea was considered to enable party states to directly address a preservation order or a preservation request to the holder of the data.[266] This – time-saving – idea did not make it.[267] Some other provisions relating to the preservation order have nonetheless been included in the Draft Convention. For instance, section 1 of Article 24 suggests that the preservation order is a temporary measure. After all, the requesting party state may only ask the requested party state to order or ensure preservation, if the requesting state indeed intends to request a search (or another form of obtaining the data), seizure (or another form of security), or disclosing the data. In order to enable the requesting state to submit such subsequent assistance requests, the data are preserved for at least forty days. The requested party state can not refuse to apply the preservation order because double criminality would be lacking, but the requirement of double criminality may indeed be posed for disclosing the data to the requesting state (see section 5.2). Only a limited number of

264 Art. 27 Draft Convention regulates an exception to this starting point: no assistance request is needed for accessing open-source data, nor for obtaining data from a person who is located in another state and who voluntarily provides those data to which he has legitimate access.

265 See art. 11.5 Dutch Telecommunications Act.

266 TK 1999-2000, 23 530, no. 40, p. 9.

267 Art. 23 para. 10 Draft Convention contains some general options for speeding up mutual assistance.

reasons allow the requested party state to refuse applying a preservation order, namely, if its sovereignty is violated, or if the security, the public order, or other essential interests are harmed.

If a request for a preservation order concerns traffic data, the requested party state must, under certain conditions, disclose without delay certain traffic data (art. 25 Draft Convention). This is the case if the requested state discovers that a third state was involved in transferring the communication. In that case, the requested party state discloses sufficient data to the requesting party state to identify the service provider and the path of the communication. Disclosure may only be withheld if it would violate the sovereignty of the requested state, or if the security, the public order, or other essential interests would be harmed.

The European Council, in May 2000, established a Convention on Mutual Assistance in Criminal Matters between the EU member states, which will enter into force once eight states have signed it.[268] This convention, among other things, creates a power to directly intercept telecommunications from a telecommunications address that is being used on the territory of another member state (from which state no technical assistance is needed). The intercepting state has to notify the other state as soon as it becomes aware of the cross-border nature of the interception. If possible, it must notify the other state in advance. The notified state is granted a certain period in which it may allow or prohibit the interception. Until this decision is taken, the intercepting state may not, in principle, use the material already intercepted. Furthermore, the convention also creates a power of cross-border interception in relation to telecommunications gateways.

The Data Protection Working Party has made recommendations for preserving traffic data by Internet providers for investigation purposes.[269] The Working Party thinks that traffic data should not be preserved merely for investigation purposes, and that national legislation should not require telecommunications and Internet providers to preserve traffic data for a longer period than is necessary for invoice purposes. The Working Party recommends the European Commission to take the appropriate measures to harmonise the preservation period within the EU, a period of three months being considered suitable by the Working Party.

The United Nations are drafting a Model Convention on Mutual Assistance in Criminal Matters. The Model Convention regulates, among other things, designating competent authorities, the content of requests, refusing assistance, protecting confidentiality, obtaining evidence, the availability of free and detained people for delivering evidence, search and seizure, certification and authentication, and costs. An expert group is studying how to keep the Model Convention as up-to-date and efficient as possible.[270]

---

[268] Council Act of 29 May 2000 establishing (...) the Convention on Mutual Assistance in Criminal Matters between the Member States of the European Union (2000/C197/01), *OJ* 12 July 2000.

[269] Recommendation 3/99 on the preservation of traffic data by internet service providers for law enforcement purposes, 7 September 1999, <http://europa.eu.int/comm/internal_market/en/media/dataprot/wpdocs/wp25en.pdf>.

[270] See <http://register.aspensys.com/nij/newmeet.htm>.

6.3 Germany

The Federal Parliament Enquiry Committee Future of the Media in Economy and Society (*Zukunft der Medien in Wirtschaft und Gesellschaft*) recognises the problems of mutual assistance in cross-border network environments, and it acknowledges the necessity of solving these at the international level. The current law for international cooperation in criminal proceedings is too complex and it works too slowly for truly effectively getting a grip on perpetrators located abroad. The legislature should therefore make an effort to simplify mutual assistance and to enhance its effectiveness. This requires international cooperation "of unprecedented magnitude".[271] The federal Ministry of Justice is actively involved in preparing the Cybercrime Convention of the Council of Europe, and it participates in the preparation – within the G8 – of internationally consistent rules on prosecuting crimes committed on international computer networks.[272]

Germany has not yet published a position on the *Crime in Cyberspace* Convention or on the issue of directly obtaining information from foreign Internet providers. On 9 June 2000, the Federal Council (*Bundesrat*) called upon the Federal Government to establish that criminal law guarantees sufficient protection against cybercrime and to enhance international cooperation in this field.[273] The preparatory works for the *Crime in Cyberspace* Convention were mentioned as a good starting point.

6.4 France

Various policy documents acknowledge the need for an international approach to address the cross-border character of e-crime.[274] In particular, cooperation within the EU, the Council of Europe, and the G8 is contemplated.

The State Council has published an elaborate position on strengthening international cooperation. They recognise that international cooperation is necessary to fight crime on the net. According to the State Council, the existing mutual-assistance instruments are, in principle, applicable in a computer-science context. After all, the current mutual-assistance treaties do not make a distinction based on the type of crimes or on the (technical) mode in which they are committed. Nevertheless, crime in cyberspace does have its specific problems. These are related to the difficulties of tracing electronic messages, the differences between states in the admissibility of evidence, the permissibility of cross-border network searches, the international implications of blocking the spread of illegal content, and intercepting satellite communications, which by their nature often cover many states. These lead the State Council to conclude that entirely new, *sui generis* forms of mutual-assistance cooperation are called for.

---

[271] Enquete-Kommission 1998, p. 24.
[272] Bundesregierung 1999, p. 45.
[273] Bundestag Drucksache 275/00.
[274] Lorentz 1998a, Conseil d'Etat 1998, and CISI 1998.

The State Council distinguishes between unofficial investigation and letters rogatory. An unofficial investigation is understood to mean preliminary investigation acts that do not require a formal competence, but that rather consist of collecting information on persons or objects, such as someone's precise identity or his or her last-known residence. In order to intensify international cooperation in this area, the State Council proposes to strengthen information exchange within the framework of Europol and Interpol.

Letters rogatory are normally handled through the respective Ministries of Justice. This procedure is especially unsuitable for the Internet environment, which is characterised by speed and fleetingness. The traditional mutual-assistance instruments will therefore have to be revised. To this purpose, it has sometimes been suggested that the Public Prosecutor or the judicial police can execute letters rogatory without prior review in court. The State Council rejects this solution, however, as contentious: intervention by a court is a fundamental guarantee for the constitutional freedoms of individuals.[275]

Effectively making mutual-assistance procedures more expedient will have to be accomplished internationally. Pending further-reaching reforms, courts should be enabled to directly address letters rogatory to each other. Investigation results would then also have to be sent directly from the requested court to the requesting court, in case of urgency by fax.

Where cross-border wiretapping or eavesdropping is concerned, France refers to the EU convention on mutual assistance between member states.[276] Moreover, mutual-assistance instruments for (network) searches and seizures will have to be arranged internationally. Here, mutual assistance remains the appropriate mechanism to provide judicial access to data located abroad.

6.5 United Kingdom

The British Home Office's Judicial Co-operation Unit published a manual on mutual assistance in criminal matters in October 1999.[277] This presents the current state of affairs for foreign authorities desiring to submit a request for mutual assistance in the United Kingdom. The document does not go into the specific problems a network environment might raise for assistance. Relevant here are the following issues. Assistance requests can be submitted in principle in every stage of an investigation or inquest. A distinction is made between requests for legal assistance and requests for investigative assistance. The former must be addressed to the Home Office, which has a multiple responsibility. It checks, among other things, whether requests for mutual assistance comply with the conditions of the British law and the UK's international obligations. Also, the Home Office considers whether executing the request is not inappropriate with a view to public-policy considerations. For instance, requests that involve double jeopardy are rejected. The Home Office is the body that passes obtained evidence on to the requesting authori-

[275] Conseil d'Etat 1998, section 4.3.5.
[276] Strauss Kahn a.o. 1999.
[277] Judicial Co-operation Unit 1999.

ties. Requests for investigative assistance can be directed to the UK National Central Bureau of Interpol. This is the case, for instance, with requests for tracing possessions or for providing data about British telecommunications subscribers for investigative purposes. The data that may be provided about a British telecommunications subscriber are the surname and initials, and the address of the telephone connection – these being the only data British telecommunications companies are able to provide.

Until recently, the United Kingdom did not have investigation powers that specifically target traffic data. Providing such data occurred either voluntarily or on the basis of a Production Order authorised by a Crown Court. The Data Protection Act and the Telecommunications Act allowed voluntary supply for certain purposes. In 1999, a bill was formulated to provide a legal basis for obtaining and supplying communications data. This Regulation of Investigatory Powers Bill applies both to supply for the sake of investigation and to supply to security services. The bill received Royal Assent on 28 July 2000 and is now known as the Regulation of Investigatory Powers Act 2000.[278]

For some activities – such as surfing through public information on the Internet – no special powers are needed.[279] In those cases, formal cooperation between enforcement authorities does not enter. Surfing the web may, however, take place within the framework of an unofficial cooperation. The UK Office of Fair Trading, for example, has participated in a surfing day organised by the US Federal Trade Commission: a day when enforcement authorities of various countries jointly comb the web looking for fraudulent websites.[280]

The report *E-commerce@its.best.uk* recommends to improve the technical capacities of enforcing and regulatory authorities, and to set up an Internet Crime Unit as proposed by the National Criminal Intelligence Service.[281]

The British government is actively involved in the preparation of the *Crime in Cyberspace* Convention.[282] They have not yet published a position on this convention, nor on directly obtaining information from foreign Internet providers.

6.6 United States

The US Ministry of Justice, in reaction to a policy document of the Federal Trade Commission, indicates that current mutual-assistance instruments are not expedient enough to secure essential data.[283] Preserving data is therefore one of the points of attention in protecting consumers from fraud. US Deputy Attorney General Holder also recognises the need of preserving data, and he remarks that privacy legislation should not obstruct ef-

---

278 See <http://www.homeoffice.gov.uk/ripa/ripact.htm>.

279 Compare TK 1999-2000, 23 530, no. 40, p. 7.

280 *Financial Times* 24 March 2000, 'Worldwide sweep for internet fraudsters: US oversees action against 1,600 suspect web sites in 28 countries'.

281 Cabinet Office 1999, recommendation 10.5.

282 Clarke 1999.

283 Department of Justice 1999, reaction to topic 16.

fective law enforcement. This could imply, in his opinion, that privacy legislation will have to be adapted in view of the problems that the new technical reality confronts law enforcers with.[284]

The President's Working Group on Unlawful Conduct on the Internet notes in the report *The Electronic Frontier* of March 2000 that further-reaching international cooperation is sought along two tracks.[285] On the one hand, more formal cooperation is sought within bodies such as the Council of Europe (the *Crime in Cyberspace* Convention) and the G8. On the other hand, forms of unofficial cooperation are being developed. Such unofficial cooperation can take place because some activities do not require formal powers; one can think, for example, of investigations restricted to consulting publicly available information on the web.

6.7 Comparison and conclusion

Other countries acknowledge the need for closer cooperation between enforcement authorities. Also, it is recognised that drastic changes in traditional mutual assistance are required to achieve this. However, this is primarily seen as an issue that necessitates an international quest for solutions. After all, mutual assistance in criminal matters is not suitable for a national 'Alleingang', as the term 'mutual' implies. Mutual assistance is provided on a basis of reciprocity. This explains why the major developments are taking place in international platforms, and why no definitive steps are taken at the national level pending the outcome of the international developments.

At the national level, countries restrict themselves to short-term measures, such as establishing central contact points accessible around the clock, and other measures available within the current legal framework. The Dutch desire to obtain data more easily is, in principle, reflected in the thinking of the other countries. However, foreign governments have not yet published positions on the specific intention to obtain data directly from foreign Internet providers.

The Council of Europe's draft *Crime in Cyberspace* Convention does not provide for this either. It does introduce a new investigation power: the preservation order, addressed to telecommunications or Internet providers, which can easily be given and which secures the preservation of data pending the execution of other investigation powers, such as search and 'seizure'. For preserving data stored in another state, however, one still has to resort to a request for mutual assistance – the Draft Convention has rejected the option of directly addressing foreign providers. Consequently, in the ILIS Memorandum, the Dutch government have not reiterated their wish to directly access foreign Internet providers.

---

284 Holder 1999.

285 President's Working Group 2000.

7. Private International Law and Online Contracts

7.1 Introduction

In the LEH Memorandum, the Dutch government notes that there are no specific choice-of-law and jurisdiction rules in national, European, or international private international law for contracts concluded online.[286] The question is whether the rules of current – off-line – private international law (PIL) can bring relief. This chapter analyses how other countries try to answer this question.

To clarify the problem, we will first provide an overview of the kinds of transactions in an online environment, since the qualification of the legal act is relevant to the issue of applicable law and jurisdiction. Subsequently, we will briefly go into the current conventional provisions and the Dutch government's position outlined in the LEH Memorandum. We will then present the views of the various countries and compare these with the Dutch government's position.

Online contracts can be divided into:

- *strict online contracts*: contracts that are concluded online and that lead to supplying the goods or services in an electronic way, and
- *indirect or partial online contracts*: contracts concluded online that relate to goods or services provided in a traditional way.[287]

This distinction is not used in the LEH Memorandum. However, it is relevant in the context of private international law issues, because with the first category, there are several legal acts in an electronic environment, which sometimes makes it difficult to determine the exact location of and the person responsible for the legal act, whereas the second category involves actual acts of delivery in a certain country. What is more, direct online contracts may involve virtual actors – intelligent agents acting on behalf of people.

The LEH Memorandum does note that specific protection rules can apply to consumer contracts, but again, no distinction is made between strict online contracts and indirect online contracts.

Absent a contractual choice of law or choice of forum, it is possible that the private international law rules lead to other results with strict online contracts than with indirect

---

[286] LEH Memorandum, p. 68.

[287] Van Esch 1999, p. 14; Prins & Gijrath 2000, p. 3.

online contracts, for example, in choosing the location of the actual delivery of the ordered goods or services.

Private international law rules

In the European Union, the Convention on the Law applicable to Contractual Obligations (Rome Convention)[288] and the Convention on jurisdiction and the enforcement of judgements in civil and commercial matters (Brussels Convention)[289] provide a conventional system of PIL rules. Both conventions are not restricted to certain kinds of contracts, which means that they apply to, for instance, purchases or licenses, and to contracts concluded by phone or in writing. Moreover, the Rome Convention has a universal scope (compare, e.g., art. 2 Rome Convention). Since the ICT-related problems with respect to both conventions are similar, we deal with them here together, and refer by way of example to the relevant provisions from the Rome Convention.

First of all, online contracts are subject to the law chosen by parties in compliance with article 3 Rome Convention. Absent a choice of law, the Rome Convention uses the basic rule that the contract is governed by the law of the country of residence of the party who provides the characteristic performance (art. 4). In consumer contracts within the meaning of article 5 para. 1, 4, and 5 Rome Convention, an explicit contractual choice of law cannot, however, deprive consumers of the protection they are entitled to on the basis of mandatory provisions of the law of their country of residence. Absent a contractual choice of law, the law of the consumers' country of habitual residence governs consumer contracts, if the contracts were concluded under the conditions of article 5 para. 2 Rome Convention.[290] Here, a distinction is made between active and passive consumers. One of the principal ICT-related problems results from this very distinction between active and passive consumers. The general idea behind the distinction is to solely protect consumers who are solicited by foreign businesses, not consumers who actively look for foreign merchants or service providers themselves. However, the question arises how to qualify consumers who are looking for the website at their own initiative. Can the website itself be considered an advertisement in the consumer's country? Does the shopkeeper's intention with respect to the scope of the website (world-wide, or limited to a certain number of countries) play a role? Can circumstances such as language, currency, and choice-of-law or choice-of-forum clauses be of relevance? There is no unambiguous answer to any of these questions. If one interprets the rules strictly, Internet consumers, in many cases, will not be protected, while protection may be especially important exactly in online situations. Moreover, legal uncertainty is detrimental to the development of electronic commerce – a development that can benefit both businesses and consumers.[291] In the Netherlands, the Consumer Association (*Consumentenbond*), by means of its Webtrader scheme, at least seems to take the position that consumers who conclude online contracts

[288] Convention on the Law applicable to Contractual Obligations, Rome, 19 June 1980, *OJ* 9 October 1980, L 266/1.

[289] Convention on jurisdiction and the enforcement of judgements in civil and commercial matters, Brussels, 27 September 1968, *OJ* 31 December 1972, L 299/32.

[290] Polak 1998, p. 88.

[291] Van der Hof 1998, p. 424; Van der Hof 2000. See also: Drion 1999, p. 84.

will in any case have to retain Dutch consumer protection, regardless of their being considered active or passive consumers.[292]

In the meantime, the European Commission has issued a draft regulation to replace and update the Brussels Convention; a revision of the Rome Convention is expected as well (see section 7.2).

The position of the Dutch government

In the LEH Memorandum, the Dutch government sets great store by clarifying the PIL rules that may apply to the electronic highway and electronic commerce. The Dutch government takes the position that developing specific PIL rules for the electronic highway deserves priority.[293] It is desirable to establish a broadly formulated framework of PIL rules that apply to online contracts. The Dutch government has a strong preference for making agreements within the framework of the Hague Conference on Private International Law.[294]

In the ILIS Memorandum, the Dutch government stresses that the choice of the Electronic Commerce Directive to apply the country-of-origin principle should be further elaborated, to make it suitable for application in a larger international setting. Such an elaboration should take place along the following lines:

- at an international level, harmonisation should take place on the basis of a set of fundamental principles;
- the country-of-origin principle should apply;
- this principle forms the basis for actually supervising requests for assistance from other states and to cooperate with such requests;
- there should be mutual recognition of such supervision.[295]

7.2 International organisations

No views are available of the OECD and the WTO on the specific issue of private international law and online contracts; the most relevant OECD documents[296] do not deal with the issue. The WTO poses that international agreements and rules are called for on the law that applies to electronic commerce, but no position was found on the direction these initiatives should take. A number of countries propose to develop a global and interna-

---

[292] See <http://www.dedigitaleconsument/webtrader.nl>, particularly the position on laws and regulations.

[293] LEH Memorandum, p. 6. The Dutch government also seems to take the position that it is desirable to further analyse and determine PIL rules for online contracts.

[294] Hague Conference on Private International Law, 1893. This Conference meanwhile also gives a high priority to the issue of the law applicable to online contracts, see <http://www.hcch.net/e/events/press01e.html>.

[295] ILIS Memorandum, section 2.5.

[296] OECD 1998c and OECD 1998d.

tional framework that all parties in electronic commerce could join, preferably the UNCITRAL Model Law.[297]

At the European level, article 12 para. 2 Distance-Selling Directive of 20 May 1997[298] contains rules that apply to a number of contracts concluded online.[299] It includes several mandatory provisions consumers can rely on. To put it briefly, a contractual choice of law cannot deprive consumers of the protection from mandatory rules of their own law. Polak rightly argues that this provision has to be reconciled with the aforementioned article 5 para. 2 Rome Convention.[300]

The Electronic Commerce Directive contained a regulation on this at first, but the final version states, in consideration 7, that it does not have the goal to provide specific PIL rules. It is a framework directive. Article 9 only states that member states have to ensure that the legal rules applicable to contractual procedures do not prevent that actual use of online contracts, without answering the question which law applies in a given case. The European Commission has decided to leave the issue of applicable law out of the Electronic Commerce Directive as far as consumer relations are concerned. For business-to-business online transactions, according to the Directive, the country-of-origin principle applies.

Finally, we should mention the draft Directive on distance marketing of financial services. Article 11 stipulates that a choice of law cannot deprive consumers of their protection under this Directive (requiring statutory consumer law of their home country to apply to the contract, if the consumers reside in a member state and if the contract has a close link with the Community).[301]

In 1999, the European Commission adopted a draft regulation on jurisdiction, recognition, and enforcement of judgements in civil and commercial matters, which is to replace and update the Brussels convention.[302] In this draft regulation, the European Commission also intends to remedy the inadequacies by including online consumer contracts in the special consumer-protection rules on jurisdiction, expressly deciding in favour of Internet consumers. Clearly, this choice is not welcomed by industry, who fear huge economic consequences as a result of this new legislation. Admittedly, the risk of being summoned into foreign courts all over the world can be expensive for companies and may not be desirable economically. In order to identify the various positions and arguments, the European Commission held a hearing on jurisdiction and applicable law in the beginning

---

[297] UNCITRAL Model Law on Electronic Commerce, General Assembly Resolution 51/162, 16 December 1996, with an additional article 5bis, 1998, <http://www.uncitral.org>.

[298] Directive 4 June 1997, *OJ* L 144, p. 19.

[299] See also Drion 1999, p. 69.

[300] Polak 1998, p. 86.

[301] Amended proposal for a European Parliament and Council directive concerning distance marketing of consumer financial services and amending directives 97/7/EC and 98/27/EC, 23 July 1999, COM(1999) 385 final.

[302] Draft Regulation on jurisdiction and the enforcement of judgements in civil and commercial matters of 14 July 1999, COM(99) 348.

of November 1999. At this hearing, consumer organisations pleaded strongly in favour of the new regulation, whereas industry fiercely opposed it.

The European Commission is also planning to prepare a draft regulation on applicable law to replace the Rome convention.

Considering the world-wide effect of a possible solution under the Hague Conference on Private International law, the outcomes of these discussions seem of particular importance for future private international law rules for online contracts. However, the adaptation of this Conference, as advocated by the Dutch government, does not appear to run particularly smoothly. At a meeting in Ottawa in late February 2000, it appeared anything but feasible to reach an agreement on the draft amendments of the current Conference text. As part of the discussions on the amendments, seals of approval for websites were proposed to address private international law problems with respect to consumer contracts. In such a system, online businesses would receive a seal of approval if they live up to a certain minimum level of consumer protection and if they offer the possibility of (free) alternative dispute resolution. Approved websites would fall under the country-of-origin principle, since disputes would for the greater part be resolved through alternative dispute resolution. Non-approved websites would still be subject to the *forum consumptoris* rule. The introduction of a website seal-of-approval system will only be successful at an international level if countries and (international) organisations can agree upon a set of minimum standards for consumer protection, since such a system requires a certain level of harmonisation.[303]

7.3 Germany

Germany is a party to the Rome Convention and to the Brussels Convention. However, with a view to ICT-related problems, it should be noted that Germany, together with the UK, Luxembourg, and Ireland, has made a declaration that they will not apply article 7 of the Rome Convention. Article 7 could be important if article 5 of this convention is interpreted as not applying to information-society issues, i.e., to online contracts (see section 7.1). In that case, consumers could fall back on article 7.[304]

According to article 27 German Civil Code, the main rule is a contractual choice of law, but, also in Germany, this choice of law can be thwarted by consumer-protection provisions.[305] The specific electronic-commerce regulations, the IuKDG and the Interstate Media Services Treaty, do not contain particular PIL rules. The German government's position on the Hague Conference is not specifically addressed in policy documents. Nor is it made clear whether the German government prefers a regulation within the framework of the Hague Conference to one within any other international organisation.

---

[303] See also Van der Hof 2000.

[304] See on the relation between articles 5 and 7 of the Rome Convention, Joustra 1997, p. 118ff.

[305] On the specific effects of this, little was found; see, e.g., Linklaters & Alliance 1999, p. 99.

7.4 France

France is also a party to both conventions, but, like the Netherlands, advocates a further-reaching harmonisation of the various consumer-protection rules. The French government does not, however, draw general conclusions from this on the necessity of establishing further choice-of-law and jurisdiction rules for online contracts, although the State Council attaches importance to a balanced approach that takes into account the interests of both consumers and vendors.[306] The French government does call it a central issue. They do not prefer a regulation within the framework of the Hague Conference to other international platforms. They do prefer a sectoral approach of the issue. Furthermore, the French government suggests that it is not by all accounts necessary to establish a regulation of PIL rules that would use the same principles online and offline.

7.5 United Kingdom

The United Kingdom has implemented the Rome Convention in national law.[307] As mentioned in section 7.3, the UK has also signed a declaration that they will not apply article 7 of the Rome Convention. In light of the planned European draft regulation on applicable law, it should be noted that the UK has made a reservation to the specific provision in the Treaty of Amsterdam on which this draft regulation is based. However, the UK government has mentioned that it will eventually adopt the regulation nevertheless.

No difference was found between article 5 para. 2 Rome Convention and the implementation of the Unfair Contract Terms Directive[308] and of the Distance-Selling Directive[309].

There is no indication that the British government advocates, like the Dutch government, a system that develops a supranational legal framework for the choice-of-law and jurisdiction rules for online contracts, but it is expected that the government will formulate an opinion on this.[310]

The UK government has not (yet) taken a position on the Hague Conference. Nor do they strictly prefer a regulation within this Conference, and they leave open the option of regulating within other platforms, such as the OECD, the WIPO, the UNCITRAL, the

---

306 Conseil d'Etat 1998.

307 Contracts (Applicable Law) Act 1990, see <http://www.hmso.gov.uk/acts/summary/01990036.htm>. This Act does not contain specific provisions for online contracts, but it can be applied to these.

308 See the Unfair terms in consumer contracts regulations 1994 (SI 1994 No. 3159). Regulation 7 contains a choice-of-law clause, see <http://www.dti.gov.uk/access/unfair/part8.htm>.

309 As implemented by the Electronic Communications Act 2000, <http://www.legislation.hmso.gov.uk/acts/acts2000/20000007.htm>.

310 See, e.g., the position on the Draft Convention on the Protection of Adults, <http://www.scotcourts.gov.uk/forms/draft_2.htm>.

WTO, and the EU. Generally, the government supports the Dutch government's adage that what holds offline, should also hold online (see section 2.5), but it is not clear whether this is also applied to the law applicable to online contracts.

7.6 United States

The US favour further harmonisation within the framework of the UNCITRAL regulation on electronic commerce.[311] The UNCITRAL regulation, however, does not include a position or shed light on PIL rules for online contracts. The topic of the law and jurisdiction applicable to international online contracts does not seem to be an issue at the federal policy level in the US. Interesting, however, are the conclusions of a draft report by the Global Cyberspace Jurisdiction Project of the American Bar Association.[312] The draft report mentions that no state or nation can hope to provide the answers to jurisdiction issues by itself. According to the Project, a global commission should be established, that is "empanelled to study jurisdiction issues and develop uniform principles and global protocol standards by a specific sunset date, working in conjunction with other international bodies considering similar issues." The report also discusses the role of technology in solving jurisdiction problems. Electronic agents and other software programs should be programmed in such a way that they allow consumers to identify the country, laws, protection standards, and remedial options that they seek when entering into a contractual relationship.

Finally, a complicating matter in the US is that the law applicable to online contracts can be determined by each state. The case law suggests a tendency that choice of law is closely related to jurisdiction.

7.7 Comparison and conclusion

The Dutch government holds the position that PIL rules applicable to online contracts should preferably be regulated as soon as possible within the framework of the Hague Conference. This position does not, for the time being, appear to be shared by the countries we studied. In the US, the question is not an issue in policy-making at the federal level. A recent US study, however, stressed that prime attention should be given to the international implications of the matter and that the problems should be handled at an international level. In Germany and the United Kingdom, no positions were found, whereas France has formulated a divergent view. So far, these countries want to tie in with the current Rome Convention and Brussels Convention rules. They all appear to await the outcome of the debates at the European level to amend the Brussels and Rome

---

311 UNCITRAL Model Law on Electronic Commerce, General Assembly Resolution 51/162, 16 December 1996, with an additional article 5bis, 1998, <http://www.uncitral.org>.

312 ABA 2000.

Conventions. Furthermore, it seems that no reconciling has occurred of article 5 para. 2 Rome Convention and the choice-of-law provisions of the Unfair Contract Terms and Distance-Selling Directives, although no indications were found either that these Directives will lead to different or contradictory rules.[313] We can conclude that the Netherlands, in the issue of private international law and online contracts, are leaning more towards a global approach than the countries we researched.

Nevertheless, we have to mention that the adaptation of the Hague Conference as advocated by the Dutch government does not appear to work out particularly smoothly. At a meeting in Ottawa in late February 2000, it appeared anything but feasible to reach an agreement on the draft adaptation of the current Conference text.

[313] On this topic, see also Van der Hof 2000.

8. Civil Liability of Internet Providers

8.1 Introduction

Internet Providers offer access to the net. They are intermediaries described as access, service, or network providers. Providing information themselves is not characteristic of their role. This does not imply that they may not sometimes be involved with information that is spread through their systems. Generally, however, the information is provided by third parties, that is to say, Internet users. Although most users use the net for spreading perfectly lawful content, some users abuse the offered facilities to spread unlawful content. Users who place such information on the net (content providers) are, of course, the first to be liable for the content. Victims of unlawful content (such as copyright owners and victims of defamation or privacy violations) could therefore hold these users liable under civil law. In practice, it often appears difficult to sue content providers. Therefore, victims often also legally target Internet Providers. In certain circumstances, these can be held liable themselves under civil law for contributing to the distribution. Besides, Internet Providers are actually in a unique position when it comes to tracing and identifying content providers. After all, they have at their disposal data files (such as subscriber and logging data), technical expertise, and good contacts with other Internet Providers. So, Internet Providers occupy a key position for citizens seeking justice when they have become a victim of unlawful content.

Nevertheless, it often appears difficult to find actual legal protection on the Internet. This holds particularly when the Internet Provider and the victim are not located in the same country or jurisdiction. In such a case, additional problems arise related to issues of foreign Internet Provider liability. Under what conditions can a foreign Internet Provider be held liable? Also, it is relevant to what extent foreign Internet Providers are able, willing, authorised, or required to cooperate with attempts to trace and identify content providers.

In this chapter, we restrict ourselves to three forms of unlawful content: copyright infringement, defamation, and privacy violation. We also restrict ourselves to civil law, for two reasons. First, substantive criminal law, more than civil law, aims at keeping up certain values, which makes it more culturally determined than civil law. In the borderless context of the Internet, criminal law therefore raises more conflict potential. The issue of criminal liability of Internet Providers in an international perspective, then, is problematic. In this study, we analyse whether civil law – where discrepancies in substantive norms are less relevant – can provide a common denominator for Internet Provider liability. This is an application of a strategy to reach international agreement on contentious issues: one starts with regulating those topics on which agreement can relatively easily be reached and, step by step, extends this to more problematic topics. A second reason to go into civil liability here is the fact that a civil party can not resort to criminal-investigation powers to trace the identity of a content provider. This raises the question whether he has sufficient opportunity to act.

The position of the Dutch government

The government has taken the following position on civil liability of Internet Provider and the related cross-border aspects. Seen from a purely national perspective, there is no reason to create a separate regulation of civil Internet Provider liability. Dutch tort law is sufficiently technology-neutral, and the open structure of the tort norm leaves open all room for the courts to further develop the issue. Nevertheless, the government supports the European Commission's view that a set of common principles must be established at the international level in order to create a level playing field.[314] After all, the government attaches importance to a good international regulation of civil liability of intermediaries. Therefore, they support the Commission's attempt to make rules on service-provider liability.[315] This does not, however, imply that they agree with all points of the regulation established in the Electronic Commerce Directive.[316] The Minister of Justice questions the soundness of the Directive's distinction of service providers into the categories of access, caching, and hosting providers. Moreover, he doubts whether it is wise to exclude in advance certain categories of service providers (in particular, access providers) from liability, regardless of their knowledge of unlawful content. The Minister has reiterated this view in the ILIS Memorandum.

The government intends to actively draw attention at the international level to citizens' and victims' interest in being able to follow electronic tracks and to trace perpetrators.

8.2 International organisations

The Ministerial Declaration of the Bonn Conference of 6-8 July 1997 lays down a number of principles on the responsibility of intermediaries.[317] For example, the responsibility should be defined in clear legal rules. These rules must be based on common principles, so that equal conditions apply to everyone. The declaration provides a basis for differentiation of responsibilities according to the various functions of providers. The declaration defines the following categories: content producers and distributors, network operators and access providers, and hosting service providers. Finally, the responsibility

[314] TK 1998-1999, 25 880, no. 7.

[315] TK 1998-1999, 25 880, no. 7, p. 9.

[316] TK 1998-1999, 25 880, no. 7, p. 10.

[317] See <http://www.ispo.cec.be/bonn/final.html>.

rules should respect the freedom of speech, take into account public and private interests, and not encumber too heavily the parties involved.

The EU Electronic Commerce Directive lays down a horizontal regulation for Internet Provider liability.[318] The regulation applies to both criminal and civil liability, and it includes, in principle, all kinds of offences. Here also, a differentiation is made based on the providers' functions. Providers who restrict themselves to 'mere conduit' are relieved from liability, if they meet a number of purely factual conditions, regardless of their knowledge. Hosting service providers are not liable, if they have no knowledge of the unlawful content (or of the circumstances that suggest unlawful content) or if they promptly remove or block access to the unlawful content at issue as soon as they acquire knowledge. Caching service providers must fulfil a large number of duties of care in order to escape liability. None of these parties are required to proactively check for irregularities in the information they deal with. The Electronic Commerce Directive does not contain obligations for parties to identify content providers. Content providers must, however, make their own identity known, if they offer an 'Information Society Service'.

The EU has published many policy documents on the protection of minors against illegal and harmful content on the Internet.[319] For information that is not unlawful but that may be harmful to minors, a different approach is taken than for unlawful information. Minors must be shielded from this information through technical and organisational measures. This may involve access control at the source (the information) as well as filtering programs, to be installed by parents, that intervene at the level of the browser. Using filtering programs requires an enormous effort in rating the content.

8.3 Germany

Internet Provider liability

Germany has a horizontal regulation of service-provider liability since 1 August 1997. This regulation is laid down in the federal Teleservices Act and the Interstate Media Services Treaty. It distinguishes between the various functions service providers can perform. Service providers are liable for their own content according to the prevailing rules. For providing information from others, they are liable only if they have knowledge of it, if they are technically able to prevent its use, and if such technical prevention can reasonably be demanded from them. Service providers are not liable for third-party content to which they only provide access. Professionally operating service providers are required to give their name and address in their offer of services. Associations also have to give the names and addresses of those who are authorised to represent them. However, service providers do not include content providers with whom editorial design for the sake of public information provision comes first (e.g., providers of opinionating content).

---

[318] Directive 2000/31/EC ("Directive on electronic commerce"), *OJ* L 178/1, 17 June 2000, <http://europa.eu.int/eur-lex/en/dat/2000/l_178/l_17820000717en00010016.pdf>.

[319] For an overview of European policy documents in this area, see <http://www2.echo.lu/legal/en/internet/internet.html>.

Conversely, providers of stock exchange information and providers of goods or services do count as service providers.

On 30 March 2000, a Munich court convicted AOL to pay damages to the owner of copyrights in MIDI music-files. AOL had offered a 'music soundforum' to its subscribers that enabled them to upload and download music files. AOL could not avail itself of the defence offered by the Teleservices Act, because AOL possessed knowledge of the infringement and could easily have stopped it.[320]

Identification of content providers

The parliamentary enquiry committee Future of the Media in Economy and Society acknowledges the identification problems that arise through the use of pseudonyms, anonyms, and encryption technologies.[321] They do not consider restricting the use of encryption as a solution, because of the many possibilities to circumvent such restrictions and because of the (privacy) drawbacks for citizens and businesses. Where anonyms are concerned, there is an outright conflict between privacy and law enforcement. To what extent this conflict can be addressed satisfactorily depends on technology. If, however, the use of anonyms were to be limited, the use of pseudonyms would by all means have to remain ensured. Data that relate pseudonyms to people's identity have to be secured well against unauthorised access. The German government's position on the extent to which Internet Providers can be expected to identify content providers is not known.

The Federal Criminal Agency (*Bundeskriminalamt*) has researched the criminal effects of the rise of e-commerce and the consequences of this for the task of the police. In the report *Electronic Commerce. Market of the Future – Also for Criminals?*, it recommends, among other things, to diminish anonymity in e-commerce.[322]

International regulation

According to the Enquiry Committee, solutions to the problems related to identifiability mentioned above should preferably be found at the international level.[323]

Cross-border aspects

Germany has attempted in the past to use access providers to get a grip on information hosted abroad. These attempts have not appeared successful. In 1998, the managing director of CompuServe Germany (Felix Somm) was convicted for distributing child pornography. CompuServe Germany provided access to newsgroups of their US parent company. The conviction caused much turmoil in Germany, and Somm was recently acquitted on appeal.[324] In 1997, the German network provider DFN, on the instigation of German judicial authorities, blocked access (from Germany) for a while to all websites hosted by the Dutch Internet Provider xs4all. The reason for this was that one of the sites

---

[320] State Court of Munich 30 March 2000, 7 O 3625/98, <http://www.netlaw.de/urteile/lgm_14.htm>.

[321] Enquete-Kommission 1998, p. 24.

[322] See <http://www.bka.de/pressemitteilungen/2000/pm000224.html>.

[323] Enquete-Kommission 1998, p. 24.

[324] See <http://www.somm-case.de>.

offered a copy of the Radikal magazine that was prohibited in Germany.[325] In due time, DFN stopped its blocking, because it had become clear that the blockade was rendered ineffective by the mushrooming of mirror sites.

8.4 France

Internet Provider liability

In the French Official Journal of 2 August 2000, Act no. 2000-719 of 1 August 2000 was published.[326] This Act modifies Act no. 86-1067 of 30 September 1986 concerning the freedom of communication. It contains provisions concerning online communications services other than private correspondence. Article 43-8 of the Freedom of Communication Act now restricts the liability of persons who offer – for free or at a charge – direct and permanent storage for the purpose of making available to the public signals, writings, images, sounds, or messages of any kind that are accessible by these services. Such persons (providers) only incur civil or criminal liability for content, if they do not promptly block access to the content, after a judicial authority has demanded them to do so. Originally, the proposed provision featured a second condition that had to be met in order to avoid liability. It read that a provider should take due care when addressed by a third party who estimated that stored content was unlawful or damaging to him. This condition was struck down by the French Constitutional Council for being too imprecise for a criminal provision.[327]

Access providers have to inform their subscribers of the existence of filtering means or they have to offer one such means to them.

In the meantime, case-law offers the following picture of Internet Provider liability under prevailing law. Defamation is covered by a 1982 act on audio-visual communications. The High Court of Puteaux, in the case of AXA/M., decided that a hosting provider is, in principle, not liable for defamation originating from third parties, because it judged the (managing director of) a hosting provider not to be a 'director of publication' (*directeur de publication*) for the purposes of the French 1982 broadcasting act.[328] This act requires that a publication is preceded by a recording,[329] which is not the case in an Internet context: almost at the same moment that the content provider uploads the information, it is available to the public. This cuts off any opportunity for the hosting provider to exercise prior monitoring of the content. So, the hosting provider is no more than a service provider who offers the technical means with which content providers can publish.

---

325 See <http://www.xs4all.nl/spotlight/blokkade_e.html>.

326 See <http://www.assemblee-nationale.fr/2/dossiers/communic/2com.htm>.

327 See <http://www.conseil-constitutionnel.fr/decision/2000/2000433/2000433dc.htm>.

328 Tribunal de Grand Instance de Puteaux 28 September 1999 (*AXA Conseil IARD et AXA Conseil Vie* v. *M. Christophe M., M. Christophe Sapet*).

329 In the same sense, Cour de Cassation, Chambre Criminelle, 8 December 1998 (*Le Procureur général c./M.R.*).

Where privacy violations are concerned, in particular violations of the personality right to one's portrait, the French courts seem to accept liability for hosting providers more readily. The High Court of Nanterre judged the liability of four Internet Providers who hosted websites with nude pictures of a model.[330] The public provision of these images violated her portrait rights. The court judged that a hosting provider is more than a mere access provider, because he enters the area of communicating ideas, opinions, information, and services. The hosting provider has a general duty of care. He therefore has to take due precautions and use reasonable means of information, vigilance, and action. This judgement is in line with the decisions in the case of Estelle Hallyday/Valentin Lacambre.[331]

For the position of Internet Providers under copyright law, a decision of the Commercial Court of Paris is important.[332] This decision involved the *sui generis* database law; given the resemblance between copyright law and database law, this judgement must be considered relevant for copyright law. T.I. Communication and M.D. offered a database through a website. This offer violated the *sui generis* database rights of Electre. The court judged that the hosting provider (Maxotex) had no duty to check the content of data he allows to 'circulate'. Maxotex had, incidentally, promptly after being notified, requested the content provider (T.I. Communication) to remove the data; when it appeared that the content provider did not accede to the request, Maxotex removed the data itself.

Identification of content providers

According to its 1998 report *The Internet and Digital Networks*, the State Council considers it necessary to strengthen the possibilities of identifying parties; it discerns various options to realise this. The Council thinks of an obligation for publishers and editors of content to include information to identify themselves at their websites. Moreover, access providers should ask new subscribers for their identity, in order to enable them to provide this information to the police or judiciary in case of an investigation. Finally, the Council points out the value that traffic data stored by access providers have for law enforcers, and the importance that these data are not deleted too quickly. However, an obligation for access providers to store traffic data for a year – like France Telecom is doing with telephone call data – is not considered realistic by the State Council, given the fact that access providers currently keep their data for a much shorter period.[333]

Also the government recognises the importance of Internet Provider logging data for law enforcement. They will therefore detail in the act on the information society under which conditions traffic data may or have to be stored.[334] In restrictions on data storing and limitations of the preservation period, three elements are taken into account: the

[330] Tribunal de Grand Instance de Nanterre 8 December 1999 (*Lynda Lacoste* v. *Multimania Company, France Cybermedia Company, SPPI, Estérel Company*).

[331] Cour d'appel de Paris 10 February 1999 (*Estelle Hallyday/Valentin Lacambre*); Tribunal de Grande Instance de Paris 9 June 1998 (*Estelle Hallyday/Valentin et Daniel Lacambre*).

[332] Tribunal de commerce de Paris 7 May 1999 (*SA Electre* v. *SARL T.I. Communication, SARL Maxotex Hébergement en M.D.*).

[333] Conseil d'Etat 1998.

[334] Strauss Kahn a.o. 1999, p. 33.

limitations of legal procedures, the costs for Internet Providers, and the need for preventing unauthorised use of files compiled on the basis of the act.

Meanwhile, an extensive regulation on the identification of Internet Providers and content providers has been included in Act no. 86-1067 of 30 September 1986 on freedom of communication.[335] Access or hosting providers are required to preserve data that allow for identification of all persons who have contributed to creating the content at issue. The State Council will determine, after having heard the opinion of the National Committee on Information Science and Civil Liberties (*Commission nationale de l'informatique et des libertés*), what identification data will have to be preserved and for how long they will have to be preserved. Judicial authorities can require providers to hand over the data in their possession (art. 43-9).

Online content providers have a direct or an indirect obligation of identification. They have to make known to the public their name, residence, and type of company, and the name of the director of publication and, if possible, the chief editor. This obligation does not apply to private correspondence. Service providers who do not act in a professional capacity can suffice with publishing their pseudonym and the name of the hosting provider. In that case, they do have to provide all the aforementioned data to the hosting provider. The hosting provider provides the technical means that allow content providers to comply with their duty of identification.

International regulation

National regulation of civil intermediary liability must fit in seamlessly with regulations at the European and international levels. Self-regulation is preferred.[336]

Cross-border aspects

Currently, there is no intention to adapt prevailing private international law rules, even if the risk would grow that conflicts have legal ties with more jurisdictions and if the difficulties of executing case-law solutions would aggravate.[337]

8.5 United Kingdom

Internet Provider liability

The United Kingdom does not have a general regulation of Internet Provider liability.

In 1996, UK defamation law was drastically reformed by the Defamation Act 1996. This act provides an 'innocent dissemination' defence to persons who are not the author, editor, or publisher of a defamatory utterance (art. 1 para. 1 sub a Defamation Act 1996). For instance, the defence can be put forward by operators or access providers of communications systems through which someone over whom they had no effective control has

[335] See <http://www.assemblee-nationale.fr/2/dossiers/communic/2com.htm>.
[336] G. Chatillon, interview.
[337] Conseil d'Etat 1998, section 4.1.2.

transported or provided the defamatory utterance.[338] For this, two conditions have to be met. The Internet Provider must have exercised due care and not have had knowledge or reasons to assume that he (also) caused or contributed to the publication of a defamatory utterance.

The Crown Court Leicester, in *Godfrey/Demon*, has now decided that an Internet Provider can, in principle, advance the defence (that is to say: he is not to be considered an author, editor, or publisher).[339] In this instance, however, the defence was not accepted, because the Internet Provider had acted negligently: he had refrained from removing the defamatory news reports after notification by the victim. The court judged that notification resulted in knowledge of the Internet Provider.

Internet Provider liability for copyright infringement is governed by the regular copyright rules (1988 Copyright Designs and Patents Act). The Internet Provider is liable, under certain conditions, as a secondary infringer. This requires knowledge. The House of Commons Trade and Industry Committee, like the government, advocates a right balance between the interests of copyright owners and information users.[340] In order to clear away legal uncertainty, the future Copyright Directive and the Electronic Commerce Directive will have to be implemented in British national legislation as soon as possible, according to the Committee.

For liability for privacy violations, one has to consider the Interception of Communications Act 1985. This act only relates to post and public telecommunications systems, and can only be enforced for licensed Public Telecommunications Operators (PTO) and the Post Office. The 1985 act does not apply to e-mail services of Internet Providers.[341] The Regulation of Investigatory Powers Act 2000 (RIPA 2000) has recently changed this.[342] The Act contains a criminalisation of unauthorised interception of a message in transmission on a public or private telecommunications system. Transmission includes temporary storage in a telecommunications system that enables the addressee to collect or otherwise access the information (art. 2(7) RIPA 2000), such as storing in an e-mail box.

Identification of content providers

In 1996, an agreement was made by the Internet Watch Foundation (IWF) – the British Internet hotline – and organisations of Internet Providers (ISPA and LINX): the Safety Net Agreement. This is the basis for Internet Provider self-regulation in the UK. This sets requirements for associated Internet Providers on, among other things, identifiability and traceability of Internet users. Internet Providers must cooperate with the IWF in order to identify providers of unlawful content, they have to research new measures against iden-

338 See art. 1 para. 1 *jo.* para. 3 sub e Defamation Act 1996. Possibly, an Internet Provider can also invoke art. 1 para. 1 *jo.* para. 3 sub c Defamation Act 1996.

339 High Court of Justice, Queen's Bench Division, Hon. mr Justice Morland 26 March 1999 (*Laurence Godfrey/Demon Internet Limited*).

340 House of Commons 1999, section 110.

341 Jabbour 1999, p. 390.

342 See <http://www.homeoffice.gov.uk/ripa/ripact.htm>.

tification gaps, and they must facilitate better traceability, for instance, by offering audit-trails and measures to improve the identifiability of users of 'free' Internet.[343]

The provision of identification information by Internet Provider to victims is governed by the Data Protection Act 1998 or takes place in the interest of arriving at the truth during legal procedures.[344]

International regulation
The government approves of the European action plan on safe use of the Internet, in which international cooperation and self-regulation are the key words. Among other things, a European network of hotlines is mentioned.[345]

Cross-border aspects
The IWF passes on notifications of child porn hosted on foreign servers to the NCIS (UK National Criminal Intelligence Service), which in turn forwards the notification to Interpol or directly to the relevant foreign police authorities. The IWF does not, however, pass on notifications of other kinds of unlawful content hosted abroad. The evaluation of IWF's functioning suggests that the NCIS has a backlog of forwarding (child-porn) notifications to Interpol and foreign police authorities.[346]

8.6 United States

Internet Provider liability
The US government does not advocate regulating Internet content itself. Only for the sake of preventing fraud do they consider government intervention appropriate.[347] The US have separate regulations for Internet Provider liability. Contrary to Germany and the European Union, the US have not opted for a horizontal approach.

The Digital Millennium Copyright Act (DMCA) contains a notice-and-take-down system. Copyright owners who discover unauthorised provision of their works on the Internet can notify the Internet Provider. If the notification meets certain formal requirements, the Internet Provider will have to block access to the information and forward the notification to the content provider. The latter can issue a counter notice within a certain period, after which it is the copyright owner's turn. If he does nothing, the Internet Provider will make the information accessible again after a period has expired. The copyright

---

343 Art. 30 Safety Net Agreement, see <http://www.iwf.org.uk/about/R3Safety.html>.

344 *E-commerce@its.best.uk* makes a recommendation that may become important for identifying content providers: the government will stimulate the use of multifunctional smart cards, likely with a broad scope of application. This contains, among other things, identification functions. Smart-card readers would in the future have to be built in in computers as a standard feature. Cabinet Office 1999, recommendation 10.3.

345 Battle 1998, p. 8.

346 KPMG & Denton Hall 1999, section 4.1.2.2.

347 Clinton & Gore 1997, p. 25-26.

owner can only prevent this by taking the matter before the court within the stipulated period. It will be clear that Internet Providers who conform with the DMCA duties of care are not liable. Before the DMCA entered into force, case law has designated the Internet Provider as a contributory infringer; this requires knowledge.[348]

The Communications Decency Act[349] drastically relieves Internet Providers from liability for defamation originating from third parties: "No provider or user of an interactive computer service shall be treated as the publisher or speaker of any information provided by another information content provider" (47 USC 230 (c) (1)). This privilege is available to Internet Providers regardless of their knowledge. The background of this is the fact that Congress feared a chilling effect on free speech if Internet Providers would be compelled to check the content they provide or transmit.[350] The well-known case of *Stratton Oakmont/Prodigy* shows that this danger is not imaginary.[351] Moreover, this regulation would stimulate self-regulation: 'Good Samaritan blocking and screening'. And liability based on knowledge would only incite Internet Providers to remain as detached as possible, as may be inferred from another well-known case, *Cubby/CompuServe*.[352]

Identification of content providers

The DMCA notice-and-take-down system includes the option for a copyright owner to request the clerk of a District Court to issue a subpoena against an Internet Provider to identify an alleged infringer. This subpoena is issued if, to put it simply, the Internet Provider has been notified in a sound way. The subpoena entails that the Internet Provider will give sufficient information to identify the alleged perpetrator, if and inasmuch the Internet Provider has that information at his disposal.

International regulation and cross-border aspects

The government is developing an informal dialogue with the major trading partners on issues of content, in order to ensure that national regulations, especially those that aim at keeping up cultural identities, will not function as trade barriers in disguise.[353] Together

---

[348] See, e.g., *Sega Entertainment Ltd.* v. *Maphia*, no. C93-04262 (N.D. Cal. 1996) and *Religious Technology Center* v. *Netcom Online Communications Services*, 907 F. Supp. 1361 (N.D. Cal. 1995).

[349] This is not the CDA provision that the Supreme Court declared unconstitutional.

[350] This is apparent from, for instance, U.S. 4th Circuit Court of Appeals 12 November 1997 (*Zeran* v. *America Online Inc.*). See also *John Doe* v. *America Online*, Case No. 97-2587, 718 So. 2d 385; 1998 Fla. App. LEXIS 1248.

[351] *Stratton Oakmont* v. *Prodigy Services Co.*, No.31063/94, 1995 WL 323710 (N.Y. Sup. Court May 1995). The court decided that Prodigy was liable for defamation by a third party; an important circumstance was the fact that Prodigy had performed some checks on the information they offered.

[352] *Cubby* v. *CompuServe*, 776 F. Supp. 135 (S.D.N.Y. 1991). The court judged that CompuServe was not liable for third-party content, since, among other things, CompuServe had outsourced all involvement relating to the content.

[353] Clinton & Gore 1997, p. 26.

with other countries, they are also looking for ways to enhance the diversity of information available on the Internet, without limiting its provision.

8.7 Other countries

8.7.1 Australia

We discuss Australia's Broadcasting Services Amendment (On-line Services) Act 1999 here, because this act (also) contains provisions on content hosted outside of Australia. The act enjoins the Australian Broadcasting Authority (ABA) with the task of having Internet content rated by the Classification Board, be it on their own initiative or in reaction to complaints. Depending on the rating result, content will be considered prohibited if the Classification Board has classified it as X (explicit sexuality) or RC (Refused Classification) (material outside of Australia will not be classified as RC). Content will also be considered prohibited if classified as R (Nudity) without being subject to a restricted access system. If prohibited content is hosted on a server in Australia, ABA will send the hosting provider a take-down notice, which he must comply with within a workday. He must also ensure that the content will not reappear on his server. If, on the other hand, content is hosted outside of Australia, the Australian service provider who offered access to it will receive a notice demanding to take all reasonable measures to block access to the content or to block the content according to the relevant rules of a (business) code. Apart from complying with notices, Internet Providers have to fulfil a large number of information duties and procedures that are to be laid down in codes of practice. The bill has heavy sanctions (fines of up to A$ 27,500 per day!).

The bill was severely criticised, not only by the Internet industry. Critics targeted the fact that the bill only establishes liability for Internet Providers without addressing content providers. Thus, it would place the costs of enforcement at the wrong link in the distribution chain, and it would encourage emigration of content. The bill entered into force in the summer of 1999, but it stipulated itself that it would only take effect on 1 January 2000. Before that date, on 30 September 1999, the Australian Senate (Upper House) carried a motion calling upon the government to attend to the industry's and public's concerns about the impossible approach taken by the government in this bill. Moreover, the government was asked to remove the major bottlenecks before 1 January 2000. The motion was also prompted by the negative effect the act – presumably – would have on the development of e-commerce and the Internet industry in Australia.[354]

8.7.2 Singapore

The Electronic Transactions Act 1998 offers a relieve, with added provisos, from liability for access providers for third-party content (art. 10). Internet Providers must register with

[354] Scott 1999, p. 21.

the Singapore Broadcasting Authority, and they have to block access to 'reprehensible' websites upon instruction by the SBA. The Singapore Broadcasting Authority (Class Licence) Notification 1996 distinguishes broad categories of content that Singapore citizens must not catch sight of. They involve general security and national defence, racial and religious harmony, public morals, and certain other content. This does not only relate to content hosted in Singapore, but also to foreign material. Cross-border Internet traffic is directed through a limited number of proxy servers, where content is filtered.[355]

8.7.3 Sweden

Since 1998, Sweden has an act on the responsibility for electronic Bulletin Boards Systems.[356] It is generally assumed that this act also applies to Internet Providers.[357] According to article 4, Bulletin Board System providers have to perform checks that are apposite in view of the extent and character of the service to be supervised. The legislative history suggests that providers do not have to check each message,[358] but they cannot refrain from checking altogether for a longer period. It depends on the content of the service how often they have to check. Commercial providers must check more intensively than private services. If the amount of checking is too burdensome for providers, they can fulfil their duty by establishing a hotline for unlawful content. The provider must remove apparently unlawful messages;[359] there are penal sanctions for not complying with this. In order to be able to comply, providers have the authority to examine message content. This supervising authority possibly also covers closed user groups.

8.8 Comparison and conclusion

The substantive criteria that the various countries use to establish Internet Provider liability (such as involvement with the content, knowledge, and care) are similar. What is most noticeable is the distinction made between providers who are involved with the content of information provision and those who only contribute to distributing information that originates from third parties.[360] The former are fully responsible for the content, the latter are liable only if they disregard standards of due care. In the Netherlands, this

---

355 Hogan 1999.

356 Law (1998:112) on the Liability of Electronic Bulletin Board Systems (*Lag (1998:112) om ansvar för elektroniska anslagstavlor*), <http://www.notisum.se/rnp/sls/lag/19980112.HTM>.

357 Palme 1998.

358 Palme 1998.

359 The duty to remove does not apply to all unlawful content, but only to the offences mentioned in art. 5: sedition, inciting racial hatred, child pornography, glorifying violence, and copyright infringement.

360 For example, in Germany, section 5 Teleservices Act; in France, proposed art. 43-6-2.II (first bullet) Law of 30 September 1986 on the freedom of communications; in the UK, art. 1 para. 1 sub a Defamation Act 1996; in the US, 47 USC 230 sub c.

distinction is endorsed both in legislation[361] and in case law. Certain regulations further distinguish, within the category of contributors, providers who only offer access services from providers who offer hosting services (e.g., in section 5 Teleservices Act (Germany), and art. 12 and 14 Electronic Commerce Directive). In the Netherlands, it is up to the court to take into account the character of the activities at stake (access or hosting), if this is relevant for judging the care a provider has observed.[362] Thus, the president of the court of The Hague, in the *Scientology* judgement, deemed Internet Providers to "only offer the technical facilities in order to enable publication by others".[363]

In the countries we studied, a – contributory – Internet Provider is only liable for unlawful content of which he has actual knowledge. There are two deviations from this starting point. On the one hand, Sweden has a proactive duty for Internet Providers to check content.[364] Because of the fact that providers can fulfil this duty by setting up a hotline, we can, however, state that Sweden does not have an obligation either for service providers to guarantee that their systems are 'clean'. On the other hand, regulations avail (in Germany and the EU) in which access providers are privileged, in that they are not liable regardless of their knowledge. In practice, to be sure, access providers will usually not have 'knowledge', nor will they be able to act against content. In the Netherlands, 'actual knowledge' is a circumstance that constitutes unlawfulness (see the Scientology verdict), also for access providers. Now that the European Directive is final, the Netherlands will have to adapt their position. The Computer Crime II Bill originally contained a provision on intermediaries, which now is removed from the bill; this regulation entailed that intermediaries would only have to act after instruction by the Public Prosecutor – mere knowledge did not oblige intermediaries to act.[365] This could be explained by the regulation's special rationale of preventing 'censorship' by intermediaries.

Finally, in all countries, service providers, when they have actual knowledge, have a duty of care to remove or block access to unlawful content as far as they are reasonably able to do so.

The countries we studied seem to recognise that Internet Providers have a special role and responsibility in identifying content providers. This responsibility need not only involve providing identification information at their disposal upon request, but it can also entail taking precautionary measures to be able to comply with a future identification request,

---

361 The immunity from prosecution, as originally proposed in the Computer Crime II Bill, applied only to the 'intermediary as such'.

362 Compare TK 1998-1999, 25 880, no. 7, p. 4. The Netherlands prefer to leave the development of law to the courts.

363 Ground 16 in Pres.Rb. 's-Gravenhage 9 June 1999, *Informatierecht/AMI* 1999, p. 100ff (*Scientology/xs4all*).

364 French case law on portrait infringement also presumes a duty to monitor.

365 Nevertheless, intention with respect to the nature of the content is relevant for the qualification under article 418 Dutch Criminal Code (DCC), which penalises violating the standards of due care of article 53 DCC. Moreover, 'knowledge' is relevant if a service provider cannot invoke the immunity from prosecution of art. 53 DCC; in that case, he is liable according to the common rules of criminal law.

such as preserving data and verifying the identity of new subscribers. However, the way these responsibilities can be reconciled with privacy interests is still giving most countries headaches. For the moment, France is taking the lead with identification regulation. A bill is pending that introduces requirements for Internet Providers with respect to providing, preserving, and handing over (traffic) data. All things considered, the Dutch position is in line with the developments one observes abroad.

The general attitude in relation to cross-border aspects is above all one of reticence. Liability of access providers is not considered a means to get a grip on the availability within the country of unlawful content hosted abroad. Australia and Singapore are exceptions to the rule in this respect.

National governments have sufficient power to effectively regulate the liability of Internet Providers residing within their territory. From the perspective of the national power to act, there is therefore no reason to regulate this at an international level. The regulation of the Electronic Commerce Directive above all serves to prevent or limit divergence between the various national regulations and case law.[366]

However, for the international problem of illegal and harmful content – dealing with unlawful content that is available within a country but hosted abroad – no solutions are at hand. A further harmonisation of substantive norms seems hardly feasible. For the time being, policies are limited to international cooperation between hotlines.

[366] See consideration 40 of the Electronic Commerce Directive.

9. Summary and Conclusions

9.1 Introduction

The results of the comparative research on internationalisation in Germany, France, the United Kingdom, and the United States lead to various conclusions. Here, we present first a summary of the general themes (9.2) and specific topics (9.3) as analysed in this report.[367] Next, we draw conclusions and make comments, based on several distinctions and trade-offs that are relevant to creating ICT policy and regulation (9.4). Finally, based on all these conclusions, we formulate an overall research conclusion (9.5).

9.2 General themes

The first notable observation in the comparative research on views about electronic-highway regulation is the fact that, unlike the Dutch government's overall analysis of ICT law of 1998 (*Legislation for the Electronic Highways*), few comprehensive legal policy documents avail in the countries researched. Only France has taken a similar effort with its *Policy Paper on the Adaptation of the Legal Framework to the Information Society* of October 1999, which is to lead to a broad legislative proposal. The other countries restrict themselves to policy documents on, for instance, electronic commerce or even more specific topics, such as taxes or illegal and harmful content.

Nevertheless, the general treatment of ICT law and internationalisation in France, Germany, the UK, and the US is roughly the same. This holds, first of all, for the first general theme researched, the principle that "what holds offline, should also hold online". Although only the UK (like Australia) has explicitly recognised this starting point, one can also infer from the policy documents and laws of the other countries that they more or less apply this principle. However, there is increasing room for deviating from this principle, because it appears that sometimes, other rules are necessary to safeguard the underlying interests. This involves both interests relating to the rule of law (such as fundamental norms and values, and consumer protection) and economic interests. The principle had therefore better be refined as the US have voiced it: the protection level in the

---

[367] Here, we summarise the outlines of the report, not repeating every conclusion of the various chapters. For that, see the Management Summary.

online world must be the same as in the offline world. In other words, for regulating the electronic highway, one must analyse the underlying interests rather than the specific realisation of these in prevailing laws and regulations. Moreover, the value of the adage seems to decrease as ICT law is being further developed: rather than transposing offline rules or interests to online rules and interests, policy should much rather be based on the singularity of the online problems.

It is striking, moreover, that the starting point is particularly affirmed at the national level. As to an international approach to ICT law, only the UK states that the principle should be respected in international negotiations. As a result, international cooperation and harmonisation, the necessity of which is recognised by all, are likely to succeed only to the extent to which the underlying national interests are shared.

Similar views can be observed when it comes to the role of self-regulation. A notable development, however, is that the preference for pure self-regulation is giving way to a more steering role for the government (co-regulation). Thus, the government must set frameworks for, e.g., electronic commerce and illegal and harmful content. This development is motivated both by strategic reasons (such as the necessity of an integrated approach – pure self-regulation leads to too many *ad hoc* initiatives, and to strengthen the competitive position by a clear ICT-law framework) and by more substantial reasons, such as legal certainty and protection of the cultural identity. Moreover, the necessity of enforcement, which all countries indeed recognise, implies a greater role for the government – self-regulation is not an adequate instrument to ensure enforcement.

Nevertheless, there are differences in the status of self-regulation or co-regulation. In Germany, the UK, and the US, self-regulation is still the starting point, whereas in France, government regulation remains paramount, with a supplementary role for self-regulation. Also, it is not at all clear for the moment what exactly *is* co-regulation: the interpretation appears to depend considerably on legislative and cultural traditions.

The final general research theme, how to ensure enforcement, appears less prominent in the official documents of the countries we researched. Although governments have put considerable thought to the necessity and options of ensuring enforcement of ICT law in the international context, so far, they have not put forward any ideas about an integrated approach to enforcement. They simply look for the best approach in each given case, which is in line with the Dutch pragmatic approach in this matter. It is also remarkable that there are few concrete ideas about how to address at an international level those issues generally considered to be potentially difficult to enforce in an international context, such as tax law, privacy, and cryptography. This finding has led the Dutch government to propose in the ILIS Memorandum to stimulate the international academic debate on enforcement, because "international legal developments could use an added boost when it comes to enforceability".

In those areas where the interests to be protected are broadly shared internationally, an international approach is most likely to succeed. The workshop suggested that it is wise to start with minor domains where there is more agreement, e.g., in combating child pornography, for which an international network of hotlines is already at work. Constructions of national contact points are the most promising in the short term to address enforcement internationally. In private-law matters, one can think of an international network of ombudspersons or Chambers of Commerce to play a central part in international alternative dispute resolution. In criminal law, for the time being, governments focus on an international network of national contact points that are available 24 hours a day and seven days a week to directly deal with and coordinate requests for mutual criminal assistance. This network can give an impetus to developing further-reaching forms of cross-border cooperation.

In conclusion, we find that the general starting points of the LEH Memorandum may be generally shared in the countries we studied, but that at the same time, developments take place that prompt a differentiation of the general starting points. Where concrete issues have to be addressed, the starting points frequently appear hard to apply. The general principles may be attractive, but as ICT law is growing up, the world appears to be more complex than that.

9.3 Specific topics

In *criminal law*, we researched the topics of double criminality and cooperation between enforcement authorities.

We found that the Dutch government's idea of abandoning double criminality in certain cases hardly strikes a sympathetic cord abroad. It is true that within the Council of Europe, it has been discussed in the preparation of the *Crime in Cyberspace* Convention, but the draft convention only abandons the requirement of double criminality for mutual-assistance requests to order a foreign Internet Provider to *preserve* data (and there is not even agreement on this: certain countries reserve the right to maintain the requirement here). But a preservation order will not help the requesting state if the requirement is subsequently preserved for being able to *obtain* the data, and the draft text does not call into question the authority of states to require double criminality for the latter. Therefore, the requesting state will not find an effective means in the treaty to obtain data (e.g., to trace a digital trail) if the fact at issue is not punishable in the other state. Likewise, the international workshop concluded that it is almost impossible to interfere with the requirement of double criminality. Countries are too much attached to national sovereignty.

Holding on to national sovereignty and national interests in criminal law implies that, at the international level, harmonisation and cooperation are the only feasible options. Even harmonisation is extremely hard to realise, given the divergence of underlying cultural values. Therefore, finding solutions in the area of internationalisation and criminal law will mostly amount to cooperation between enforcement authorities (and here, one also has to be aware of the fact that differences in substantive norms will, through the requirement of double criminality, affect the potential of investigation powers). Several international initiatives aim at strengthening cooperation, the main one being the draft *Crime in Cyberspace* Convention. The countries do agree on the outlines of the regulation, but drafting the convention has been a slow process, and it has, so far, taken place with little publicity and public opinion-making – not until April 2000 was a first text published. We can therefore conclude that criminal-law policies and regulations with a view to internationalisation will be hard to bring about. The only option to achieve something in this area is to start with topics on which there is considerable international agreement, especially where underlying interests are shared, such as in the financial sector. Slowly, and step by step, more difficult and contentious topics can then be dealt with.

In *private law*, we researched private international law for online contracts and Internet Provider liability. Besides, at the international workshop, a lot of attention was paid to electronic signatures.

The topic of private international law and online contracts is not an issue to regulate at the national level; it above all requires discussion within international organisations, such as the EU and, world-wide, within the Hague Conference on Private International Law. The European Electronic Commerce Directive originally contained a regulation on this, but the final version states it does not aim at providing specific private international law rules. The Commission decided to leave the issue of applicable law outside of the Electronic Commerce Directive as far as consumer relationships are concerned. For business-to-business online transactions, the Directive adopts the country-of-origin principle. Furthermore, the adaptation of the Hague Conference that is advocated by the Dutch government does not appear to work out particularly smoothly. At a meeting in Ottawa in late February 2000, it appeared anything but feasible to reach an agreement on the draft adaptation of the current Conference text. It turns out that the Netherlands, in the issue of the law applicable to online contracts, are leaning more towards a global approach than the countries we researched.

Internet Provider liability is a hot issue in all countries. Legislation and case law have everywhere fashioned the policy in this area, with all countries applying largely similar substantive criteria. Even though some elements of the Swedish and German regulations are divergent, in practice, the civil liability of Internet Providers amounts to the same position everywhere. Thus, the regulation of Internet Provider liability provides a solution to unlawful content on the Internet. However, one must note that, for the time being, this is only a solution to unlawful content that is hosted *nationally*; the countries prove extremely cautious in holding national Internet Providers liable for content hosted abroad. So, the *international* problem of illegal and harmful content is not solved in this way. For now, no initiatives attempt to address this problem internationally, other than the market initiative of international cooperation between hotlines.

In private law, it is moreover striking that the general policy preference for self-regulation does not at all result in refraining from legislating. This is especially apparent in the legislative torrent in the area of electronic signatures (only in the US, 252 e-signature bills have been launched in the 50 states). An explanation for this is the fact that this is an issue of legal certainty: the market wants to have a concrete answer to the question whether e-signatures are legally valid. At the national level (and in federal states, at the state level), legislation aims at giving an answer; at the same time, at the international level (within the EU and UNCITRAL), it is attempted to make the national regulations consistent. The bottom-up and top-down approach have, for the time being, not resulted in uniform regulations, but it is certainly possible that the initiatives will converge to an internationally consistent policy.

Such convergence is less conceivable in issues that require not only answers but also steering, such as privacy. After all, market parties are much more ready to accept legislation that primarily answers than legislation that also aims at influencing their behaviour. This explains the protracted struggle between the EU and the US in the area of privacy. The legislative traditions related to the different views on how steering should be constructed have the effect that agreement between the EU and the US in this area is much harder to bring about than in areas that mainly call for 'answers', such as electronic signatures.

9.4 Distinctions and trade-offs

Looking at the separate conclusions, we discern various distinctions and trade-offs that play a part in formulating electronic-highway policy. For example, there is a trade-off between government regulation and market regulation, and there is a distinction between answering questions and influencing behaviour. Here, we present the conclusions on the basis of these and other dichotomies, analysing the implications for the theme of ICT law and internationalisation. Notwithstanding the dichotomies, we will also stress the subtleties and shades of meaning of each distinction and trade-off.

9.4.1 Offline – online

One can discern a recent tendency in all the countries we studied towards differentiation of the general starting point "what holds offline, should also hold online" that was so eagerly used in the past. When concrete topics have to be regulated, the adage of several years ago often appears difficult to apply. It seems to have been a useful concept in the embryo stage of ICT regulation, but as ICT law is growing up, the world turns out to be more complex than that. Attention should be paid to the interests underlying the concrete rules.

For the theme of internationalisation, this implies that the major factors that influence the interests underlying the rules (such as cultural values) will have to be scrutinised. Often, this will necessitate explicit attention to the *why*: why does the offline world have certain rules, and why should these rules be preserved in the online world? Policy-makers must not so much attempt to transpose the offline rules and interests to the online world, but rather, they must heed and examine the specificity of the problems in the online world.

9.4.2 Government regulation – market regulation

We have already indicated that the regulation scheme of market leadership is everywhere giving way to a scheme with a conspicuous part and function for the government. In this scheme of co-regulation, government and the market join forces in developing policy. As indicated, we also note that the term co-regulation may be interpreted differently in the various countries.

Although as a general policy line, the starting point of co-regulation is being advocated, the analysis of specific topics and positions of the separate countries shows that there are also remarkable differences in the views on regulation. We find that some countries (notably France), are leaning more towards the government end of the spectrum of government regulation – market regulation, whereas other countries (Germany, the UK, and the US) are positioned more at the market end. Moreover, the preference for government regulation or for market regulation depends considerably on the specific issue to be regulated. The research shows that for a number of topics, the countries generally consider a certain level of government intervention definitely desirable, for instance, consumer protection, privacy, and cybercrime. The interests at stake here are legal certainty, safeguarding fundamental rights and duties related to the rule of law, and the national competitive position.

In choosing a certain level of government intervention (such as posing preconditions), the question is whether one opts for a system of voluntary compliance with the rules or a system of mandatory compliance. The countries we researched show a difference in the extent to which compliance with, for example, a certification system is made voluntary (UK) or mandatory (France). Experiences in the United Kingdom indicate that a government policy based on voluntary private-sector cooperation can definitely be effective: enterprises and organisations seem to want to comply with the policy because it offers competitive advantages. It is precisely this aspect of competitive profits, combined with the global Internet market, that may make an international policy based on voluntary cooperation advantageous for certain problem areas.

For the theme of internationalisation, this implies that international harmonisation is likely to succeed to the extent that one has a clear view of the issues and areas with agreement on a supranational level. It is important to be definite about the desired level of approach (government intervention, co-regulation, pure self-regulation), as well as sympathetic to the various interests and traditions that underlie the separate national governments' views on the appropriate level of intervention.

In view of the theme of internationalisation, the countries we studied do not detect a potential negative effect of policies that lean too much towards market regulation. Complete market regulation could, after all, risk creating (unintentional) trade barriers. For example, if many countries were to apply different conditions for carrying a seal of approval for secure electronic commerce, some countries could impose upon businesses a higher level of consumer protection than other countries, thus impeding international trade.

9.4.3 Overall principles – specific solutions

This brings us to the following distinction. Both the analysis of the various countries' policy documents and the international workshop suggest that the government had better concentrate on finding tailor-made solutions for every specific regulatory issue, rather than attempt to formulate general guidelines and starting points for the broad field of ICT law. A blanket approach in the sense of applying uniform starting points in thinking about regulation (such as an overall preference for self-regulation and the adage 'online = offline') does not do justice to the specific problems of the matter at hand.

This does not mean that one cannot voice a preference in general terms for certain starting points. In order to clarify the national government position when a problem is tabled for international discussion, it can definitely be useful to formulate general positions (such as co-regulation) that mirror the national cultural and legislative interests and traditions; as a result, people in international discussions will know where they stand. However, the diversity of problems and national positions in internationally addressing the problems requires an exceptionally open attitude that is more sympathetic to other valid approaches and starting points than that it should hold on to its own starting points.

9.4.4 Answering – steering

When it comes to the rationale of things, there is also a conceptual distinction between, on the one hand, regulations that primarily try to answer practical questions in order to create legal certainty (e.g., "can I use a digital signature to sign a contract?") and, on the other hand, regulations that aim at influencing behaviour (e.g., "do not use encryption that hampers investigation"). With 'answering issues', the addressees, in principle, care less about the particular outcome as long as a choice is made by the government, whereas with 'steering issues', addressees have a clear preference for a particular outcome. Therefore, governments have to ask themselves *why* it is desirable to intervene in a certain way in social and economic life.

For the theme of internationalisation, this implies that governments must be aware to what extent an intended regulation is answering and to what extent it is steering. In the short term, primarily answering regulations are called for in order to establish legal certainty; more steering regulations should only be undertaken once it has become sufficiently clear what 'steering goals' are envisioned and what are the best means to achieve those goals.

It is true that regulation is never completely answering or completely steering (thus, rules on the liability of Internet Providers may be partly answering and partly steering), but it is nonetheless desirable for governments to consider in any case on which side of the spectrum answering – steering the emphasis lies with a possible regulative intervention. This will help them to estimate the likelihood of compliance, the enforcement options, and therefore the effectiveness of the regulation.

9.4.5 Top-down – bottom-up

Certain topics, such as Internet-provider liability and electronic signatures, are essentially national issues that can be addressed at a national level. Because of internationalisation, however, this is not enough: the national regulations must be made consistent. This is facilitated in international platforms. The result is an interaction between the parallel processes of national and international policy-making. The interaction is not always optimal, however, as electronic-signatures policies illustrate: some national governments (such as Germany) have first chosen a national solution that they subsequently presented as a model law internationally, while at the same time the solutions of other platforms (such as the UNCITRAL) moved in a different direction. Thus, the bottom-up approach in this instance was too little appreciative of the dimension of internationalisation, forcing Germany to adapt the regulation a few years later. In such cases, policy making would become more effective if the bottom-up and top-down approaches are better fine-tuned at an early stage.

Contrary to this, other topics call for an international approach by definition, such as private international law for online contracts and cross-border investigation. In these areas, policies are made nearly only at the international level, within international organisations. A notable effect of this may be that national governments do not make explicit their contributions in these platforms or indicate their positions in policy documents, as is illustrated by the lack of explicit positions taken on the Hague Conference or the draft *Crime in Cyberspace* Convention. The result is that public opinion and public discussion at the national levels are less developed than with issues that have a primarily national component. Ultimately, this could also affect the quality of international policy-making. Also here, a better interaction between top-down and bottom-up approaches is desirable.

This means that the answer to the question which topics appear on the international agenda at an early stage is related to the (inter)national power to act. Where separate countries are able to address a problem, at least for the time being, at the national level, the discussion at the international level will not readily evolve. This entails the risk that national policies are being developed too quickly. To adequately deal with the theme of internationalisation, governments must be much more aware of the international dimension of the problems, and they must optimise the interaction between national and international policy-making.

9.5 Variety in unity

What general conclusions can be drawn from the many specific conclusions? What does all this imply for the central research theme of internationalisation and the national and international attention paid to this theme?

We discern a desire for a uniform approach of the various problems, but at the same time a need to be aware of the specific dynamics of each issue, the range of interests involved, and the variety of cultural and legislative national traditions. In short, there must be variety in unity.

This means that in various areas, international agreement is problematic. The creative approach that is needed implies in the first place a search for areas where the interests are shared and where it is relatively easy to reach an agreement. Once governments have agreed upon the outlines in such areas, topics could be addressed where the positions diverge more. The broad field of ICT law in view of internationalisation must thus be addressed step by step.

It is of primary importance that each issue is indeed addressed from an *international* perspective. Our research indicates that governments are still to a large extent thinking about ICT law from a national perspective, because they want to first clear things up nationally and only then start to think of international fine-tuning. This is not surprising in the light of the 'growing-up' of ICT law, but it is undesirable to keep the international perspective out of sight any longer. Questions of internationalisation are so intrinsic to policy-making in the area of ICT law, that the national and international perspectives can not do without each other.

We think the time has come to take the next step in regulating the information society. Five years ago, policy concentrated on addressing national problems. Now that this approach is well on its way, it is time for including the international dimension of the problems. Although the various governments currently do proclaim that policies must be consistent at the international level, our analysis shows that in reality, few things come off the ground; all too often, it is noted that problems should first take shape at a national level. The topics discussed in the various international platforms are often not the most fundamental problems of internationalisation, and if such problems do appear on the international agenda (such as private international law), agreement turns out to be far away. There are many initiatives by international organisations, but these have so far yielded mainly policy intentions and vague principles, yet few concrete results. In short, both at the national and at the international level, there is little effective progress in policy-making in the area of internationalisation.

Governments should therefore urge the international community to pay express attention to the perspective of internationalisation in all the platforms that discuss ICT-law issues. Also, governments should make a case for better fine-tuning the policy-making in all the various international bodies and platforms. In order to facilitate the international discussions and policy-making in which they take part, the formulation of general principles that support the national positioning, such as the Dutch working principles of the ILIS Memorandum, may be useful. These starting points can help to determine interests that are broadly shared internationally; from that basis, one can identify topics that might be addressed at the international level with a reasonable chance of success. For now, the focus should be on 'answering' issues rather than on 'steering' issues.

However, general principles for positioning and policy-making in issues of internationalisation can only serve to *start* discussing. First and foremost, and even more so than with traditional law topics, governments must have a flexible and particularly open attitude that is sympathetic to all the subtleties of the issue at stake and to the variety of national positions that are intrinsic to the internationalisation problems of ICT law.

The final conclusion is that governments should incorporate the international dimension more explicitly in the national and international policy-making in the field of ICT law. ICT law has by now outgrown the infancy stage of general starting points and national interim solutions. A grown-up ICT law calls for structurally incorporating the perspective of internationalisation.

Appendix I

A Bird's Eye View of Governments on ICT Law and ICT Policy

	Germany	France	UK	US
general view	international approach, in which national approach can (or should) serve as a model	international cooperation, with room for national multiformity	international cooperation is necessary	international approach, with high priority for self-regulation
interests	legal certainty, public interest (among other things, consumer protection, protection of minors)	market competition and stimulating business, human rights, consumer protection, cultural tradition	public interest, in particular fighting obscenity, market competition and stimulating business	Information multiformity, stimulating market competition, consistent legal framework, consumer protection, protection of minors
goal and strategy	national legislation as a model; Europe must guide and influence international platforms more, in order to enhance Europe's influence; 2002 global summit (ITU) very important, close involvement with agenda	active participation in international platforms in order to safeguard French interests; Europe must take consistent position in international platforms and guide and influence more; find right balance between EU harmonisation and remaining national legislation	leading role in international platforms; European Commission must participate more actively in Global Business Dialogue in order to enhance the influence of Europe and European enterprises	removing foreign trade barriers; convincing foreign countries that self-regulation mechanisms best promote e-commerce

	Germany	France	UK	US
e-commerce	particularly focused on tax, consumer protection (transparency is important) and privacy; at international level, a single international body should issue website seals of approval according to internationally consistent criteria	achieve more consistency between fragmented initiatives in various international bodies; establish a single European framework, with consumer protection as important basic principle; if trade barriers emerge, legislation must be simplified and harmonised	a coordinated approach must result in a framework for e-commerce; focus on issues, not on institutions	promoting market competition, consumer protection, high priority for security, fighting identity fraud, broad access for the public to e-commerce services

Appendix II

Composition of the Monitoring Committee

T. Heukels, Europa Instituut, Leiden University, the Netherlands (chairman)

H. Hijmans, Ministry of Justice, the Netherlands

W.M. de Jongste, WODC Research and Documentation Center, the Netherlands

J.A. Peters, Ministry of the Interior and Kingdom Relations, the Netherlands

Appendix III

Foreign Correspondents

Georges Chatillon, Université de Paris (France)

Christopher Kuner, Morrison & Foerster (Germany)

Henry Perritt, Illinois Institute of Technology (US)

Stephen Saxby, University of Southampton (UK)

Ulrich Sieber, Universität Würzburg (Germany)

Appendix IV

Report of the Workshop On Internationalisation

Amsterdam, 29 March 2000

Chairman *Coen Drion* opened the workshop by referring to his bike ride – closing the lock reminded him of the difficulty of solving international legal problems in ICT law. *Jan-Tom Bos* welcomed the participants on behalf of the Dutch Minister of Justice. He outlined the background to the workshop: the Ministry of Justice will present a report to parliament on internationalisation and jurisdiction with respect to ICT law, as a follow-up on the 1998 memorandum *Legislation for the Electronic Highways*. The workshop is to discuss the main themes of this topic, and it will assess the draft working principles that will guide Dutch representatives in international negotiations.

Subsequently, *Corien Prins* presented the first conclusions of the comparative-law study on France, Germany, the UK, and the US by Tilburg University that the Ministry of Justice commissioned. The study covers three general themes and four specific subjects, all of which are on the agenda today. The main findings were that governments' preference for self-regulation is increasingly giving way to various forms of co-regulation, that the adage "what holds offline should also hold online" is becoming more difficult to apply as legal problems become more sophisticated, and that enforcement is an issue that, although considered extremely important, governments have no overall solution to. On the specific themes, the research found that governments are largely waiting for the *Crime in Cyberspace* convention of the Council of Europe to update judicial cooperation in criminal matters, that the Dutch suggestion to abandon the requirement of double criminality for content-related offences has not been discussed abroad, that governments consider the Rome Convention the main way of settling the issue which law applies to online agreements, and that most countries have similar, nationally-centred systems for civil liability of ISPs.

Three general themes and the working principles

In the morning session, the three general themes and the Ministry's draft working principles were discussed, each introduced by a participant.

The discussion on **self-regulation**, introduced by *Thomas Smedinghoff*, confirmed the tentative conclusion by Tilburg University that co-regulation is gaining ground. Nevertheless, self-regulation is still important to give the private sector the opportunity to experiment; government interference could hamper innovation. This is particularly stressed in the US, where paradoxically, looking at recent practice, an enormous amount of legislation has been issued (on electronic signatures: 252 laws in 50 states). Moreover, the US private sector increasingly stresses the need for legal certainty, which may call for regulatory steps. Likewise, consumer organisations more and more make themselves heard, asking for government intervention to secure their interests. These developments have led to the clear US preference for self-regulation shifting towards a tendency to co-regulation, which can better safeguard compelling interests (consumer protection, privacy, legal certainty). The same tendency is seen in France and the UK. The latter country views co-regulation as a partnership in which the government defines minimum conditions. It seems that the exact meaning of the term 'co-regulation' differs in each country.

A useful distinction was made between two types of government intervention: regulation that aims at answering practical questions ("Can I use a digital signature to make a transaction?") and regulation that aims at influencing behaviour ("Don't use encryption that hampers law enforcement!"). The first kind of regulation is generally called for and welcomed by the market, whereas the second kind is generally not favoured.

Of primary importance in the theme of self-regulation is the issue of enforcement. Practice shows that regulation based on voluntary participation can be effective: private parties appear to abide by the rules in order to gain competitive advantages (as in the UK with the official recognition of Certification Authorities).

The discussion on the **adage "what holds offline, should also hold online"**, introduced by *Corien Prins*, likewise confirmed the finding of Tilburg University that it is becoming increasingly difficult to apply this to specific issues, since it turns out that in order to safeguard the basic principles underlying 'offline law' in an online environment, regulations may have to diverge from this starting point. It was felt that the adage was a useful one in the 'early days' of ICT law (in the mid-1990s), when it had to be made clear that the Internet was not a legal vacuum. Some participants stressed that we have to look ahead and see what is happening in Cyberspace, rather than stick to this romantic, outdated basic rule. Practice shows that the problems in the online world differ from those in the offline world; in those cases, it is not useful to apply the rules of the offline world.

The most important thing is to identify *why* we have and wish to have certain rules. If we know the goals and rationales of our rule systems and identify the underlying principles, we can analyse to what extent these can hold for both the online and offline worlds. If technology introduces specific differences, we should assess how these affect or should affect the current rules, taking into account the underlying goals of these rules. Rather than rely on transposing traditional rules or principles, governments had perhaps better forget the adage and be simply creative in finding solutions.

It was also pointed out that we have to be aware of the possibility that the adage "what holds offline, should also hold online" may be turned into its reverse: "what holds online, should also hold offline". Thus, the relationship between offline rules and online rules will likely become an interactive one. And, like with self-regulation, a basic issue is the question to what extent the online rules can be enforced.

The third general theme, **enforcement**, introduced by *Bert-Jaap Koops*, had already emerged from the previous discussions as a pivotal issue. This contradicted the research by Tilburg University, which had found very few remarks or ideas in official documents about addressing enforcement of ICT law in an international context as such. This paradox was explained by the comment that governments do think about enforcement a lot, but that they do not have ready-made or overall solutions to it, and consequently refer to it relatively little in official documents.

Various tentative suggestions were made to find ways of safeguarding enforcement. It was felt that finding these ways will depend a lot on the specific problem and the law area. It is easiest to start with areas in which there is a relatively large international agreement on basic principles, such as in the financial-regulations sector. Also, in private law, where common principles may be found on a multinational or international level, agreements will help ensure enforcement, perhaps through Alternative Dispute Resolution mechanisms. This could take the form of international mediation through national contact points, e.g., by ombudspersons and Chambers of Commerce.

By far the largest enforcement problem is in the area of criminal law. Here, it is less likely to agree upon shared basic principles on an international level, because there are major cultural differences in countries' views on crime and crime fighting. Nonetheless, governments should start on a modest level and see whether agreement can be reached on specific issues that most countries share an interest in, like in combating international financial crimes. Like in private law, international contact points such as hotlines could serve as a starting point. It was stressed, however, that addressing international enforcement in criminal law will be a long and slow process.

To finish the morning session, *Hielke Hijmans* presented the Dutch government's **draft working principles** that will guide Dutch representatives in international negotiations. These working principles will form a recognisable common position in the many international forums that discuss ICT (self-)regulations, enabling the Netherlands to gain more influence and be more effective, being the small country it is. The draft does not have any official status, but when Parliament accepts the document, the working principles will become official policy.

The working principles were viewed as generally uplifting. Some informative questions and critical remarks were made on various details and on the wording of some principles, e.g., on the preference for functional equivalence (it depends on your starting point where this leads you) and on ISP liability (where applying the adage 'online equals offline' depends on how you view an ISP).

Specific private-law and criminal-law issues

In the afternoon session, specific private-law and criminal-law issues were discussed in more detail.

***Private-law issues**, introduced by Patricia Fry*

As regards private law, the discussion in the United States shows that we can distinguish between two lines of reasoning: those who argue that quick action is required for the sake of legal certainty, and those who argue that we first need to understand ICT better before taking any legislative action. In general, one could say that the freedom of contracting should prevail also online, unless this leads to abuse. Contract rules should be default rules instead of minimum standards.

The specific private law topics currently debated in the US are:

- validation of e-contracts;
- enforceability of e-contracts;
- electronic signatures (including authentication questions);
- data(base) protection;
- privacy;
- consumer protection;
- jurisdiction;
- intellectual property.

As regards consumer protection, the consumer organisations tend to lobby for rules that force electronic suppliers to stay in the paper world. Also, arguments are being raised that in order to safeguard consumer protection, new rules for the online world are needed. Thus far, the US government have shown no particular interest in developments outside the US, since the debates raging domestically keep them busy. As a result, there is no strong push or force that deals with internationalisation of e-commerce issues.

Experience shows that the problems are mitigated once the relevant parties have come to the table to discuss the issues and the special interests.

As regards intellectual-property law, there remains a natural tension between the protection of intellectual-property rights and freedom of information.

As regards private international law issues and cross-border online agreements, no coherent view has emerged so far.

Finally, mention was made of the importance of alternative dispute resolution (ADR) mechanisms. In the US, ADR systems are not seen as favouring consumer interests, because the people involved in the decision-making process are less capable, less informed and often staffed by industry.

The discussion then focused on the United Kingdom. In general, one could say that the UK government takes a 'soft-law approach'. From this perspective, the government takes a special interest in the basic framework of the OECD guidelines on electronic consumer protection. DTI, together with industry, is promoting the introduction of Codes of Conduct.

At present there are no specific initiatives in UK on online consumer protection. The government is closely following the developments on ADR initiatives in the EU.

Although not directly linked to private law, mention was made of an issue that has come up recently in the UK: the relationship between citizens and the government. How far do you allow the citizen to contact the government and what opportunities do you give consumers and businesses to e-contract with the government?

Finally, the discussion showed that there are diverging opinions on the relevance and practicability of a solution for private international law issues by means of 'compartmentalisation'. Such a solution, which uses technological facilities to exclude consumers from jurisdictions with which the supplier does not want to contract, is seen as unrealistic and undesirable in light of technological developments.

***Criminal-law issues**, introduced by Stephen Saxby*

The UK Law Commission has given a concise outline of UK law on criminal jurisdiction.[368] "The general rule is that the exercise of criminal jurisdiction does not extend to cover acts committed on land abroad. Jurisdiction over a crime belongs to the country in which it was committed. So, in general, English subjects who commit acts abroad are not amenable to the jurisdiction of the courts in England and Wales. Under the present law, the English courts do not have jurisdiction to try a criminal offence unless the last act or event necessary for its completion occurs within the jurisdiction. This general principle applies to both common law and statutory offences, but as Parliament is supreme it may extend the territorial limit of a particular offence." A good example of the reluctance to laws with extraterritorial effect is the Sexual Offences (Conspiracy and Incitement) Act 1996, which is, inter alia, targeted at sex tourism to the Philippines. It does so by criminalising the preparation for sex-tourism holidays (the preparation takes place in the UK). The government pointed out that there are three reasons for not having laws with extraterritorial effects: (1) criminal law has a territorial base, (2) there are practical difficulties in gathering and presenting in British courts evidence of acts that have occurred abroad, and (3) it is better to have effective laws in the countries where the offences are committed. Therefore, extraterritorial reach should be the exception to the rule. See, e.g., a recent ruling: UK bribery law is not applicable to British executives who bribe foreign officials abroad (*Financial Times*, 28 March 2000).

An interdepartmental review of the Sexual Offences (Conspiracy and Incitement) Act 1996 has provided some guidelines on when extraterritorial reach of British law might be applied:

a. it concerns serious offences;
b. evidence and witnesses must be likely to be available in the UK;
c. there is international agreement that the conduct in question is reprehensible and that concerted action is needed to deal with the problem;
d. action is needed because of the vulnerability of the victims;
e. action is in the interest of the standing and reputation of the UK in the international community; and
f. there is a danger that if nothing is done, the offenders will not be brought to justice.

It should be stressed that these are not guidelines for the abandonment of double criminality.

What instruments should governments use to enforce criminal law internationally? First of all, there are international conventions, such as the UN Convention on the Rights of the Child, which was ratified by the UK in 1991. Five years later, this led to the en-

[368] The Law Commission, *Legislating the criminal code: corruption*, Consultation Paper 145, <http://www.lawcom.gov.uk/library/lccp145/cp145.pdf> (visited 30 March 2000), sections 9.2 and 9.3, p. 102, and The Law Commission, *Legislating the criminal code: corruption*, Report 248, <http://www.lawcom.gov.uk/library/lc248/lc248.pdf> (visited 30 March 2000), sections 7.3 and 7.4, p. 105.

actment of the Sexual Offences (Conspiracy and Incitement) Act 1996. A drawback of international conventions is that it is second best to improving national laws themselves.

In practice, informal cooperation between enforcement authorities and private organisations – such as the Internet Watch Foundation – in different countries is invaluable. Whether or not this requires (international) regulation is a good question. It is also an open question. As an illustration, one can mention the 'World Wide Sweep for Internet Fraudsters', a surf day organised by the US Federal Trade Commission, in which numerous international organisations participated. The sweep exposed some 1600 suspicious websites (see *Financial Times*, 24 March 2000).

We ought to be aware of the secondary areas of law that in themselves create the concept of multinational crime. In the UK, taxation law has created problems with regard to the illegal import of cigarettes and spirits. The British government has decided that it wants to increase the monitoring and prosecution of these activities rather than reduce the taxes to a level where the incentive to commit these crime is reduced. That is a perfectly reasonable policy choice for the British government to take.

The discussion took up the issue of the relation between double criminality and extraterritorial jurisdiction. The UK has extraterritorial jurisdiction with respect to offences such as murder, bigamy, and child sex. The execution of extraterritorial jurisdiction holds a certain risk of imposing one's own norms to foreign countries: a risk that is even more real in a computer network, such as the Internet, that encompasses the entire world. The best solution to this would be a harmonisation of (some?) substantive norms in the field of public-order law. Because such a harmonisation is something that will not happen in the foreseeable future, the requirement of double criminality remains, in principle, a necessary means to avoid imposing a country's own law on foreign countries.

The discussion then addressed the question of whether the requirement of double criminality ought to be met for the cross-border exercise of each and every coercive power, or whether one could discard it for certain powers under certain conditions – in the words of the chairman: "Is there something between black and white?" There was no discussion about the necessity of the requirement when it comes to extradition or cross-border searches and seizures. There was more discussion over the question whether the requirement has to be met when coercing foreign ISPs to trace and identify Internet users. Although some cases could be envisaged in which such a power without the requirement of double criminality could be useful, the overall opinion was that relinquishing the requirement would 'open the floodgates' and make criminal (procedural) law go down the way of censorship. It was pointed out, however, that if a power does not have a coercive element, the requirement need not be met.

Given the idea that a state can not (and may not) impose its norms to a website that is hosted abroad, there could be a shift towards liability of local Internet Access Providers: if they could be required to block access to certain foreign sites, much of the problems surrounding diverging normative claims to the world-wide Internet could be alleviated. The participants declined an obligation to block access to foreign material, because it militates against the very essence of the Internet: the free, uninhibited flow of information. Moreover, blocking measures are costly and probably ineffective.

Overall conclusions

- There is an obvious tendency away from pure market self-regulation in the direction of 'co-regulation', a cooperation by government and business as 'partners' in regulation.
- It is far from clear what exactly should be understood by co-regulation as a starting point. The way this starting is given shape in practice will differ per country, depending on the regulatory tradition. For co-regulation to work in an international context, countries will have to clarify what exactly they take 'co-regulation' to mean.
- In discussing possible government regulation, it is useful to distinguish regulation aiming at influencing behaviour on the one hand, and regulation aiming at answering questions (e.g., to create legal certainty) on the other hand.
- In co-regulation, the government has an obvious task of defining a minimum level of protection and of indicating interests that have to be taken into account.
- The effect of self-regulation and co-regulation will ultimately depend on enforcement: the rules must be enforceable, and they will indeed have to be enforced in practice.
- It is not useful to take rules as a starting point in the adage "what holds offline, should also hold online". Rather, one must identify the (social) function of the rules in the offline world, in order to create rules in the online world that have an analogous function. Resulting rules should thus be functional equivalents.
- The rationale of the adage "what holds offline, should also hold online" lies in creating similar levels of protection in the offline and online worlds. The relationship between offline and online regulation will thus be an interactive process.
- Of primary importance in applying this adage will be the question to what extent enforcement can be sufficiently ensured in the online world. The government will also have to take into account people's trust in the online rules.
- Ultimately, rather than abide by the slightly outdated adage "what holds offline, should also hold online", governments will have to be creative in addressing new problems and issues.
- Enforcement is considered the main problem with respect to ICT law in the international context. However, there are few ideas about safeguarding enforcement in general.
- Enforcement is most likely to be agreed upon in those areas where governments agree upon basic principles, e.g., in the financial sector.
- In private law, enforcement could be safeguarded by international mediation through national contact points (such as ombudspersons or Chambers of Commerce).
- In criminal law, enforcement will be a slow and long process; here also, national contact points can be used to facilitate international enforcement.
- The requirement of double criminality is a fundamental requirement; it is hard if not impossible to find acceptable ways to make exceptions to this.
- The Dutch draft working principles are welcomed with a fundamentally positive attitude.

- The overall conclusion is that, generally, procedural rules are relatively easy to agree upon (governments and businesses agree how they should agree upon things), whereas substantive rules (reaching specific agreements) are more contentious.

List of participants

Erwin ARKENBOUT	NL	Ministry of Justice
Jan-Tom BOS	NL	Ministry of Justice
Patricia BRUMFIELD FRY	USA	Wm. Mitchell College of Law
Georges CHATILLON	FR	University of Paris
Lars DAVIES	UK	London University, Ashurst Morris Crisp
Robbie DOWNING	UK	Baker & McKenzie
Coen DRION (chairman)	NL	Kennedy van der Laan
Serge GIJRATH	NL	Tilburg University
Nigel HICKSON	UK	Department of Trade and Industry
Simone VAN DER HOF	NL	Tilburg University
Hielke HIJMANS	NL	Ministry of Justice
Cyril VAN DER NET	NL	Leiden University, Ministry of Justice
Bert-Jaap KOOPS	NL	Tilburg University
Tomas OUDEJANS	NL	Tilburg University
Corien PRINS	NL	Tilburg University
Stephen SAXBY	UK	University of Southampton
Maurice SCHELLEKENS	NL	Tilburg University
Florence SCHMIDT-PARISET	FR	OECD, Ministry of Justice
Thomas SMEDINGHOFF	USA	Baker & McKenzie
Guido TIELMAN	NL	Ministry of Foreign Affairs
Frederique VAN ZOMEREN	NL	Ministry of Justice

Abbreviations

ADR	Alternative Dispute Resolution
AOL	America OnLine
CALEA	Communications Assistance for Law Enforcement Act (US)
CIA	confidentiality, integrity, and availability Central Intelligence Agency (US)
CISI	Comité Interministériel pour la Société de l'Information (Interministerial Committee for the Information Society) (F)
DMCA	Digital Millennium Copyright Act
DMSA	Netherlands Association for Direct Marketing, Distance Selling and Sales Promotion
DPWP	Data Protection Working Party
DTI	Department of Trade and Industry (UK)
EC	European Commission
ECP.NL	Electronic Commerce Platform Netherlands
EK	Eerste Kamer (Upper House) (NL)
EPIC	Electronic Privacy Information Center (US)
EU	European Union
FBI	Federal Bureau of Investigations (US)
FCC	Federal Communications Commission (US)
FIDNET	Federal Intrusion Detection Network
FTC	Federal Trade Commission (US)
G8	Group of Eight
GBDe	Global Business Dialogue on electronic commerce
ICANN	Internet Corporation for Assignment of Names and Numbers
ICC	International Chamber of Commerce
ICT	Information and Communication Technologies
IIA	Internet Industry Association (Aus)
ILETS	International Law Enforcement on Telecommunications Seminar
ILIS	Internationalisation and Law in the Information Society
INHOPE	Internet Hotline Providers in Europe Association
ISP	Internet Service Provider
ISPA	Internet Services Providers Association (UK)
ITeR	InformatieTechnologie en Recht (National Programme for Information Technology and Law) (NL)

IuKDG	Gesetz zur Regelung der Rahmenbedingungen für Informations- und Kommunikationsdienste (Law to Regulate the Framework Conditions for Information and Communications Services; Multimedia Act) (G)
IWF	Internet Watch Foundation (UK)
LEH	Legislation for the Electronic Highways (NL)
LINX	London Internet Exchange
MDStV	Mediendienste-Staatsvertrag (Interstate Media Services Treaty) (G)
MLAT	Multi Lateral Assistance Treaty
NAI	Network Advertising Initiative (US)
NLIP	Netherlands League of Internet Providers
OECD	Organisation for Economic Co-operation and Development
OFTEL	Office of Telecommunications (UK)
OIE	Office of Internet Enforcement (US)
OJ	Official Journal
OPTA	Onafhankelijke Post- en TelecommunicatieAutoriteit (Independent Post and Telecommunications Authority) (NL)
PAGSI	Programme d'Action Gouvernemental pour la Société de l'Information (Government Program for the Information Society) (F)
PICS	Platform for Internet Content Selection
PIL	private international law
RIPA	Regulation of Investigatory Powers Act (UK)
SBA	Singapore Broadcasting Authority
STOA	Scientific and Technical Options Assessment programme office (European Parliament)
TK	Tweede Kamer (Lower House) (NL)
Trb.	Tractatenblad
TTP	Trusted Third Party
UK	United Kingdom
UN	United Nations
UNCITRAL	United Nations Commission on International Trade Law
US	United States of America
VNO-NCW	Confederation of Netherlands Industry and Employers
WIPO	World Intellectual Property Organization
WRR	Wetenschappelijke Raad voor het Regeringsbeleid (Netherlands Scientific Council for Government Policy)
WTO	World Trade Organisation
WWW	World Wide Web

Bibliography

ABA 2000
ABA Global Cyberspace Jurisdiction Project, *Achieving Legal and Business Order in Cyberspace: A Report on Global Jurisdiction Issues Created by the Internet. London Meeting Draft*, <http://www.kentlaw.edu/cyberlaw/docs/drafts/draft.rtf>.

Asscher 2000
Lodewijk Asscher, 'Naar een eEurope van de burgers!', *Nederlands Juristenblad* 2000, p. 762-763.

Battle 1998
John Battle, *HMG Strategy for the Internet*, 18 March 1998, <http://www.dti.gov.uk/Minspeech/btlspch3.htm>.

Bertelsmann 1999
Bertelsmann Foundation, *Self-regulation of Internet Content*, Gütersloh 1999, available at <http://www.bertelsmann-stiftung.de/internetcontent/english/content/c3200.htm>.

Blair 1998
Tony Blair, *Our Information Age, The Government's Vision*, May 1998, <http://www.number-10.gov.uk/textsite/info/releases/publications/infoagefeat.html>.

BMBF 1999
Bundesministerium für Bildung, Wissenschaft, Forschung und Technologie, *Multimedia möglich machen. Deutschlands Weg in die Wissensgesellschaft*, February 1999, <http://www.iid.de/mmm_bmbf/mm_p4.htm>.

BMWi 1996
Bundesministerium für Wirtschaft, *Info 2000: Deutschland's Weg in die Informationsgesellschaft*, February 1996, <http://www.bmwi-info2000.de/archive/berichte/info2000/index.html>.

BMWi 1999
Bundesministerium für Wirtschaft und Technologie, *Evaluierungsbericht des IuKDG*, 16 June 1999, <http://www.iid.de/iukdg/pm160699.html>.

Bundesregierung 1999
Innovation und Arbeitsplätze in der Informationsgesellschaft des 21. Jahrhunderts – Aktionsprogramm der Bundesregierung, 1999,
<http://www.iid.de/aktionen/aktionsprogramm/deckblatt.html>.

Cabinet Office 1999
Cabinet Office, *E-commerce@its.best.uk*, September 1999, <http://www.cabinet-office.gov.uk/innovation/1999/ecommerce/index.htm>.

CISI 1999
Comité Interministériel pour la Société de l'Information, *Mise en oeuvre du Programme d'action gouvernemental pour la société de l'information – Etat d'avancement après un an (janvier 1998 – janvier 1999)*, 19 January 1999,
<http://www.internet.gouv.fr/francais/textesref/cisi190199/sommaire.htm>.

Clarke 1999
C. Clarke, *Speech to the International Hi-Tech Crime and Forensic Conference*, 4 October 1999, <http://www.infowar.com/law/99/law_100799d_j.shtml>.

Clinton 1997
William J. Clinton, *Presidential Directive*, 1 July 1997,
<http://www.whitehouse.gov/WH/New/Commerce/directive.html>.

Conseil d'Etat 1998
Conseil d'Etat, *Internet et les résaux numériques*, 2 July 1998,
<http://www.internet.gouv.fr/francais/textesref/rapce98/synthese.htm>, English version at <http://www.internet.gouv.fr/francais/textesref/rapce98/accueil.htm>.

Council of Europe 1995
Council of Europe Recommendation No. R (95) 13 of the Committee of Ministers to Member States Concerning Problems of Criminal Procedure Law Connected with Information Technology, 11 September 1995,
<http://www.privacy.org/pi/intl_orgs/coe/info_tech_1995.html>.

Council of Europe 1999
Council of Europe Recommendation No. R (99) 5, Guidelines for the protection of individuals with regard to the collection and processing of personal data on information highways, 23 February 1999, <http://www.coe.fr/cm/ta/rec/1999/99r5.htm>.

Council of Europe 2000
Council of Europe, *Crime in Cyberspace. First Draft of International Convention Released for Public Discussion*, 27 April 2000,
<http://conventions.coe.int/treaty/en/projets/cybercrime.htm>.

Den Boer 1999
M.G.W. den Boer, 'Internationale politiesamenwerking', in: C.J.C.F. Fijnaut, E.R. Muller & U. Rosenthal (red.), *Politie. Studies over haar werking en organisatie*, Alphen a/d Rijn: Samsom 1999.

Den Haan 1998
Reinoud den Haan, *Internationale organisaties en de elektronische snelweg*, November 1998 (report for the Dutch Ministry of Justice, unpublished).

Department of Commerce 1997
Department of Commerce, *Privacy and Selfregulation in the Information Age*, June 1997, <http://www.ntia.doc.gov/reports/privacy/privacy_report.htm>.

Department of Commerce 1998
Department of Commerce, *The Emerging Digital Economy*, April 1998, <http://www.ecommerce.gov/emerging.htm>.

Department of Justice 1999
Justice Department comments to the FTC on Consumer Protection in the Global Marketplace, 29 March 1999, <http://www.usdoj.gov/criminal/cybercrime/ftcconsu.htm>.

DPWP 1999
Data Protection Working Party, *Recommendation on the Respect of Privacy in the context of Interception of Telecommunications*, 3 May 1999, <http://europa.eu.int/comm/internal_market/en/media/dataprot/wpdocs/wp18en.htm>.

Drion 1999
C. Drion, 'Internationale ontwikkelingen in materieel recht met betrekking tot e-commerce, over botsende rechtsstelsels en het "compartimenteringsbeginsel" en enkele specifieke vragen van internationaal privaatrecht', in: *Meester over 2000, Meester over IT* (Jonge Balie Congres 1999), Den Haag: Sdu 1999, p. 67-85.

Electronic Commerce Directive 2000
Directive 2000/31/EC of the European Parliament and of the Council of 8 June 2000 on certain legal aspects of information society services, in particular electronic commerce, in the Internal Market ("Directive on electronic commerce"), *OJ* L 178/1, 17 June 2000, <http://europa.eu.int/eur-lex/en/dat/2000/l_178/l_17820000717en00010016.pdf>.

Enquete-Kommission 1998
Schlußbericht der Enquete-Kommission Zukunft der Medien in Wirtschaft und Gesellschaft – Deutschlands Weg in die Informationsgesellschaft zum Thema Deutschlands Weg in die Informationsgesellschaft, 22 June 1998, Drucksache 13/11004.

Eijlander a.o. 1993
Ph. Eijlander, P.C. Gilhuis, J.A.F. Peters (red.), *Overheid en zelfregulering*, Zwolle 1993.

FCC 1997
Federal Communications Commission, *Digital Tornado: The Internet and Telecommunications Policy*, March 1997, <http://www.fcc.gov/Bureaus/OPP/working_papers/oppwp29.pdf>.

FTC 2000
Federal Trade Commission, *Fair Information Practices in the Electronic Marketplace*, 22 May 2000, <http://www.ftc.gov/os/2000/05/index.htm#22>.

G8 1999
Ministerial Conference of the G-8 Countries on Combating Transnational Organized Crime, Moscow, October 19-20, 1999, *Communiqué*, <http://www.library.utoronto.ca/g7/adhoc/crime99.htm>.

G8 2000
G8, *Okinawa Charter on Global Information Society*, July 2000, <http://www.g8kyushu-okinawa.go.jp/e/documents/it1.html>.

Hogan 1999
S.B. Hogan, 'To Net or Not To Net: Singapore's Regulation of the Internet', *Federal Communications Law Journal* 1999, p. 429-447, <http://www.law.indiana.edu/fclj/pubs/v51/no2/v51no2.html>.

Holder 1999
Eric Holder, *International Conference "Combating Pornography on the Internet". Remarks of U.S. Deputy Attorney General Eric Holder*, Vienna, 29 September 1999, <http://www.usdoj.gov/criminal/cybercrime/dagceos.html>.

House of Commons 1999
House of Commons, *Tenth Report of the Select Committee on Trade and Industry*, August 1999, <http://www.parliament.the-stationery-office.co.uk/pa/cm199899/cmselect/cmtrdind/648/64802.htm>.

House of Lords 1996
House of Lords, *Information Society: Agenda for Action in the UK*, 23 July 1996, <http://www.parliament.the-stationery-office.co.uk/pa/ld199596/ldselect/inforsoc/inforsoc.htm>.

Hugot 1999
Rapport numéro 154 de M. Jean-Paul HUGOT, fait au nom de la commission des Affaires culturelles, 22 December 1999, <http://www.senat.fr/rap/l99-154/l99-154.html>.

ICANN 1999
ICANN, *Uniform Domain Name Dispute Resolution Policy*, 24 October 1999, <http://www.icann.org/udrp/udrp-policy-24oct99.htm>.

ILIS Memorandum
TK 1999-2000, 25 880, no. 10 (*Internationalisering en Recht in de Informatiemaatschappij*), May 2000, English version *Internationalisation and Law in the Information Society*, p. 21-68 of this book.

ISI 1999
The Government's policy for the information age, <http://www.isi.gov.uk/isi/infosoc/govpolicy.htm> (accessed 15 July 2000).

Jabbour 1999
V. Jabbour, 'Comment on the interception of communications in the UK Consultation Paper', *Computer Law & Security Report* 1999, p. 389-391.

Jansen & Janssen 1999
Buro Jansen & Janssen, *Luisterrijk. Een gids over afluisteren*, Amsterdam: Jansen & Janssen/ Papieren Tijger 1999.

Jospin 1997
Prime Minister, *Preparing France's Entry into the Information Society*, 25 August 1997, <http://www.premier-ministre.gouv.fr/GB/INFO/HOURT.HTM>.

Jospin 1999a
Le Premier Ministre, *Société de l'information: discours du Premier ministre à l'Université d'été de la communication*, Hourtin, 26 August 1999, <http://www.internet.gouv.fr/francais/textesref/pagsi2/discourspm.htm>.

Jospin 1999b
Le Premier Ministre, *Allocution du Premier ministre lors de la réception concluant la conférence mondiale des régulateurs sur l'internet*, Paris, 1 December 1999, <http://www.premier-ministre.gouv.fr/PM/D011299.HTM>.

Joustra 1997
C.A. Joustra, *De internationale consumentenovereenkomst*, Deventer: Kluwer 1997.

JRC 2000
Joint Research Centre, *Out-of-court dispute settlement systems for e-commerce. Report of an exploratory study*, 20 April 2000, <http://dsa-isis.jrc.it/ADR/Reportv20apr.pdf>.

Judicial Co-operation Unit 1999
Judicial Co-operation Unit, *Seeking Assistance in Criminal Matters from the United Kingdom. Guidelines for judicial and prosecuting authorities (Second Edition)*, October 1999, <http://www.homeoffice.gov.uk/oicd/jcu/guidelns.htm>.

Koops 2000
B.J. Koops, *Crypto Law Survey*, version 18.1, August 2000, <http://cwis.kub.nl/~frw/people/koops/lawsurvy.htm>.

KPMG & Denton Hall 1999
KPMG en Denton Hall, *Review of the Internet Watch Foundation. A report for the DTI and Home Office by KPMG and Denton Hall*, <http://www.kpmgiwf.org/iwfrevu.pdf> (accessed 26 April 2000).

LEH Memorandum
TK 1997-1998, 25 880, nos. 1-2 (*Wetgeving voor de elektronische snelweg*), English Management Summary: p. 3-20 of this book.

Linklaters & Alliance 1999
Linklaters & Alliance, *Telecommunications and electronic business: doing business in the electronic age. A legal overview*, Deventer: Kluwer 1999.

Lorentz 1998a
Ministère de l'Économie, des Finances en de l'Industrie, Francis Lorentz, *Commerce électronique. Une nouvelle donne pour les consommateurs, les entreprises, les citoyens et les pouvoirs publics*, 7 January 1998, <http://www.finances.gouv.fr/lorentz/rapports/index-d.htm>.

Lorentz 1998b
Ministère de l'Économie, des Finances en de l'Industrie, Francis Lorentz, *Rapport sur le commerce électronique – Addendum*, 15 March 1998, <http://www.finances.gouv.fr/lorentz/rapports/forum.htm>.

Lorentz 1999
Ministère de l'Économie, des Finances en de l'Industrie, Francis Lorentz, *La nouvelle donne du commerce électronique. Réalisations 1998 et perspectives. Synthèse*, February 1999, <http://www.finances.gouv.fr/lorentz/travaux/synth_generale.html>.

OECD 1997
OECD, *Recommendation of the Council concerning Guidelines for Cryptography Policy*, 17 March 1997, < http://www.oecd.org/dsti/sti/it/secur/prod/e-crypto.htm>.

OECD 1998a
OECD, Working Party on Information Security and Privacy, *Ministerial Declaration on the Protection of Privacy on Global Networks*, DSTI/ICCP/REG(98)10/FINAL, 18 December 1998, <http://appli1.oecd.org/olis/1998doc.nsf/linkto/dsti-iccp-reg(98)10-final>.

OECD 1998b
OECD, *Ministerial Declaration on Consumer Protection in the Context of Electronic Commerce*, DSTI/CP(98)12/FINAL, 18 December 1998, <http://www.olis.oecd.org/olis/1998doc.nsf/LinkTo/DSTI-CP(98)12-FINAL>.

OECD 1998c
OECD Ministerial Conference Ottawa, *A Borderless World: Realising the Potential of Global Electronic Commerce*, 7-9 October 1998.

OECD 1998d
OECD Ministerial Conference Ottawa, *A global action plan for electronic commerce prepared by business with recommendations for Governments*, 7-9 October 1998.

OECD 1999
OECD Forum on Electronic Commerce, *Report on the Forum*, Paris, 12-13 October 1999, <http://www.oecd.org//dsti/sti/it/ec/act/Paris_ec/pdf/forum_report.pdf>.

PAGSI 1998
Comité Interministériel pour la Société de l'Information, *Programme d'action gouvernemental. Préparer l'entrée de la France dans la société de l'information*, 16 January 1998, <http://www.internet.gouv.fr/francais/textesref/pagsi.htm>.

Palme 1998
J. Palme, *Swedish Law on Responsibilities for Internet Information Providers*, updated 3 June 1998, <http://www.dsv.su.se/~jpalme/society/swedish-bbs-act.html>.

Paul 2000
Christian Paul, *Du droit et des libertés sur l'internet. La corégulation, contribution française pour une régulation mondiale*, 29 June 2000, <http://www.internet.gouv.fr/francais/textesref/pagsi2/lsi/rapportcpaul/rapcpaul2intro.htm>.

Polak 1998
M.V. Polak, 'Internationaal privaatrecht: vangnet voor het Internet', *Nederlandse Juristen-Vereniging 1998-I*, Deventer: Tjeenk Willink 1998, p. 59-118.

President's Working Group 2000
President's Working Group on Unlawful Conduct on the Internet, *The Electronic Frontier: the Challenge of Unlawful Conduct Involving the Use of the Internet* , March 2000, <http://www.usdoj.gov/criminal/cybercrime/unlawful.htm>.

Prins & Gijrath 2000
J.E.J. Prins & S.J.H. Gijrath, *Privaatrechtelijke aspecten van elektronische handel*, Deventer: Tjeenk Willink 2000.

Prins & Van Kralingen 1997
J.E.J. Prins & R.W. van Kralingen, 'De invloed van informatie- en communicatietechnologie op het recht', in: *Volatilisering in de economie*, Den Haag: WRR 1997, p. 105-123; English version 'To Regulate or Not to Regulate: Prevalence and Impact of a Virtual Society', *The EDI Law Review* 1997, p. 91-111.

Scott 1999
B. Scott, 'An Essential Guide to Internet Censorship in Australia', *World Internet Law Report* 1999/10, p. 16-21.

Sieber 1998
U. Sieber, *Legal aspects of computer-related crime in the Information Society – comcrime study* , 1998, <http://www2.echo.lu/legal/en/comcrime/sieber.html>.

STOA 1998
Steve Wright, Omega Foundation, *An appraisal of technologies for political control. Working document*, Luxembourg: European Parliament B STOA, 6 January 1998, <http://jya.com/stoa-atpc.htm>.

STOA 1999
Duncan Campbell, *Interception Capabilities 2000. Report to the Director General for Research of the European Parliament (Scientific and Technical Options Assessment programme office) on the development of surveillance technology and risk of abuse of economic information*, April 1999,
<http://www.iptvreports.mcmail.com/interception_capabilities_2000.htm>.

Strauss Kahn a.o. 1999
Dominique Strauss Kahn a.o., *Une société de l'information pour tous. Document d'orientation*, November 1999, <http://www.internet.gouv.fr/francais/index.html> English version: *Policy Paper on the Adaptation of the Legal Framework to the Information Society*, <http://www.finances.gouv.fr/societe_information/anglais/sommaire_ang.htm>.

Van Esch 1999
R.E. van Esch, *Electronic Data Interchange (EDI) en het vermogensrecht*, Deventer: Tjeenk Willink 1999.

Van der Hof a.o. 1997
Simone van der Hof, Bert-Jaap Koops a.o., *Netiquette of Wetiquette. Zelfregulering of overheidsregulering van de elektronische snelweg in Frankrijk, Duitsland, het Verenigd Koninkrijk en de Verenigde Staten*, November 1997, <http://cwis.kub.nl/~frw/schrdijk/cri/pdf/netofwet.pdf>.

Van der Hof 1998
S. van der Hof, 'De Internetconsument en het internationaal privaatrecht, *Tijdschrift voor consumentenrecht*, December 1998, no. 5, p. 415-421.

Van der Hof 2000
S. van der Hof, 'De Internationale on-line overeenkomst', in: *De e-Consument. Consumentenbescherming in de Nieuwe Economie* (preadvies NVvIR), Elsevier 2000.

Van der Net 2000
C.B. Van der Net, *Grenzen stellen op het Internet. Aansprakelijkheid van Internet-providers en rechtsmacht*, Deventer: Gouda Quint 2000

Clinton & Gore 1997
William J. Clinton & Albert Gore, Jr., *A Framework for Global Electronic Commerce*, 1 July 1997, <http://www.whitehouse.gov/WH/New/Commerce>.

White House 1998
The White House, *Memorandum for Heads of Executive Departments and Agencies. Designation of Interagency Committees to Facilitate and Encourage Agency Use of Alternate Means of Dispute Resolution and Negotiated Rulemaking*, 1 May 1998, <http://www.npr.gov/library/direct/memos/disputre.html>.

White House 1999
The White House, *Memorandum for the Heads of Executive Departments and Agencies. Facilitating the Growth of Electronic Commerce*, 29 November 1999, <http://www.dot.gov/ost/m60/eleccomm/ecgrowth.htm>.

White House 2000a
The White House, *National Plan for Information Systems Protection*, 7 January 2000, available at <http://www.epic.org/security/infowar/resources.html>.

White House 2000b
The White House, *Statement by the President*, 30 June 2000,
<http://www.pub.whitehouse.gov/uri-res/I2R?urn:pdi://oma.eop.gov.us/2000/7/3/
5.text.2>.

White House 2000c
The White House, *Assuring Security And Trust In Cyberspace*, 17 July 2000,
<http://www.pub.whitehouse.gov/uri-res/I2R?urn:pdi://oma.eop.gov.us/2000/7/17/
15.text.1>.

WRR 1998
Wetenschappelijke Raad voor het Regeringsbeleid, *Staat zonder land*, WRR report no. 54, The Hague 1998

Authors

Hielke Hijmans works at the Dutch Ministry of Justice. All other authors work at the Center for Law, Public Administration and Informatisation (CRBI) of Tilburg University, the Netherlands.

Serge Gijrath
Serge Gijrath is an attorney in Amsterdam, a partner with Caron & Stevens/Baker & McKenzie, and, since 1999, he has been a research fellow with the CRBI of Tilburg University. He specialises in the legal aspects of information technology and telecommunications, with a further specialisation in intellectual-property law.

Hielke Hijmans
Hielke Hijmans is counsellor at the Department for Legislation of the Dutch Ministry of Justice in The Hague. In this capacity, he is specialised in subjects concerning the legal aspects of the development towards an information society. He is responsible for the policy documents *Legislation for the Electronic Highways* and *Internationalisation and Law in the Information Society*. As of November 2000, he will be working at the Court of Justice of the European Communities in Luxembourg, as a member of the cabinet of Advocate General Geelhoed.

Bert-Jaap Koops
Bert-Jaap Koops has been a senior research fellow with the CRBI since 1998. He studied Mathematics as well as General and comparative literature in Groningen, and from 1994 to 1998, he was a PhD student at Tilburg University and Eindhoven University of Technology. In January 1999, he received his PhD for his dissertation *The Crypto Controversy*. Koops researches the field of IT and law, in particular, criminal-procedure law and ICT, computer crime, encryption, digital signatures, and TTPs. In 2000-2001, he focuses on the borderline between criminal investigation and privacy in the light of ICT, with a personal grant from the Netherlands Organization for Scientific Research (NWO).

Corien Prins
Corien Prins has been a professor in law and informatisation with the CRBI since 1994. From 1980 onwards, she studied Slavic Languages and Literatures as well as Law at Leiden University, where she received her PhD in 1991. In 1993, she was invited visiting professor at Hastings School of Law (University of California, San Francisco). Prins is an editor of various national and international journals and loose-leaf reference books. Her

research currently focuses on electronic commerce, privacy and anonymity, intelligent agents, and regulatory principles with respect to ICT.

Maurice Schellekens

Maurice Schellekens has been a senior research fellow with the CRBI since 1999. Before, he was a PhD student with this centre. In early 2001, his PhD thesis will appear on the liability of Internet Providers in criminal and copyright law. In 1999, he published a study, financed by the National Programme for Information Technology and Law (*ITeR*) into offences on the electronic highway. Maurice Schellekens studied Dutch Law at Maastricht University and Technical Information Science at Eindhoven University of Technology.

Eric Schreuders

Eric Schreuders has been a research fellow with the CRBI since 1996. Earlier, he worked at the Ministry of Justice and at the Data Protection Authority (*Registratiekamer*). He is preparing a PhD thesis on the legal aspects of knowledge discovery in databases (KDD) and data mining, financed by the National Programme for Information Technology and Law (*ITeR*). He gives graduate and post-graduate courses in the field of privacy.

Index

www.ingramcontent.com/pod-product-compliance
Lightning Source LLC
Chambersburg PA
CBHW071244230926
51849CB00001B/227